I0816896

Morriconeʼs music?
Itʼs like listening to the light.

Anonymous

ENNIO MORRICONE

Master of the Soundtrack

Maurizio Baroni

TEXTS BY
Germano Barban

CONTRIBUTIONS BY
Dario Argento
John Boorman
John Carpenter
Liliana Cavani
Edda Dell'Orso
Roberto Faenza
Christopher Frayling
Daniele Furlati
Lisa Gastoni
Giancarlo Giannini
Guido Lombardo
Mauro Maur
Giuliano Montaldo
Franco Nero
Gino Paoli
Nicola Piovani
Quentin Tarantino
Giuseppe Tornatore
Carlo Verdone

GINGKO PRESS

ennio
morricone
e la sua orchestra
musica
sul
velluto

CANZONI
AL
CINEMA

successi
da
cinelandia
volume 1

UN'ORCHESTRA PER TANTI SUCCESSI

PATHOS BELLICO

RCA
ITALIANA
I GRANDI TEMI DA FILM DI ENNIO MORRICONE
ENNIO MORRICONE
E LA SUA ORCHESTRA

CANZONI AL CINEMA
JOHNNY
YUMA
ARIZONA
COLT
ALGERI
AMERICA

RCA
ITALIANA
the feed-back

RCA
ITALIANA
IDEATO, SCRITTO E DIRETTO DA
ENNIO MORRICONE

colori
ENNIO MORRICONE

E. MORRICONE
CONTRO
FASE

RCA
INTERNATIONAL
i western
ennio
morricone

STEREO
CINEMA
PARADE

ENNIO MORRICONE
GESTAZIONE
TOTEM SECONDO

LA MUSICA
NEL CINEMA
ENNIO MORRICONE

i film della
VIOLENZA
ENNIO MORRICONE
colonne sonore originali

RCA
LE COLONNE SONORE ORIGINALI DI
ENNIO
MORRICONE
UN FILM
UNA MUSICA

I GRANDI WESTERNS ITALIANI
ENNIO MORRICONE
COLONNE SONORE ORIGINALI
RCA
SERGIO LEONE

Stereo
Gruppo Di Improvvisazione
NUOVA CONSONANZA
improvvisazioni a formazioni variate
Mario BERTONCINI Walter BRANCHI Franco EVANGELISTI
John HEINEMANN Egisto MACCHI Ennio MORRICONE

GRUPPO D'IMPROVVISAZIONE NUOVA CONSONANZA

Ennio
Morricone
fotogramma
per
fotogramma
Vol.2

nova musicha n.9
GRUPPO DI IMPROVVISAZIONE
NUOVA CONSONANZA
MUSICA SU SCHEMI
FRANCO EVANGELISTI
EGISTO MACCHI
ENNIO MORRICONE
ANTONELLO NERI
GIOVANNI PIAZZA
GIANCARLO SCHIAFFINI

Contents

MAURIZIO BARONI

You Never Forget Your First Love

I can't read music. I have never played a musical instrument. I have never studied music. Nonetheless, I can still sing in tune. I like to sing and I absolutely love music that moves me until tears well up in my eyes. *West Side Story* set the 'tone' for my discovery of movie soundtracks, thanks to the genius of Leonard Bernstein. But what mesmerized me most was the whistle and crack of a whip that are the unmistakable prelude to *A Fistful of Dollars;* truly a masterpiece. And that is how I discovered Maestro Ennio Morricone.

And there wasn't just his music for the movies. I know that I might be accused of heresy as I dare to say that I wished *Sapore di Sale* and *Se Telefonando* had been songs only written in orchestral versions, despite the voices of Gino Paoli and the unbeatable Mina. I was still a kid when I started buying vinyl 45 rpm and LP records with money that I saved from my weekly allowance and I became a member of that small group of collectors of soundtracks. Besides Morricone, my knowledge of music grew to include other composers: Armando Trovajoli, Piero Piccioni, Carlo Rustichelli … as well as some foreign artists like John Barry, Michel Magne, and John Williams. All of them are outstanding musicians, and I am well aware of that special touch each one of them has, but 'you never forget your first love.' There is no other composer who makes me feel the way I do as when I listen to music by Morricone.

Around the late 1960s, I was especially taken by the score written for *The Lady of Monza* directed by Eriprando Visconti. For years, I desperately tried to find the recording; those pieces got inside my head and have never abandoned me. When an LP was produced in the late 1980s, I was overjoyed. And what can I say about how I felt while listening to *Deborah's Theme* on the soundtrack of *Once Upon a Time in America* by Sergio Leone? Feeling so deeply, I wanted to share this piece with my friends and relatives so much so that I had it played during Mass at my daughter Valentina's wedding. I was able to crown this passion on many visits to the Maestro's home in Rome. Although I am used to interacting with actors, filmmakers, and musicians with whom I share friendship and esteem, each time I meet Morricone I feel emotional and intimidated; even though he is always very courteous and patient with me. For years I had been planning to pay tribute to the Maestro with a book featuring the album covers for all of his movies; a huge task seeing his vast production. I succeed in doing this with *Ennio Morricone*, thanks to the help of so many friends and professionals in the film business who were honored to be a part of this celebration of his genius.

I took a draft of the book to acclaimed director and screenwriter, Giuseppe Tornatore, who not only encouraged me to keep working to finish the job, but also suggested that I show it to Morricone himself, who would undoubtedly appreciate it. He was prophetic, and in fact, during our encounter, the Maestro took great pains to look at each page; he was so interested in it that he asked me for a copy of the draft! One can't say no to Maestro Morricone.

Many of the most talented names in Italian cinema were pleased to participate in this project, sending me their own accounts of the personal relationship that ties them to Morricone. One that I would like to mention is John Carpenter, whom I was able to contact through a mutual friend in the United States. Within a few days of contacting him, he sent me his memories, with a separate note that said he was proud to have worked for the Maestro. A great help, yet, came from Sir Christopher Frayling, who enthusiastically sent me over not only his interview to Morricone, but also suggested and kindly gave us his permission to republish part of the long conversation he had with Quentin Tarantino in 2018. That part, when Tarantino talks about Morricone, looks like it was done specially for this book. So, I'd like to express my gratitude to both of them. And my deepest thanks to Giuseppe Tornatore for his contribution as well; he replied to my call straight away and wrote his tribute by return, in the name of the Maestro.

GERMANO BARBAN

The Soundtrack of a Lifetime

For all of us born in the 1950s, we inevitably found ourselves growing up at a time when there were no computers, videogames, or smartphones. In our free time, we played ball in a field right across the street from where we lived, read comics, scuffled while playing five-a-side soccer, and listened to popular music: Gino Paoli, Nico Fidenco, Mina, Edoardo Vianello. We also went to the movies to see Sergio Leone's Spaghetti Westerns, and after that the first thrillers, and erotic films, which in those days were strictly X-rated. It dawned on us at a certain point that in all of this, there was often the hand of someone named Ennio Morricone: musician, composer, and arranger, whose lovely, melodious arias reached everyone's ears evermore persuasively.

For me, as someone who was besotted with the music of America's blockbuster movies, Miklós Rózsa was already a legend with his scores for *Quo Vadis*, *Ben-Hur*, *El Cid,* and the *King of Kings*; so, it was easy for me to be trained to appreciate Ennio Morricone. Then came *The Doors, Pink Floyd,* Jimi Hendrix, the student protests, Woodstock, and, lastly, the rock music of *Led Zeppelin, Deep Purple, and Black Sabbath*. I embraced that music not so much because it had become the favorite music of my generation, but because the electric power triggered by that sound reminded me of the powerful, epic compositions of the movies I loved so much; and especially the multicolored, "inventive" musical arrangements for the Spaghetti Westerns; in other words, those soundtracks written by Maestro Morricone himself. And to anyone who might ask me, puzzled upon seeing me emerge from a record shop with the unmistakable blimp on the cover of the *Led Zeppelin* album; and the soundtrack to *The Big Gundown*, "D'ya really listen to this stuff?", I'd answer, "You bet. You can't have one without the other."

And so, in the midst of studying and working, hanging out with girls, and my free time divided among seeing friends, reading, traveling, and listening to music, the soundtrack that accompanied my life was soon clearly outlined as epic fanfares, wild guitar music, and the sounds of Morricone. It was in Morricone's music that I managed to discover some unexpected nuances: besides the whole assortment of musical styles and genres, there seems to be lots of rock music in Ennio's compositions. Whether hidden or latent, it's there. All you have to do is want to glimpse, or, better still, hear it. To this end, it is certainly worthwhile listening to *The Ecstasy of Gold,* a wonderful piece from the soundtrack of *The Good, the Bad and the Ugly*, in the hard-rock version by *Metallica*, for a better understanding about what I'm saying. It is part of the universality through and through of the Maestro's music, of his genius, which can effortlessly range from any type of musical expression without ever forsaking his commitment, professionalism, and great, brilliant, extraordinary creativity. And now that I am no longer young, now that my hair has turned gray and I have aches and pains in all my joints, I don't have to rewind the tape of the soundtrack of my life. It has continued to play non-stop since those now distant years of my youth, and on this fateful, timeless tape, is always *Led Zeppelin, AC/DC,* Miklós Rózsa's work, and him – Ennio Morricone. His is an unmistakable music, made from purity of sound and assembled with harmony and beauty.

Ennio Morricone: the man, the musician, the composer; 'our' illustrious fellow Italian, of whom we are especially proud of in the eyes of the world. The possessive adjective 'our' becomes inappropriate and outdated because Ennio Morricone's music has come to be considered a heritage beyond Italy's, and a gift for the whole world.

DARIO ARGENTO

I Started with Morricone

I met Morricone through my father on the occasion of my first movie, *The Bird with the Crystal Plumage*. We were introduced a few days before filming began. Watching him create was an amazing experience: Morricone, along with his collaborators, would watch the scenes as they moved along on the screen and composed by improvising. I don't think that music composed in an impromptu manner had ever before been used for a movie! After that, the Maestro set other films that I directed to music too: *The Cat o' Nine Tails* and *Four Flies on Grey Velvet*; but the soundtrack he wrote for *The Bird with the Crystal Plumage* is the one that I'm fondest of. He put all his skill and inventiveness into it, and every time I hear it, tears come to my eyes.

To be able to make *Deep Red,* I had to go to London to find groundbreaking musical groups like *Pink Floyd* and *Genesis* because I hoped that they would do something new for a movie that was so dreamlike, bizarre, and different from ones that I had made before; and I was determined to find new music for it. I returned home disappointed, and not having found what I was seeking, I turned to TV producer Carlo Bixio. He had me listen to a promo made by a group of very young musicians who had just graduated from the conservatory.

Their music impressed me and, trusting my intuition, I was crazy enough to choose them. *Deep Red* was at the top of the charts for almost a year; which is unusual for a soundtrack.

I worked with Morricone again in later years. Sometimes I would go to his house and he would play on the piano some of the pieces that he was composing. We had a great professional relationship. It was an honor for me to work with him, and I think he's still one of the greatest musicians alive.

JOHN CARPENTER

Love of a Fan

I knew of Ennio Morricone from the Sergio Leone Westerns. I was in my teens when I watched them and I remember the music – genre-changing, distinctive, evocative. I was 21 when I saw *Once Upon a Time in the West*, a masterpiece for both Leone and Morricone. Ennio's score was, in my case, life-changing. *Once Upon a Time* … was a widescreen, Western opera, and the music stunning. I fell in love with this composer.

Thirteen years later, I was hired to direct *The Thing* for Universal. They didn't want me to score the movie (they never asked me). Stuart Cohen, the cinema-knowledgeable associate producer, recommended Ennio. It was a brilliant idea and I said, "Hell yes"!

I met Ennio for the first time in Rome, I believe in 1982. He spoke no English and I spoke no Italian. Our interpreter was my assistant editor. He had composed several trial pieces for me and played them on the piano. It was incredible music. I asked for a main title theme "using fewer notes"; and Maestro Morricone complied.

Besides the main theme, Ennio composed a couple of absolutely beautiful, totally desolate orchestral pieces. *The Thing* was about the end of the world; about mankind being lost to a superior alien species and Ennio brilliantly provided the theme music to mankind's demise.

I loved my collaboration with the great Ennio Morricone. I cannot sing his praises enough. I am a 'hopelessly-in-love' fan. He has composed some of the greatest cinematic scores ever; and some of my favorite movie music.

From experimental music to *Cinema, Maestro!*, Ennio Morricone's life and work is 'Hall of Fame' brilliant. I am in awe of this man's talent.

JOHN BOORMAN

"What you like, John?"

I went to Rome to try to persuade Ennio to write a score for *The Heretic*, a sequel to *The Exorcist*. I had been asked to direct the original film. I read the book and when I found that it was a story about torturing a child, I declined. The film turned out to be just that, the torturing of a child; and it was a huge success.

I set about making a riposte – a response to that horrible film – a Manichean story in which goodness overcomes evil. My film was a disaster for audiences who craved more blood and horror. They threw things at the screen and demanded their money back.

But that would all happen in the future. First, I described the film I intended to make to Ennio and asked the Maestro if he would score it?

While I was there in Rome, I arranged to meet Sergio Leone with Morricone. Like everyone else, I loved their collaborations. In some of those Spaghetti Westerns, if you stripped out the music, there was little story. In fact, Ennio was at his best when there was not too much story.to get in the way of the music. It is often said that the film score is like an extra character. In films by these two men, the score was often the leading character. This is not to disparage Leone. His *Once Upon a Time in America* is one of the greatest pictures ever made. Yes, these scores were like a form of opera. Morricone was drawing on an Italian tradition.

So, I asked how they did it. At first, they trotted out the guff that they fed critics? Was Ennio consulted at the script stage? Not really. They would watch the film together, talk, and then somehow it would just happen. As the music grew, Sergio would open up the film to give the music more space. It would start with a phrase, perhaps a female voice. Ennio would sit at the piano and sing the phrase. It would grow like that.

I went back to Burbank to shoot the movie. After many months and much pain, I took the cut picture to show Ennio. He fell in love with the locust swarm. I said that I liked the sound of thousands of wings vibrating together. No music. "I write you something, anyway. What you like, John?" That became his mantra – What you like, John?Ennio would sketch the themes on the piano and augment them with sounds of French horns or flutes that he could simulate with his voice. In those days it was all a composer could do, and when you heard the orchestra it was often not how you imagined it; and hasty changes would be made.

As we talked, I became aware of his great musical possibilities. It was like gaining access to an enormous musical mind that could create infinitely. At the end of our discussions, Ennio had developed three dissonant themes that would merge together at the end into one harmonious whole. It sounded too intellectual to me. When I left I said, "Feel free to go with your gut, Ennio." "What you like, John?"

Eventually, Ennio arrived at Warner Brothers and began to work with a 60-piece orchestra, except instead of assembling the orchestra, he called the musicians one by one. Each musician would listen on ear phones to a guide track and record his part. Ennio's 60-piece orchestra now existed on 60 separate tracks! We sat by side and he began mixing. "What you like, John?" I finally understood what that meant. He could mix it any way we wanted; and we did!These days all composers have samples of every instrument. They can put the score on a computer and a director can listen to how it will sound.

This dance between director and composer is now much better choreographed.

I did a score with Hans Zimmer. We sat side by side at the piano and put up the first sequence that needed music on the screen. It was about a woman who had lost a child. "What instrument do you hear," he asked? "Not strings," I said. "Too sentimental." He suggested woodwinds and blended some together. "Now play me a phrase on the piano." I experimented and finally came up with one I liked and the woodwinds played it. Hans took over and developed the theme. We worked that way all through the score.

I am sure Ennio that works this way now. It was a great privilege to have been with him and to experience his great talent first hand.

LILIANA CAVANI

The Music that Completes the Movie

At times, music is more important than words. When movies were silent, the images were exalted by a pianist in the room – to create atmosphere, to underscore joy, pain, glory, or victory.

For the cinema, music gives voice to feelings. Not all composers know how to create music that works for the cinema. Morricone on the other hand, has always known how to, to the great advantage of the images. There are films in which musical commentary is an interference; it can be a distraction, even annoying. But Morricone is one of the few musicians to elevate the emotional richness of a plot to engage an audience. He has been awarded some important prizes, all of which he has truly deserved.

I have many memories of his collaboration on my own movies; wonderful memories of hours spent in the recording booth while he conducted musicians and simultaneously watched the sequences moving past on the screen. Absolutely marvelous hours, when a grateful director finally saw images intensified by the soundtrack. Discoveries were made when a scene that appeared lacking when watched through a viewing machine, took on its full meaning when Morricone's influence came to the fore.

This type of occurrence helps us to better understand just how important musical commentary is to a movie. At other times, music that's beautiful when listened to without images can, on the contrary, be damaging when it accompanies a film sequence. The musician's task is as important as it is delicate. If he or she makes a mistake, it might not only strip the cinematic story of its meaning, but could even weigh it down.

I believe that Morricone helped many films be more loved by the audience; be more beautiful. While a filmmaker tends to always work with the same musician, sometimes as the date nears to start filming, which is often just hypothetical, a particular musician may be working elsewhere. This happened to me for *The Night Porter*, and so I also worked with Maestro Daniele Paris, a legend, to whom I owe some amazing soundtracks.

When I go to the movies, I listen to the music carefully, and it's safe to say that Italy's cinema has some great musicians, truly outstanding ones, especially if you compare Italian soundtracks with those of other international films.

ROBERTO FAENZA

When It's the Music that Makes the Movie

This is a chance for me to remember my work alongside an extraordinary genius, having been fortunate enough to enjoy his collaboration for my first eight movies, from *Escalation* to *According to Pereira*. Unfortunately, our collaboration ended in 1997 due to a misunderstanding, which caused both of us much pain.

What we're talking about here is a kind of talent that elevated the film score to its highest splendor. Musical scoring for film is not, as many musicians themselves believe, a lesser genre; in the same way that chamber music or sacred music are not minor.

With Morricone, there's the legacy of the composers who made the history of Italy great – from Frescobaldi to Puccini, all the way to the artist whom I believe he considers his own maestro, Goffredo Petrassi. With respect to other musicians who have bestowed emotion on the cinema, with Morricone there's always that extra "note," the one that makes all the difference. And indeed, Morricone took a big step forward. His work was no longer music accompanying action, but rather an integral, necessary part of a movie; for instance, in the manner of photography. This type of accompaniment is so closely intertwined with the storyline that sometimes for some movies, the first thing that comes to mind is Ennio's soundtrack, even before the plot. A case in point is *Investigation of a Citizen Above Suspicion,* where the music is so perfectly a part of the movie that it lingers in the mind almost as though it were itself an image. The same can be said of his collaboration with Sergio Leone. Something similar happened with Fellini's movies and Nino Rota's music – a partnership so intimate that you can't think of one without the other.

Does Morricone have an heir? Right now, I don't see one and I think we're going to have to wait a while longer. He himself explains why he doesn't have a successor when he warns that the commodification of music in popular culture engenders "a generalized standardization of musical culture, of listening, of understanding: today we 'consume' music, and it is often no more than the background noise in a store." How true that is.

GIUSEPPE TORNATORE

The Historical Role of Album Covers

During public ceremonies, when Ennio Morricone is surrounded by people asking for his autograph on their program for the event, or on a book, or on a photograph, he always selects first the fan who holds out one of his old album covers. The gesture is an instinctive one. I don't think it has anything to do with nostalgia for the vinyl age, a feeling that the Maestro has never given signs of nurturing in any special way. I believe it's an impulsive tribute to the historical role of album covers.

There was a time when you would look at records on display in shop windows; or see them stacked one behind the other in music store bins. And you could let your curiosity be piqued by an image, by the graphic design, by a title, by the face of your favorite singer, or by the name of a musician you liked.

At that point, you would ask a sales assistant if you could listen to something on the record you had chosen. The sales assistant would slide the record out of the sleeve being careful not to scratch it. The platter would be placed on the turntable of the record player sitting in plain sight on the counter. Raising the tonearm to position it, the person would then lower the stylus onto the groove. You could listen to several albums, whichever ones you chose, and then decide which one to buy.

And even after leaving the store, after the cover had exhausted its role as an attraction, it acquired other tasks. For instance, you could use it to write the date it was purchased, or someone's phone number; or you could use it to write a dedication to the person you wanted to give it to for their birthday, or just to express how much you loved them. How many love stories have started this way, with the gift of a record album?

And then, when you went through your own collection of records or those at your friends' homes, you could tell how much a song, a concert, a soundtrack was loved by how worn the cover was. Some covers ended up wrinkled, stained, torn, covered in hearts and arrows or flower drawings; or repaired with glue or Scotch tape that was more or less transparent.

When covers such as these thread their way through all the hands offering makeshift pieces of paper to obtain the Maestro's autograph, those are the ones he chooses first – the covers of his vinyl LPs and 45s. He has recorded so many of them, especially if you include his popular tunes and his contemporary music. But even limiting ourselves to the musical themes of the West for his film scores, it would seem like an impossible job to find all the covers, considering the countless number of movies that Ennio Morricone has worked on in over seven decades of activity. Yet, Maurizio Baroni, thanks to the patience and determination that he is famous for, has miraculously managed to find each and every one of them. And not as some collecting fetish, but rather as an impassioned and loving way to trace back over Morricone's long road as a composer of soundtracks by way of the humblest symbols that mark the life of a prolific composer. It is a path made up of images and musical echoes in which it is easy for all of us to rediscover the footsteps of our own story.

GIULIANO MONTALDO

In conversation with Maurizio Baroni

Ennio Taught Me to Give Space to Music

Your work with Maestro Morricone began in 1967 for the movie *Grand Slam*. Before that, you'd made other movies with other Italian musicians, like Piero Umiliani. On that occasion, was it the producer who told you to work with Ennio Morricone, or did you seek him out on your own?

At the time, Morricone was working with the producers Georgio Papi and Arrigo Colombo on *A Fistful of Dollars;* and Sergio Leone would talk about this person named Ennio in superb terms. Leaving aside the fact that Leone was a marvelous figure himself, and that he also produced a movie for me, *A Dangerous Toy*, the way that Sergio described the film was unbelievable. He would imitate the sound of a gunshot and the music that followed, or the fact that the noise made by horses' hooves turned into a rumbling sound, and the rumbling sound into music. This was what Morricone had shared and suggested to him. I was enraptured right then and there, and absolutely had to meet him. When I did eventually meet him, I discovered a wonderful person, a generous and attentive one, quite the opposite of a star, and that was how our collaboration all began. In the first movie I made with him, *Grand Slam*, filmed in Brazil, there was a robbery scene that took place during the Carnival in Rio. We obviously couldn't do the filming during the actual Carnival, so, thanks to the help of a samba school, we managed to reconstruct one of the moments. Ennio had composed some wonderful sambas, and I had all my recordings with me. During one of the rehearsals, at the start of the scene and the music, the dancers got going and couldn't stop! They absolutely loved the music, and just couldn't stop dancing and singing. I had to call everyone back the next day to do the scene over again. I was really struck by this. It made me realize that Ennio had penetrated the very heart and soul of the country's music.

So, your friendship with Maestro Morricone began while you were making this movie?

Our work together got off to a very friendly start, a very pleasant one. That was when we first became friends, and our friendship continues to this day with great affection. I've learned so much from him. When I gave him the script so he could read it, for instance, Ennio explained to me that already during the writing phase you have to keep the spaces for the music in mind. When you're making a movie, there's no point inserting the music during an air raid, while tanks are rolling by, or when there's a scene of chaos. If you want to add music to a scene you have to make sure it has the proper space. This was food for thought. For example, if you rev up your car you hear the sound of the engine, but then the sound fades away. We all know what the vroom of an engine sounds like, and that's when you make room for the music.

I love music, though I can't say I'm an expert. However, whenever Ennio would invite me to his home to choose among the pieces he had composed and he would sit down at the piano to play them, I knew exactly which one of the pieces he was more committed to, the one he loved the most, and that was the one I always chose, of course.

You've made two memorable works, *Sacco & Vanzetti* and the series *Marco Polo*, for which Ennio Morricone went to China to get a sense of the mood and the history of the place. The compositions he wrote for those two movies are wonderful and famous everywhere. To what extent do you think they contributed to the movie's success?

As concerns *Sacco & Vanzetti,* I have to say the song sung by Joan Baez had a great pull; it was sung all around the world. I remember being in Berlin to talk to a producer about doing a movie on the dramatic, historic event of the Reichstag fire. It had been a life-long dream of mine to make a movie about it. There was a huge student protest going on, and just as I was about to pass by, a policeman put his hand on my stomach and stopped me. I could see those kids in Berlin moving forward, and what were they singing? "Here's to you, Nicola and Bart." It was amazing. I kept thinking to myself, "if only the policeman knew ...". I've also heard it sung in lots of other parts of the world, especially in America and in South America.

How did Joan Baez's name come up for the song?

It's a crazy story. It took me three years to convince a producer to make that movie. In Italy, the story of Sacco and Vanzetti wasn't that well known, and in America, in all the places where the story had taken place (1920-27) not a single brick was still standing. In Boston and the surrounding area, everything had been demolished, so any producer was immediately alarmed at the idea of having to reconstruct the scenes. In the end, we filmed part of the movie in Dublin, because it was the people of Ireland who had built Boston. To be sure we were right, we even ran a test: we showed pictures of Dublin to an old cab driver in Boston and asked, "Can you drive us here?" To which he answered, "I've seen this place before." So, we knew it would work. When the movie had already been edited and Ennio was working on the music, I said, "Ballads are in these days," to which he answered, laughing, "Are you going to sing it?" but then adding more seriously, "We'd need Baez for that." Soon afterwards I went to the United States to look for archival material to include in the movie, and I stopped off in New York to visit a friend who might help me out. One morning as I was leaving my hotel, I bumped into Furio Colombo who was working there at the time. I told him about the Sacco and Vanzetti project – it was a story he was very familiar with – and about the problems we'd run up against; but also about the idea and faint hope of meeting Joan Baez. His eyes opened wide, and then he said, "She's coming to my house for dinner tonight!" Three years had passed, and finally a stroke of luck. I went up to my room, grabbed the script in English, and asked him to give a copy to Baez. The next day she called me and said, "I'll do it." When I told Ennio he could hardly believe it! Many of the words in the text came from the letters written by Sacco and Vanzetti, which she adapted. The letters were in Italian, but some of them, the ones they wrote from prison to the Defense Committee, were in English.

In your movie *And Agnes Chose to Die*, there's a piece by Morricone that's called *Canzone della nostalgia*. It's melancholy, and so sweet it breaks your heart.

I'm very fond of that movie, because it was really produced by the people of Romagna. They brought everything – the clothes, the bicycles; their participation came from the heart. A movie about women's contribution during the Second World War, women known as 'staffette,' runners or bikers, had never been made before. When a woman rides her bike across those immense plains, the Comacchio Valley, the music has all the space it deserves.

Whenever you commission Morricone to work on one of your movies, at what point does he start composing the soundtrack?

Sometimes I haven't even made the movie yet. Obviously, before he starts composing he's read the script, like that time with Baez. The movie hadn't been made yet, but the music was already inside his head. Then there's the editing phase, and there, along with figuring out the timing, the music is selected. I would go there and I'd see him directing.

Has it ever happened that, when the music has been written and added to the context of the scene, you've particularly liked it?

More than once! On a few occasions I've asked him to choose between two pieces because they were too close musically speaking; and he said no problem at all. He's a very patient man. On that subject, I have two anecdotes for you. While doing the sound mixing for one of his movies, for which Morricone had composed the music, Elio Petri decided to play a trick on him. For the opening credits, he played music that Ennio had composed, but for a different movie. Petri invited him to the screening. I was invited there too. And as we watched, we saw Ennio gradually grow smaller and smaller in his chair. At the end of the roll he said, "Well, I guess if that's how you like it you can leave it." The other story was told to me by my friend Gillo Pontecorvo, a great lover of music. One night he had an idea for a piece and he started whistling it, and to avoid interrupting his idea he continued to whistle, got into his car still whistling, and when he got to Ennio's house, as he rang the doorbell, he kept whistling. Ennio heard him, opened the door and could hear him whistling as he climbed up the stairs. Upon entering Ennio's home, Gillo said, "Ennio, listen to this," to which he replied, "No, you listen," and sat down at the piano to play the same music! Gillo was blown away!

The soundtracks of almost all your films are by Morricone, so you can link the name Montaldo to the Maestro's, the same way that you think of Fellini and Rota, Scola and Trovajoli…

It's a comparison that makes me tremble, but I have to say that I've always had absolute faith in Ennio as a person who has never shown off, never acted like a famous star. What moves me the most is his great generosity at helping you out, giving you advice, always being there for you.

QUENTIN TARANTINO

The Best Ending

[This is an extract from a long conversation between Quentin Tarantino and Christopher Frayling, which took place in Los Angeles at the end of January 2018, and which became the Foreword to Frayling's book, *Once Upon a Time in the West: Shooting a Masterpiece* (Reel Art Press, 2019). Thanks to Christoper Frayling for permission to re-print this extract.]

[…] I think a case can easily be made that Ennio Morricone and Sergio Leone are the greatest composer/director collaboration in the history of film. Even a collaboration as wonderful as the Hitchcock/ Bernard Herrmann collaboration isn't comparable to how important Leone was to Morricone and Morricone was to Leone. You can't even imagine the Leone movies without Ennio Morricone's music. When you think of the *Dollars* trilogy, the whole combination of Leone, Eastwood, and Morricone, those three men came along and changed Westerns – changed the face of cinema with that operatic style, that use of music that was so important ... and completely unheard of at that time. There's an 'opera-ness' about the Leone movies.

[…] Now, with regard to how collaboration between Morricone and Leone affected my films? It affected them in every way, shape, and form that it could. First, think of surf music, Dick Dale [the surf rock guitarist of the early 1960s], and the song *Misirlou*. I never understood what surf music had to do with surfing. To me, it always sounded like a rock'n'roll Spaghetti Western – Morricone music with a guitar-driven beat. I've always said that *Pulp Fiction* was a modern day Spaghetti Western. I started using bits of Morricone music that he'd written for other movies. Then eventually I worked with him as my composer – which I'd never done before with *anyone;* working one to one on music. From surf music, I went to using bits of his music and he did not get it; and then he did – he literally saw it my way – and then we worked together on *The Hateful Eight;* and through all this, our relationship changed.

I had never just worked with one composer before … Ennio Moricone and I have become really good friends. He's been very warm to me, to such a degree that people who know me say 'My God, it's really *obvious* how much he likes you' and it's just an incredibly sweet thing. But for years he didn't get what I was doing when I would use his bits of music from other movies. He thought 'What is the meaning of that?' But then two things happened to change his mind. Initially, he was happy to license the bits to me even though he thought it was nonsense. With *Kill Bill*, he said 'I don't get this. What is this?' He probably didn't like his work being mixed in with other Italian composers. That's the way he felt about it. Then, for two reasons, he basically changed his mind. One, he loved *Inglourious Basterds*; he really liked that movie. And then I think it's obvious that I used *Un Amico* better in *Inglourious Basterds* than Sergio Sollima had used it in *Blood in the Streets* or *Revolver*. And even Ennio saw that: 'Oh, okay. Well, that's a scene worthy of this piece of my music.' And also, since he liked the movie, he understood what I was doing with the music. That's one reason. The other thing that changed his mind is that while conducting concerts, he realised that when he played his music that I had used in my movies, the audience recognised it. They recognised it more from my movies than from the original films; and their response affected him. The fact was 'Hey, they know this song now. I can actually play stuff from *Navajo Joe* and the audience fucking gets it.' And *Inglourious Basterds* was a special one, because he really liked the movie and the way his music worked in it; and also compared to say *Django Unchained* and *Kill Bill*, it wasn't all over the place. Well, that's not even true. There was *The Green Leaves of Summer*, *White Lightning*, *Slaughter,* and Gianni Ferrio's music from *One Silver Dollar* (1965), but I think he ignored that His music was a piece of that movie (music from *A Gun for Ringo*, *The Big Gundown*, *The Battle of Algiers*, *The Return of Ringo*, *A Professional Gun*, *Death Rides a Horse*, *Allonsanfàn,* and *Un Amico*).

[…] I have a cool Morricone story about working with him on *The Hateful Eight*. I think *The Hateful Eight* is one of my best movies – and the end of the movie might be, if not my best ending, one of my best endings of the eight movies I've done. It comes just after the scene where a big deal is made of the Lincoln letter, and then while reading it, two guys who hate each other become bloody brothers as they die. They're gonna die; they're not living through this, right? They're going to freeze to death, bleed to death, something. So, I'm in a different world now. I can't just use any piece of music I want – so I was nervous going into a deal with Morricone because I had never worked with just one composer before. I couldn't just go through my record collection and say 'Hey, let's try this. Let's try that. Let's try this,' which is what I'd done before.

We had already worked out that I was going to use some of the tracks from *The Thing* (1982) and I did tell him that I wanted to use *Regan's Theme/Floating Sound* from *Exorcist II* (1977); and he was cool with that. Again, I'm only using his music; I'm not using other people's stuff. So, everything's fine but then I decide I need a piece of music for that sequence and I know exactly what piece of music I want to use, except it turns out that it's not an Ennio Morricone piece. It's Maurice Jarre's theme from *The Life and Times of Judge Roy Bean*. It's the end piece from that soundtrack album and of course, naturally, it works. In that movie, Lillie Langtry (Ava Gardner) reads the letter from Judge Roy Bean (the 'Miss Lillie Langtry' theme). The Maurice Jarre music works perfectly; it's someone reading a fucking letter. So we try it and, yes, it's amazing. It works magnificently and I'm there with my editor, Fred Raskin, and I say'I can't use it, can I?' I have to give Ennio the chance to do it, otherwise it's disrespectful to him. We made a deal and I can't believe I'm looking at something that works so magnificently and I'm going to discard it but I have to. I made a deal with Ennio and I have to give him the opportunity. If I can't stand what he does, we'll deal with it then but, as great as this is, I've got to give him the opportunity. By the way, my editor Fred is saying this even louder than I am. Fred is saying it works great and I'm saying 'Of course it works great. It's a fucking letter-reading piece of music. Of course it works great.' I say 'Well, let's send it to him with the Maurice Jarre music so that he has an idea about what we like.' We wouldn't say copy the Maurice Jarre music. We just thought we'd send it to him to give him an idea about how it's supposed to work.'

And what he sends back – what he writes for *The Hateful Eight* is closest to a 'Western' piece. It's not like horror movie music that he has written. It's like an old military theme and actually sounds like it could be from *The Good, the Bad and the Ugly*. It's not like the Maurice Jarre piece at all; it is sentimental like the Maurice Jarre piece, but sentimental in a completely different way. It sounds almost like ghostly dead soldiers playing and it really is the most Spaghetti Western piece of music he's written in probably thirty years. But with no words from me; and just hearing it and seeing the scene – everthing else he did fit into the piece. This was a new thing. Oh, and by the way, it wasn't me choosing where to put the music. It was 'I need a piece of music for this, for this emotion.' Everything else in the movie was me laying it in. But with this music, Ennio thought 'No. I have to supply Quentin with this emotion.' And it came to be what I think is one of my best endings; and one of the best pieces of music in the movie, especially in relation to the scene itself.

CARLO VERDONE

"What About the Musician?"

It was June 1979 and I was at Sergio Leone's home to discuss final details before starting to make my first film, *Fun Is Beautiful*. Sergio seemed happy with the crew, whom he had chosen painstakingly. In the previous months, every morning I had to be at his house because he wanted to teach me "the geometry of the shooting." He knew I had graduated from the Corso di Regia at the Centro Sperimentale di cinematografia in Rome, but he still wanted me to learn the many details that a good film director must be familiar with before approaching a movie.

Those were unforgettable days because my teacher was one of the most intelligent film directors Italy has ever known. On the last day I spent the morning at Leone's house; I embraced and thanked him. I was now ready to occupy my production office and move on to choosing the actors. But as I headed for the door leading out of his villa at the Eur, he shouted: "Where do you think you're going?" I stopped short and answered, intimidated, "Well … I thought I'd go to production." To which he replied, "Do you think we have all the collaborators we need? Think again." I shrugged my shoulders and started listing all of them. From the director of photography, to the film editor, to the set designer, to the costume designer, to the props master, and so on. It was an endless list but I knew the first and last names of each one of them. After five minutes I had finished. Frankly speaking, I didn't think anyone was missing. He walked over to me, opened the door, and looking at me in a light-hearted manner he said: "Come with me."

We walked for ten minutes and I didn't ask him anything because he seemed mysterious and resolute. We arrived in front of a large, beautiful villa. Sergio rang the doorbell. At that point I asked, "Whose doorbell are you ringing?" In a low voice Leone replied: "What about the musician, the one who composes the soundtrack?" I was speechless. He was right. We had never discussed the composer for the movie. I said: "Do you have any ideas?" "The idea is the person who is going to open that door."

Another second went by and there at the door to the villa was Ennio Morricone. I could hardly breathe. Morricone knew nothing about the offer that Leone was there to make him. Sergio forced me to tell him about the whole movie, even having me imitate the voices of the characters in all three episodes. I had never been so overwhelmed and embarrassed. Standing before me was the composer I appreciated and loved the most in those years, to the point that I was convinced he would never work for a novice and his budget movie. Instead, he liked the idea. And Sergio's authority almost convinced him right away. After Ennio finally read the script, he accepted unreservedly. It was a special day for me, one of those rare days that you think everything must be a dream.

I didn't feel like suggesting anything to him. I realized that he had perfectly understood the poetry and melancholy of my first work. The first two pieces Ennio played on the piano were already brilliant. He was even more so when I sat in on the final recordings with the orchestra. The arrangements were sublime and classy.

When I came to know him better, I learned that Ennio is a humble man but one who is also very tough when it comes to his work. This absolute professionalism and enchanting inspiration are, I believe, the fruit of his having had a teacher like Goffredo Petrassi; and of having become a member of the *Nuova Consonanza* improvisation group, which stimulated him to compose some of the most avant-garde, most intellectual, and finest music of the 1960s. His all-encompassing musical culture has resulted in an ingenious familiarity with various musical genres, including easy listening. Immense culture, a sense of irony, and creative sensitivity have made him the composer who, more than anyone else, manages to bring out the best in the films that he decides to work on. Still today, I myself am indebted to him for the great success of my first two movies: *Fun Is Beautiful* and *Bianco, Rosso & Verdone*. His music has always been, and will always be, at one with the image. This is the greatness of this mild, kind, funny, curious, and profoundly cultivated man.

GUIDO LOMBARDO
President of Titanus

Ennio and Titanus: An Extraordinary Relationship!

My father told me about the first time he worked with Morricone, on the occasion of Paolo Cavara's docu-film, *Malamondo*, which he produced in 1964. He told me that the music composed by the Maestro was perfect, that it backed and underscored the inquiry into European youths represented in the documentary. The connection between Ennio and Titanus was truly extraordinary, and it added that "extra something" to every film or series that had the honor of being accompanied by the composer's soundtracks.

Three moments can still make my heart beat faster and bring tears of joy to my eyes: one was in 1995, when my father and Ennio were given the Golden Lion Lifetime Achievement Award; another was the time we were all in the small screening room at Titanus and I had the privilege for just a few seconds of hearing Ennio humming the music he had just thought of for *The Law of the Desert*; and the third moment was the morning when, having gone to pick up Giuseppe Tornatore who was making a documentary about my father (*The Last Leopard: Portrait of Goffredo Lombardo,* 2010), Peppuccio asked me to come upstairs for a minute because he wanted me to hear something. As soon as the music began playing, I was enraptured by so much beauty, and Giuseppe said to me: "Guidì, if you like it, Ennio will give it to you with all his heart for your Papa's documentary!"

Many of Titanus' most successful films were commissioned to Maestro Morricone so that the music would always be unforgettable: *The Bird with the Crystal Plumage* and *The Cat o' Nine Tails* by Dario Argento; *Metello*, *La venexiana,* and *The Inheritance* by Mauro Bolognini; and *Property Is No Longer a Theft* by Elio Petri.

DANIELE FURLATI

The Sound of Strings

I met Ennio Morricone for the first time in 1991, in the courtyard of the Accademia Musicale Chigiana in Siena. I was there because the following day the first edition of the 'Composing for Film' course was going to begin; taught by both the Maestro and Professor Sergio Miceli.

I was a seventeen-year-old student at the Conservatory, and I loved Morricone's music, not just the kind he composed for the movies, but his absolute music and his arrangements. In particular, I was fascinated by the sound of the strings, which I thought was a recurring motif in his compositions. Whatever it took, I wanted to understand how he wrote his music. I was obsessed with it, and when I finally had the chance to enroll in those summer courses, I was so happy that I attended the other sessions too, until the last one that was held in 1995.

As soon as I had the chance, I asked the Maestro to explain how he wrote the parts for the strings – sounds that seemed to hover in the air as you listened to them. To my great joy, he went to the blackboard and showed me an example, harmonizing a fragment of the descendant scale of D major with his technique of creating leaps in the voices. Little by little, he revealed his rules: each tension should never resolve and should leap to a distant interval each time. In the end, I was astonished to discover that such an effect could be achieved thanks to a counterpoint of just three voices that moved with those leaps, and without ever coming together.

Of course, I wasted no time trying to imitate him, and later, I brought him my composition for a film to score as a test for the course.

That same year, Sergio Miceli's monograph, *Morricone, la musica, il cinema* was published. I still have a copy of it, with the Maestro's dedication: "For Daniele Furlati, thinking about his composition that I share (too much), with fondest regards." I was convinced that I was going to win the highest award for my creation. But I didn't. Instead, the explanation was that it would have been "like awarding the prize to himself." I remember how angry I was when I read the Maestro's words, how they made me want to throw away the inscribed book. Today, I know that his greatest teaching lay in those very words: to seek my own rules, to find my own way.

NICOLA PIOVANI

Maestros Aren't Born, They're Made

"Maestro" is a term that we Italians use with different meanings beginning in elementary school. I personally enjoy using the word to talk about "master artisans" as a title for those who are in charge of art workshops and sites – master carpenter, master of music, master of dance. In theater, maestro has always been used to refer to the person who directs a musical performance, whether it's the maestro in the orchestra pit, or someone like Herbert von Karajan in the mystical experience of Salzburg.

Maestro is also the word that we Italians use to describe the artist who shows us the way, the person who leads a form of art toward new horizons. It's someone who has young imitators and followers who glean knowledge from his or her teachings; a maestro alters the course of an art genre.

A maestro is also someone who, outside the narrow field of their profession, sets an example for others because of their ethical consistency, and who makes their own strict rules and sticks to them. It is a person who coherently binds their musical score, canvas, or poem – to organicity that is not just aesthetic.

So, when I say Maestro Ennio Morricone, I am using the title of Maestro in every sense of the word: artisanal, artistic, ethical. To me he is all these things and one doesn't need to explain what is common knowledge about the greatness of his art on a global scale – the utmost quality of his music and the communicative power of his miraculous inventions. And these are not just results that have fallen from the sky, the fruit of inspiration – a word that Morricone utters humbly – but also the product of constant and difficult research work, of tireless study, and no doubt, of innate genius. There's an Italian saying, "Maestro non si nasce, si diventa." (Maestros aren't born, they're made.) and I am convinced that this Maestro shares such a belief.

I want to bear witness to the quality of the man, Ennio Morricone, from my own experience. On many occasions, I was struck by his behavior toward me and other young composers. His gestures debunked the stereotype of a super-competitive, jealous artist who envies other people's successes. When Ennio acknowledges the accomplishment of a "colleague," he expresses his approval with joy in his eyes before he proceeds to voice his praise.

I owe him more gratitude than he knows. I learned so much from his work, from the days when, already an affirmed master, he recorded music for Elio Petri and I, a rookie musician, watched him secretly. I would "bribe" the projectionist in the Fono Roma recording studio, near Piazzale Flaminio, and spend hours watching the Maestro at work from the projection porthole – to learn from him, to steal a few tricks. When I say steal I mean it nicely. (As for stealing his music, I'm not the only thief on the planet.) And while I tried to steal some of his approach to the musical task, later it was actually Morricone himself who disclosed to me and taught me intricacies of his fine craft.

Ennio Morricone is famous for his frankness. If he doesn't like what you've written or done, he lets you know. He is direct but more than through words, he expresses his support through deeds. For example, whenever he was the director of a concert season, he always helped his younger, less famous colleagues, including me, by commissioning concerts from us.

We are talking about an artist who, as everyone knows, has touched upon practically every genre and every possible field with his music – and who always excelled at it. His diversity includes symphonic work such as *Le voci dal silenzio*, songs for Mina and Joan Baez, music for Pier Paolo Pasolini's or Carlo Verdone's movies, and also music for his beloved experimental group, *Nuova Consonanza*.

As we celebrate the Maestro's 90th birthday, we see that when he pens a manuscript, he still surprises us with a combative freshness for his composing and a yearning to experiment. He does not repeat himself and amazes us with the beauty of his creativity. If anyone wants to know Ennio Morricone's artistic age with respect to his birth certificate, they should analyze the magnificent score he wrote for Quentin Tarantino's film, *The Hateful Eight*. The Maestro won an Oscar for its Best Original Score in 2016. He continues to demonstrate his capacity to pave new roads for all of us who make music and beyond.

MAURO MAUR

An Inhabitant of Other Marvelous and Diverse Universes

Dug deep down and well-arranged beneath the Basilica del Sacro Cuore in Piazza Euclide, located in Parioli, one of Rome's most elegant quarters, is the Forum Music Village recording studio. It is a piece of history focused on the creation of Italian and international soundtracks. This is where I was rather unexpectedly summoned one morning in 1985 to record a solo for a film. I had just returned after a long period of time spent in France, almost a decade, where I had studied and managed to acquire some valuable experience playing with French orchestras and soloists.

Naturally, I had heard of Ennio Morricone, but I had no idea what he looked like. And so that morning I saw the Maestro looking straight at me from the podium as I put on my earphones, hunted for the right page, and waited for the tap of the baton, the orchestra, and the go-ahead. I played the solo once, a rather long one, and when I had finished, the Maestro took off his earphones, came down from the podium, and walked in my direction. He was staring at me and I remember wondering what I might have done wrong. He walked up to my music stand, looked at me a moment without saying anything, and then asked me: "Do you speak Italian?" to which I replied, "Of course I do!" Maybe he thinks I'm French, I thought to myself, and so I explained: "I'm from Trieste, Maestro. If you want, I can do the solo over again right now. I can do it better," to which he answered, "No, no, it's fine as it is." But I insisted, "Maestro, let me do one more take." In my earphones, they were already announcing the next scene, saying, "Maestro Morricone, it's good, we can go ahead!" That was when I found out the type of person he was. His reply to them was, "Well fine, but let's let him do it over again."

It was the start of many marvelous years spent recording countless splendid movies with him. L'Unione Musicisti di Roma would phone to give me a schedule for so-called "shifts." It took me a while to realize that they were checking my engagements beforehand with the Orchestra Del Teatro Dell'Opera Di Roma, where I was First Trumpet. I was always surprised that it fit right in with my schedule and told them so. Years later I found out how they would laugh about it.

I saw Maestro Morricone work with names such as Franco Zeffirelli, Clint Eastwood, and Giuseppe Tornatore. The man was a genius who was totally immersed in his world, in his grand profession as a pure, true composer like no one else, without settling for second best and without limits, resolute and absolute. I especially loved the tension he created during recording sessions. In those years, there was still a huge movie screen at the Forum. The lights would be dimmed, we could hear the tapping of the baton, the Maestro would give us our cue, and we'd start performing in a fantastic, beautiful, and truly magical way.

After a recording of the opening credits for *In the Line of the Fire* with Clint Eastwood, I told him that he had composed truly magnificently, and that it was as difficult as a trumpet concert. Six or seven months later, I received a call from him. His calls always started like this, enunciating clearly: "Ennio Morricone speaking." But this time what followed was different: "Mauro, your concert is ready." He had written a concert for solo trumpet and orchestra! Magnificent, extremely difficult, historic. I have played it in many parts of the world, and even under his directorship.

It has been a privilege to know him – to work together in extraordinary conditions, to have been given the gift of his friendship. Still today, I think about the fact that I have been able to witness a complex yet simple, extremely profound and totally familiar man; and to act and create from close up with a man who is also undoubtedly an inhabitant of other marvelous and diverse universes.

EDDA DELL'ORSO

The Lady Sings the West

I have a diploma in piano and I studied singing at the Conservatory of Santa Cecilia in Rome under the direction of Maestro Ernesto Brancucci. After two years, I joined the *Cantori Moderni di Alessandroni,* which gave me the chance to make lots of vinyl 45s at RCA studios. During those recordings, Ennio Morricone, who was often there as an arranger, heard my soprano voice. Since I could extend my voice as many as three octaves, he decided to assign me the solo part on his soundtracks.

In my life I have always done what I like, and that is to sing. My soul needed music and I put joy and sorrow into my singing. But because of this passion, I neglected my children. I was lucky to be living with my parents who were like a mother and a father to our kids, because both my husband, Giacomo Dell'Orso, and I were totally devoted to our musical work.

I was fortunate to live at a time with many excellent composers – Piero Piccioni, Armando Trovaioli, and Piero Umiliani, but my name will inextricably be tied to the music of Maestro Morricone, who was particularly close to my way of feeling. One of my favorite titles is, of course, *The Invisible Woman*. Morricone had immense respect for me, so much so that whenever he handed me the score he'd say: "This is the piece…". I'd read it as though I were reading the newspaper, interpreting it on the spot, because the compositions always touched my sensitivity as a singer. Interpreting pieces came naturally to me. It took no effort at all; my voice flowed naturally. Even for the movie *Ecce Homo*, where the score was really complex, I had no difficulty singing it.

I remember asking the Maestro to let me do a piece with lyrics, to which he replied: "Signora, if you sing a song you're going to be like everyone else. This way, you're unique!" I will probably forever be remembered as 'Lady Once Upon a Time in the West', even though it was my performance for *The Good, the Bad and the Ugly* that introduced me to the public at large. In 1971, my voice entered the history of music for films for the main title of Sergio Leone's movie, *Duck, You Sucker*, that everybody knows as *Sean Sean*.

My working relationship with Morricone was exclusively that – it was always about the work, but we still nurtured great mutual esteem; and I was very fortunate to be able to offer my voice to a genius.

GINO PAOLI

The Talent of the Person Who Sings Off-Key

Ennio Morricone was my one-way ticket to freedom when I decided to leave Dischi Ricordi to follow record producer Nanni Ricordi to RCA Italiana. The record company's condition for terminating my contract was that I record one last LP for them. I had my own conditions too, which was actually just one: to have Ennio Morricone arrange the music. I had literally been blown away by some of his work; and I really wanted him to do this. My proposal was accepted, and in 1962 we worked together for the first time, breathing life into *Le Cose dell'Amore*.

From the first time we met, we were always on the same wavelength, except for the fact that the Maestro is terribly out of tune. Whenever he'd mention a piece that he'd listened to, and tried to give me an idea of the melody or hum the refrain, it was horrible. And he's also a very messy person, a genius surrounded by chaos, but still really messy. Whenever a chord or a few notes popped into his head, he'd stop to jot them down on whatever he could find at hand, even a paper tissue. Unfortunately, he wrote the scores for all the instruments not just all together but also sideways. He was the only one who could read them.

Then came the huge success of *Sapore di sale*, success that was mostly due to Ennio's violin arrangement and the sax solo which contributed to making the piece unforgettable and played by Gato Barbieri. I've always been grateful for everything Ennio created for and with me. We have always shared unique harmony when it comes to our aims and ideas. So much so that when I was given an award in Taormina for the sales of *Sapore di sale*, I broke the golden plaque that I was handed onstage in half and gave one half to Ennio. The next assignment that we did together was *Before the Revolution* directed by Bernardo Bertolucci, which introduced us together to the world of cinema. For Morricone, this was followed by movies with Sergio Leone, Duccio Tessari, and others. He invited me to collaborate on the soundtrack for *A Pistol for Ringo*, starring Montgomery Wood, alias Giuliano Gemma. Together we wrote *Angel Face*, a new *Sapore di sale* in Western style; same chords, same melody – another big hit.

GIANCARLO GIANNINI

Music: Universal Language

In 1966, I was supposed to play the part of a singer in a movie made for television called *Lo squarciagola* and directed by Luigi Squarzina. On that occasion, I met Ennio Morricone, who by accompanying me on the piano, taught me to sing and to be on-key when performing two songs that he had written for me.

To my mind, Morricone is one of the greatest musicians ever: he composes, he arranges, and I have often seen him direct music for soundtracks while watching the scenes on a screen. *Mission* is one of his most amazing compositions and it really struck a chord in me. But Morricone is not just a composer for the movies. I read in one of his interviews that he has never liked to write music for the movies, that he actually prefers to experiment.

When filmmaker Gillo Pontecorvo asked him to write the music for *The Battle of Algiers*, the Maestro accepted on the condition that he could compose asynchronous music at an experimental level. He did this and succeeded marvelously.

Asynchronous music was conceived in Russia and is based on contrast. It is different from music that accompanies dialogues and images, and creates a new, unusual and interesting sensation. Few have had the courage to use this format. Morricone was among the first to do so with *The Battle of Algiers* in 1967 and his decision was a far-sighted one.

In my opinion, Italy has had two truly great composers: Nino Rota and Ennio Morricone. Great geniuses often begin with Beethoven and Stravinsky and then elaborate on what they've learned. In Morricone's case, he used his wonderful personality, imagination, and inventiveness to generate masterpieces like the soundtracks written for important films directed by Elio Petri such as *Investigation of a Citizen Above Suspicion*; and Sergio Leone's *Once Upon a Time in America*. For Mauro Bolognini's *Drama of the Rich*, the musical score contributed significantly to the movie's success, accompanying the beautifully poignant images of the Murri family's dramatic tale.

Beethoven believed that music is "the language of God" and therefore, a universal language. While actors have the ability to change the sounds of their voices, music has the power to emotionally penetrate people's sensitivity with notes. Michelangelo and Leonardo da Vinci were both Italians, and fortunately, other geniuses were also born among us. One of those geniuses is Ennio Morricone; and we are proud of him. The Maestro has given us some of the most beautiful music ever written.

LISA GASTONI

Just Get It Done!

Ennio and I were at the start of our respective careers when we first met. He taught music; I believe in Frosinone. Many of the most important movies I acted in were set to music by Ennio.

While making Salvatore Samperi's movie, *Come Play with Me,* I had to leave the set due to a funding problem. When I finally returned to the set, since the money problem still hadn't been solved, I had to wear clothes from my own wardrobe, and do my own makeup and hair. This sacrifice was well worth it if you think of the success with the public and the critics that continues today to accompany *Come Play with Me*. The rhyme that Ennio wrote for the soundtrack is difficult to forget: *Guerra e pace, pollo e brace*.

My first acting success was in *Wake Up and Die* directed by Carlo Lizzani, whom I absolutely adored. He was like an elder brother to me; we were the closest of friends until the day he passed away. Ennio and I met in Lugano, and in the basement of the hotel where we were staying, we attempted the song, *Una stanza vuota*; playing it on an out-of-tune piano. Nevertheless, thanks to his patience and professionalism, Ennio helped me to just get it done!

It was 1966 and I had been summoned to receive the award *La noce d'oro*. Since I couldn't attend in person, I asked Ennio whether, while passing through, he might pick it up for me. And he did as proof of the humility and kindness that are part of his soul! That is perhaps the first thing I remember about Maestro Morricone. The song, *Chi mai*, that the Maestro wrote for the movie, *Maddalena,* was beautiful and poignant. I recorded it in several languages. It's so beautiful that it was also used for the movie, *The Professional*, starring Jean-Paul Belmondo. It wasn't difficult to perform the song and convey all the sensuousness of the character.

In 1975, with Lizzani as director, I also played the part of Claretta Petacci in *Mussolini*. Playing that character took considerable effort and was rather stressful, but it was also something I felt very strongly about because those events of 1945 were not long past. Once again, Ennio's musical commentary accentuated and underscored the drama of the story.

Ennio Morricone is an outstanding talent; and I am happy to say that our relationship is based on great friendship and mutual respect.

FRANCO NERO

"Vamos a matar Franco Nero": Ennio and I

How often can we boast of having met a genius, of having benefited from his friendship? Sometimes never. I, a humble actor who has had a bit of luck in this world, have met more than one genius of the arts, and Ennio Morricone is among them. We go way back, as does his collaboration as the author of soundtracks in over 15 movies I've been in. And when so much time has passed, choosing an anecdote to tell becomes a rather thankless task because there are lots of things I could say about a "monstre sacré" of Italian culture like Ennio; a composer who plays multiple instruments, who added unusual sounds like the bell, the whistle, the Jew's harp, and the cracking of a whip to the musical themes of the West; who created a new style borrowed by his fellow composers from America.

So, I prefer to tell an amusing story that proves how, behind that sublime mind, there's also a wonderful sense of humor. When Ennio composed the music for *Vamos a matar compañeros*, Sergio Corbucci's movie starring myself, Tomas Milian, and Jack Palance, he had me listen to the piece that included the title sung by the chorus. One day, while fooling around with the rhyme between "Compañeros" and "Franco Nero," he said to me, while humming, "You know, at this point they could say, "Vamos a matar, vamos a matar, companerooos, vamos a matar, vamos a matar, Franco Ne-rooo." (Let's go kill, let's go kill, partners. Let's go kill, let's go kill, Franco Ne-rooo). It was perfect!

When the Maestro was given a star on the Hollywood Walk of Fame in 2016, "I was there," as people like to say. Quentin Tarantino was there too. Ennio was the 13th Italian artist to have his name put onto the Walk of Fame, preceded by Rudolph Valentino, the soprano Renata Tebaldi, Toscanini, Anna Magnani, Andrea Bocelli, among others. But even without that star, even without the two Oscars and all the others prizes that he has won over the course of his 500 movies as a composer, he had received the most important award: public appreciation.

Ennio is like Mozart: erudite but popular. And like Mozart, he's also a "madman." Mad because of his imagination, his courage to break away from all the conventions and invent something new. That's the only way that art can move forward. So, God bless the madman! God bless Ennio Morricone!

CHRISTOPHER FRAYLING

The Morricone Affair

[This conversation originated as a Whistledown production for BBC Radio 4, produced by Sarah Cuddon, first broadcast on Saturday 1st November 2008 to celebrate Ennio Morricone's eightieth birthday. It has been specially edited for this book. Thanks to Sarah for her permission.]

CHRISTOPHER FRAYLING [on location in the Piazza Venezia] I've walked past this part of Rome many times – the Piazza Venezia – and people have said to me, 'Ennio Morricone lives somewhere round here.' Well, we're quite close now, with that huge Victor Emmanuel monument next to us, that out-of-scale marble giant known locally as *the typewriter* … Our entry ticket to Ennio Morricone is our interpreter Roberta Rinaldi, who has told us that she has long blonde hair and that she will be standing on the steps leading up to the Campidoglio, the great Michelangelo monument … Let's hope we find her …

Ennio Morricone is the most important – and prolific – living composer of scores for films. In the last 47 years, he has composed and arranged over 400 scores for every possible type of film and worked with 150 directors from Argento to Zeffirelli. In the United Kingdom, he's best known for his work with Sergio Leone on a series of Spaghetti Westerns, or rather Westerns all'Italiana, in the 1960s: this became one of the closest and most innovative partnerships between director and composer in the history of the movies. I've been to Rome many times, researching Sergio Leone and his works, but have never so far managed to pin down the famously shy and elusive Maestro Morricone. A few years ago, when I recorded the radio programme *Desert Island Discs*, I selected his theme 'The Ecstasy of Gold' from *The Good, the Bad and the Ugly* as my one record to take onto a desert island with me, and I've been dying to tell him this for years. Well, at last here we are in Rome to make a radio programme about Ennio Morricone for his eightieth birthday. After some cloak-and-dagger stuff about exactly where he lives, we finally locate our interpreter Roberta Rinaldi, who gives us a few helpful 'dos and don'ts'. Quite a few, it turns out, including don't ask to go anywhere near his soundproofed study with its tight-fitting door.

ROBERTA RINALDI Yes, the key is always in his pocket, and that's the room where he actually composes everything – and if he needs something from the room, he gets the key, opens the door, fetches something, locks the door again and puts the key back in his pocket once more. And he doesn't want his wife to dust the place …

Roberta gives us another gentle warning … about the word 'spaghetti', as in Spaghetti Westerns.

ROBERTA RINALDI He won't answer if you ask him, 'Who is your favourite actor?' And 'Spaghetti Western' is *totally prohibited* in his place – no way, no way. It is not a restaurant, you see. Spaghetti is something that we eat. 'I don't compose things that we eat.'

Christopher arrives at Ennio Morricone's apartment, and is greeted by Ennio.

ENNIO MORRICONE I've always lived in Rome. I've never really been tempted by America, I have to say, although I have recorded in Los Angeles and in New York quite a few times, and I recorded *The Mission* in London. I'd be a supporter of Roma football team even if I went to live in Australia …!

CHRISTOPHER FRAYLING Can I start with something you said about film music: 'The best film music should reveal something which cannot be seen or told. It should illustrate what a film does not express …'

ENNIO MORRICONE Music has its own flexibility. What I mean by this is that it adapts to the cultural sensibilities of the listener. Each listener brings his own ear to a piece of music so it can be interpreted in many different ways, depending on your culture. What I look for as a composer for cinema is the underlying story in a film, the story that cannot be told through images or through dialogue.

CHRISTOPHER FRAYLING So does this understanding of the 'underlying story' depend on a close relationship with the director?

ENNIO MORRICONE Well, the relationship with the director is very important, but what's also important is the need for a cultural exchange between the composer and the director – in any case you need to find common ground, a mutual understanding – either that or the director simply accepts what the composer suggests, which happens sometimes.

Ennio Morricone started his musical career at just nine years old when he enrolled to study trumpet, then harmony, then composition at the Conservatorio of Santa Cecilia in Rome under the composer Gofreddo Petrassi. His father Mario, also a trumpet-player, encouraged this classical training. As a young man Morricone played in his father's nightclub band – while simultaneously composing concert pieces – and then gravitated towards arranging songs, including many for the Italian-American tenor Mario Lanza. He had a big hit with 'Se telefonando' sung by Italian popstar Mina.

MUSIC
Se telefonando

Was his training useful to him as a professional composer?

ENNIO MORRICONE Studying is fundamental for anyone who wants to become a high-level professional, to rise through the ranks – however, my own experience was that, having completed the training, a composer nevertheless has to start from year zero. The course teaches you to write like the greats of the past. I know how to write like Bach, Mozart, Beethoven, Monteverdi because I've learned those techniques, but after that I have to apply what I know. If I'm a slave to what I learned, I won't be a good composer – a good musician, for sure, but not a great composer. However, if I manage to free myself and put in my own blood, my own style, then it will go well. The best composers are the ones who really find their own way.

CHRISTOPHER FRAYLING I can see how such musical versatility would be very useful to a composer for films. You mention Bach, and I know you made a deep study of Bach's music when you were at the Conservatorio – but are there any particular historical periods which continued to appeal to you in your own work?

ENNIO MORRICONE Well, I have a deep love of Gregorian chant, absolutely, yes, I'm in love with Gregorian chant and I study it profoundly even now, and I understand very well what road the Gregorian chant has taken – I understand its origins. It came out of Hebrew chants, which in turn came from Middle Eastern and Greek chants – then from Roman music, the music of troubadours, from the Middle East to Greece to Italy to Germany to England to Ireland and then across the ocean, where it met and mixed with African chants, which led to gospel, negro spirituals … it's a musical journey that starts from ancient music and becomes music that works even now. I'm very much in love with Gregorian chant because I feel it reflects my nature – even when you can't hear it in my work, when I'm writing there is always a bit of ancient mystical music in there.

Morricone started to experiment with writing music for Italian films in the late 1950s, with his first credit in 1961. When Sergio Leone was seeking someone to write the new-style music for his first Western, he discovered he had been at primary school with Morricone in the mid-1930s, and the two men were meeting again for the first time in 28 years. They hit it off immediately and Morricone was hired to compose the music for *A Fistful of Dollars*. This was the start of an extraordinary creative partnership which produced a whole series of legendary film scores by Morricone for what came to be known (by some) as 'Spaghetti Westerns'. These were larger-than-life Westerns, from an Italian perspective, made by young cinéastes who loved the old Hollywood movies but didn't buy their ideology, and they tended to be filmed in Rome, for the interiors, and Almería in Southern Spain for the exteriors. A case of chilli con carnage, as someone said. Morricone's scores were unlike anything cinemagoers had heard before.

CHRISTOPHER FRAYLING What was your working relationship with Sergio Leone …?

ENNIO MORRICONE I have to say it was entirely loving and supportive. Every once in a while, it's true, he would get angry for a minute or I would, then his wife would come over and say, 'Shut up, you two, stop it.' There was total trust between us, and that's what you need to work well together.

Now, I must admit that I was personally responsible for popularising the term 'Spaghetti Westerns' – when I wrote a book with that title – and some people think I invented it, so discussing these films with the great man is a little like walking on eggshells. A case of don't mention the spaghetti.

Because although these Western film scores remain some of Morricone's most famous and best-loved pieces of music, the composer himself feels that this has led to much of his other work being side-lined … and the word 'spaghetti', as we'd been told, is regarded as a putdown in the Morricone household. 'I only wrote the scores of 35 Westerns out of 400,' he tends to say. Only 35! Sounds like a lot to me. Anyway, being very, very careful not to mention the 'S' word, I asked Morricone about the unique sound of his Western scores and where it came from …

CHRISTOPHER FRAYLING You were part of a seminar with John Cage, in 1958 …

ENNIO MORRICONE John Cage was a massive influence on many composers at that time – and I'm talking about avant-garde music but also music in general. For example, he gave importance to the *pauses* in music – the absence of sound – that's something that came from Cage. He also made the *isolated* sound very important … all this led to a correction and therefore Cage influenced all composers, traditional and avant-garde.

CHRISTOPHER FRAYLING Did these ideas have any influence on your Western scores, do you think?

ENNIO MORRICONE This is a lot simpler than it might seem. There's a Swedish Musicologist at the University of Liverpool who said my Western music is Celtic music. I never thought this was true because I didn't really know that kind of music, but coming back to what I was saying earlier about Hebrew chants passing through to England and Ireland, there you may have my love of Gregorian chants again. Therefore to me it seems that this music doesn't have characteristics that are so different from my other music. There is a kind of interior sacredness in killing a person, an infernal sacrality, the devil, a personality but also God, if you like. Pragmatically I tried to translate these experiences into music for the Western. *What a mess I made of this answer.*

CHRISTOPHER FRAYLING But I think you also created an Italian sound for the 'Western all'Italiana' – the maranzano, the arghilophone, these are Italian folk instruments, aren't they, which had never been used in that context before – and it's a whole world away from Aaron Copland and his students Elmer Bernstein and Jerome Moross and all those big symphonic scores for American Westerns …

ENNIO MORRICONE You can find the arghilophone in Korea and Germany as well as Italy! No, if Leone's Italian Westerns had been set in China I would have written the same music. I wasn't influenced by the place and therefore neither by American or Italian folklore, so I just put in the tones, the sounds that felt right …

MUSIC
From the *'Dollars'* films

Whatever Ennio Morricone now says about the sound he produced for the Westerns all'Italiana, I believe it *was* in some ways a distinctively Italian sound – with rural folk instruments which were unusual in a Western setting, and an Italian sense of irony, a down-to-earthness, altogether a more direct musical experience. I also believe that the use of concrete sounds in his scores – whipcracks, bells, anvils, grunts and manly choruses with incomprehensible lyrics – relates to the experiments of John Cage in the 1950s, exploring a variety of sounds and silences in concert settings. As well as attending one of Cage's seminars in 1958, Morricone belonged to an avant-garde music group called Nuova Consonanza in the 1960s and later agreed that this changed his thought processes about making music. Morricone had also been passionate about choral music, since Santa Cecilia days – and one of the very striking things about the Italian Western scores is his choral work with a singing group called the Cantori Moderni led by Alessandro Alessandroni. This was the man who became celebrated as the whistler in Leone's Westerns – and many others besides. Human whistling is used on thirty of Morricone's scores.

ENNIO MORRICONE I can't really remember how it came up. I just came upon the idea and Sergio liked it and decided to use it in the first film, and then he wanted it in the second movie as well, and by the third one I had to say 'That's enough now, no more whistling, we've used it too much now,' and so we used the coyote howl instead for *The Good, the Bad and The Ugly*. In the concert version of this, though, I didn't have the voice or the arghilophone so I simply gave the part to the clarinet.

Such musical punctuation sometimes tells us about what the characters on screen are thinking, sometimes gives us information about their pasts, and always enhances the experience of the visual image. Sergio Leone once said that, 'If it is true that I've created new-style Westerns, then it is the music of Ennio which has made them talk.' Music and image in complete synchronisation. Morricone also used the soprano Edda Dell'Orso – a member of the Cantori Moderni – to take the female vocal line, with her voice used as a musical instrument – and this was yet another revolutionary idea at the time. It started with *For a Few Dollars More* and since then it's been very influential on soundtracks such as *Gladiator* or *Troy*, where the sound of a wailing woman is strongly featured.

ENNIO MORRICONE … because the human voice is the most amazing instrument that exists! We don't need an instrument; we are the instrument – it's us, our body. That's the possibility we have. I'll make some sounds that seem … they're human sounds. [*He makes a variety of sounds.*] The voice can do anything and it's the most amazing instrument that exists. That's why I use it and that's why I love the voice as the principal instrument. We're used to beautiful, sweet voices, but then there are terrible voices, subhuman, dramatic: of evil people, of terrible people. The voice represents all the good and all the bad in human nature: in its tone the voice can represent either. That's why I made for you those horrible sounds just now, *but I would ask you to edit them out because people may not understand the reason why I made those sounds!*

In 1968 Morricone took his work on Westerns up a few notches with the richer, more textured score for the film *Once Upon a Time in the West*. This was the full package – with a soaring soprano voice, clever orchestration of strings, heavy-metal guitar – plus banjo and whistling, all written *before* the film was shot, and played on the set. Leone wanted 'a fresco on the birth of a great nation', and that's what he got. When in the film Claudia Cardinale, as Jill McBain, first arrived at the train station, the speed of the camera crane was exactly governed by the musical crescendo Morricone had already written. And there was that opening at Cattle Corner, with three *pistoleros* waiting for a train. The idea of using amplified natural sounds rather than music originated in a concert in Florence – where a performance artist created music out of a metal ladder held close to the microphone …

ENNIO MORRICONE I did tell Leone about that concert in Florence and the idea came from that – but it was *his* idea to start with those twenty minutes of sounds, everyday sounds; real sounds, when taken out of context, out of their reality, or isolated, become something else.

Part of this fearlessness, this exuberance, was the use of strange musical sounds to embellish a character on the screen – often in playful ways – much in evidence in his score for *A Fistful of Dynamite*, made a couple of years after *Once Upon a Time in the West*. One of the centrepieces is 'The March of the Beggars', which includes a jaunty march played on a pennywhistle, some bars of music borrowed from Mozart and burping sounds – 'wap, wap, wap'. I'd often wondered if it was Morricone himself who supplied the burps – so I asked him.

ENNIO MORRICONE Yes. It was me. As it was a march of the beggars, I had to create the musical symbol of people with full bellies, fat stomachs because they've just eaten after being so hungry for such a long time. I wanted to include that rhythm of a hiccup, and that's what I wanted to show – but it was just a bit of fun …

Sometimes playful, sometimes threatening – with childlike melodies building up to something much more sinister – which you don't see but you hear. In the late 1960s and 1970s, he collaborated with director Dario Argento on some of his films known as *Gialli* – films with yellow covers, like the books – which included *The Bird with Crystal Plumage* and *Four Flies on Grey Velvet*. Again, Morricone developed a distinctive sound which revolutionised the use of music in thrillers and horror films: people groaning or gasping in the background, or a soprano singing 'la la la la' like a spiteful little girl, or even music which sounded religious. In *Four Flies*, the piece called 'Like a Madrigal' – which sounds as if you might hear it in a church – accompanies a decapitation in slow motion!

ENNIO MORRICONE In those first three films by Dario Argento, I did experiment with those strange, traumatic noises. I was trying to transmit through music what I felt about those characters' sufferings, about their distorted states of mind. They were the sounds of that time, they seemed right. I told Argento what I wanted to do and he didn't try to influence me at all; I worked in tranquillity and serenity. And he accepted these experiments. But the films were commercial, so the music couldn't be an obstacle – I invented some very original music then.

CHRISTOPHER FRAYLING What about the use of childlike sounds, or children's voices …

ENNIO MORRICONE Children's voices have such a special sound – from their tone you can infer aspects of their personality – innocence, simplicity. I've written for children's voices and I've used them for more revolutionary purposes, for devilish, infernal, bestial things as well.

One of Morricone's best-known scores, again beyond his work in the Western, is for Gillo Pontecorvo's award-winning film of 1966 *The Battle of Algiers*, about the Algerian war of independence of ten years earlier. Pontecorvo chose Morricone as a composer, because he loved what had been achieved in *For a Few Dollars More*. *The Battle of Algiers* included a minimalist march with percussion, horn and piano for the arrival of the French paras, Gregorian chant for the torture sequences, a mixing of sound effects and music, and a simple, lyrical four-note theme for freedom-fighter Ali La Pointe. This score was Morricone's first really high-profile non-Western soundtrack – but the credits mysteriously said 'music by Ennio Morricone and Gillo Pontecorvo'. A unique shared credit.

ENNIO MORRICONE Gillo Pontecorvo called me up and said, 'I've got a contract with this producer to compose this music but I want *you* to compose the music. My name will still have to be on the credits, though …' But I have to say that the suggestions Gillo gave me for *The Battle of Algiers* were very important, not just for this film but for the rest of my career. In fact that theme 'dah da da dah da', he actually wrote that and then I worked on various variations of it. [*We sing the theme together.*] He gave it an ethnic value, and its repetition gave it a harsh, primitive sonority. This was minimalism before minimalism had been invented.

CHRISTOPHER FRAYLING I once asked Gillo how much he had composed of *The Battle of Algiers* and he replied 'Four notes.'

ENNIO MORRICONE Yes, that's about right. He was telling the truth. [*Laughs*] On that occasion!

By the mid-1970s, Morricone already had an astonishing number of film scores to his name. Bernardo Bertolucci joked that it was impossible to see a major Italian film at that time without music supplied by Ennio. Westerns, thrillers, historical epics, romances, horror movies, costume dramas, mafia stories, comedies, erotic films, agitprop, A movies and B movies – everything from the Old Testament and the *Arabian Nights* to films with bizarre titles such as *What Did Stalin Do to Women?*. It has to be said that some of the Maestro's musical themes have become so popular and ubiquitous that they can be heard in elevators and waiting rooms across the globe.

MUSIC
Chi Mai

This tune, which is so instantly recognisable as Muzak, has worked its way into just about every corner of international pop culture – the neo-baroque melody on strings; the astonishing use of the drum-kit, almost the star of the show. It is a beautiful, irritatingly catchy piece known as 'Chi Mai' – originally written for the film *Maddalena* in 1971, recycled for *Le Professionnel* ten years later, and in Britain used for the television series *The Life and Times of David Lloyd George* … What did Ennio Morricone think about this kind of musical recycling?

ENNIO MORRICONE I've already talked about the flexibility music has and how its interpretation depends on the musical culture of the listener. I can't really judge how it's used – if you do it just because it's a nice tune, that's superficial; if you do it because you think it means something, it might be right, it might be wrong … The piece has its own strange sensuality. I'm pleased that it's used – it can be very powerful – but then I also ask myself if they were right to use it.

When I mentioned that his iconic tune 'Chi Mai' had also been used as the main theme for a BBC drama series about the life of a well-known Welsh prime minister, he just rolled his eyes and shrugged. There certainly came a point in the mid-1970s when he had become so famous and prolific that he had to be careful to retain his hard-won credibility. He was also bringing up three sons and a daughter. But he always remained aloof from the celebrity circuit, shied away from media attention, led a quiet, utterly studious life – a life which was always deeply attached to the Catholic Church – an influence which is clearly present in his music. For example, there's his continuing affection for Gregorian chant – and his admission that 'there is always a bit of ancient mystical music in there …'

This sense of the 'mistica musicale antica' became a powerful element in one of Morricone's most celebrated scores of the 1980s, for Roland Joffé's film *The Mission* – a film which the composer has always said he feels particularly attached to. It's about a Jesuit priest, played by Jeremy Irons, in 1750s South America – and it's also about the healing power of music, when the Jesuit high command and the Guarani Indians find themselves on opposing sides. The resulting score should have won an Academy Award.

ENNIO MORRICONE It's a film in which I certainly recognise myself technically and spiritually. Because I was working within three elements, so I wrote a theme for the oboe that took account not just of the language and culture of the Jesuits but unfortunately also of the fact that Jeremy Irons couldn't really play the oboe – to start with, he just moved his fingers at random. The second element I took into account was 'Palestrinian Polyphony'. Because before the Council of Trent and the Counter-Reformation people used to casually combine sacred texts with profane melodies and sacred melodies with profane texts – which is something that's still done now! – according to the Second Vatican Council, anyway. The Council of Trent, according to some accounts, tried to bring some coherence to this … and the finest exponent of the polyphonic treatment of sacred texts at that time was Palestrina, who was involved in the debates. Where the folk music in the film was concerned – the third element – I was creating an illusion because I had none of the indigenous musicians or instruments. I wasn't even familiar with the music of the Indios – so I had to invent something that I felt was right, that I felt could have been. These were the three main elements.

MUSIC
The Mission: *Gabriel's Oboe* and *The Falls*

Ennio Morricone has no time for composers who pick out a tune on the piano and send it off to be arranged by someone else. They aren't composers at all, he says. He sees composition and orchestration as parts of a single process, and he writes every single note on the manuscript paper himself – in that soundproofed study with just one key. He sits in front of 32-stave manuscript paper and fills it in from out of his head – without the use of a piano or any other reference point. A truly remarkable gift.

CHRISTOPHER FRAYLING [on location at Forum Studios] Since the 1960s, Ennio Morricone has nearly always recorded in Rome, and when in Rome, since 1969, has always recorded here at the Forum Music Village, this recording studio which he co-founded, situated beneath the Sacro Cuore di Maria. It has a very special acoustic, and is particularly well-known for accommodating the rich, full sound of a church organ. Morricone has usually worked here with the same musicians – the Rome Sinfonietta, which used to be known as the Unione Musicale di Roma (The Music Union of Rome). And he would use this orchestra, sometimes augmented with students from the Santa Cecilia Academy, or teachers, and also virtuoso trumpet-players, harmonica-players, or the whistler Alessandro Alessandroni and members of his choir. You can imagine him sitting here at the console – there's the chair and the desk – directing operations, getting all those strange sounds happening at the same time as the orchestral music. It is really very evocative being here.

CHRISTOPHER FRAYLING Gabriele, you work here in the studio [as a recording engineer]: is Ennio Morricone a hard taskmaster to work with; I imagine he is an absolute perfectionist in everything he does …?

GABRIELE Yeah, he is – the music must really be perfect. And he is very fast, I have to say. One of the most impressive things about Ennio Morricone is that he comes into the studio knowing *exactly* what he wants to do: every take, every overdub. He comes into the studio at eight o'clock in the morning and by seven o'clock in the evening he is done.

CHRISTOPHER FRAYLING Ennio, you have composed over 400 film scores, 500 arrangements of popular songs and about 100 concert pieces. If you do the math, this works out to about 40-45 years of solid work without a break …

ENNIO MORRICONE … because this is all I know how to do, it's what I do, I do it every day, I have a strict routine, I'm a very diligent person. When someone actually counted up everything I've done and gave me the figures, I nearly fell off my chair – I had no idea.

MUSIC
Once Upon a Time in America
and *Cinema Paradiso*

Ennio Morricone is particularly good, in his music from the 1980s onwards, at capturing nostalgia – without falling into the usual sentimentality. He has been called 'a composer who is always coming to terms with his own past … as if he has lost something and is trying to find it again'. I had to ask him what *he* remembered of his own experiences as a child and teenager in Rome, growing up during the Second World War – when Mussolini was in charge, then the Nazis occupied Rome, then the victorious Allies came to liberate the city. He played the trumpet with his father … was this something to be nostalgic about …?

ENNIO MORRICONE I have to say that, on the contrary, that era was a sad time for me. Because the English and the Americans were in Italy, and the Canadians … the Germans had been there as occupiers. When I played for the Germans, the Americans, the Canadians, the English, the South Africans, it wasn't a happy time for me – I never said that, I never thought that. If anything, it was an unhappy time because I had this instrument which I had studied, and I was using it only to earn money. It was a very hard time – because of the war, things hadn't gone well, times were hard and so I had to earn money. So I played just to be given a few cigarettes, which I then sold for food to bring home.

CHRISTOPHER FRAYLING [on location in a Roman record store] Here we are, under 'Colonne sonore' – M for Morricone – there's a whole rack of CDs here. The Platinum Collection, the Supergold edition of six CDs, 100 tracks, the Greatest Hits, the Love Themes, the Westerns … Ennio may say that his music for the Westerns all'Italiana wasn't particularly significant – but all those anthologies of tracks include the '*Dollars*' films, *Once Upon a Time in the West*, *The Big Silence*, *Companeros*, and others … At least half the selections here are from the Western soundtracks – they are evidently the most popular ones even in Italy, just as they are in England …

In recent years, Ennio Morricone has given more time to writing classical pieces for performance – still working regularly with the Rome Sinfonietta. He likes to combine in his concerts a sonata or concerto – or even a cantata – with his better-known film pieces, which doesn't always go down too well with *The Good, the Bad and the Ugly* crowd. When I was in Rome to see him, he had a big concert in honour of the Olympics at the Auditorium. I have to admit I'm not as familiar with all his classical work as I am with his film scores – but I did take time to buy a copy of the 28-minute orchestral piece 'Voci dal Silenzio' ('Voices of Silence'), which he originally wrote in response to September 11th – 'Concerto contro tutte le stragi della storia, dell'umanità' – which was recorded live at the Arena di Verona on September 11th 2004 and which is a very moving piece of choral music, featuring music and voices which are usually silent.

MUSIC
Voci dal Silenzio

ENNIO MORRICONE I immediately wanted to write the piece after 9/11, but then I extended the dedication to all the tragedies and massacres of the modern world. Why 'silent voices'? Because that American tragedy in New York was talked about a lot, it got a lot of exposure in the media, but other tragedies and massacres that happen every day are not heard about so much. That's why I wanted to dedicate it to all those who die in silence – also our silence because we know nothing about it. So I expanded the original dedication and added other voices of silence to it.

But I must say – and so must a lot of other listeners – that it is his film scores we hold most dear. Morricone is still uneasy about this reputation, even after all these years. He still talks about feeling ostracised by the elite classical music establishment in Italy and especially Rome. Like many people who achieve the heights, they still feel there is something that means a lot to them – which they *haven't* yet achieved. For the rest of us, his astonishing achievements as a composer for film speak for themselves …

CHRISTOPHER FRAYLING I know Ennio doesn't like being asked what his favourite piece of his own music is, but I want to tell him what *my* favourite piece of film music that he has written is – and that is the three minutes and twenty seconds of 'The Ecstasy of Gold' from *The Good, the Bad and the Ugly*, with Tuco running round and round Sad Hill cemetery. I think this is the finest piece of film music he has ever composed …

ENNIO MORRICONE Well, it's a piece of cinema that pleases me too. That music suffered from one of the difficulties of film-scoring, the timing of the film and the need to synchronise. Nobody ever cares about these things, but in those three minutes and twenty seconds there was so much action, and in this piece I succeeded in giving the music a unified feel whilst still respecting the timing and synchronisation of the images.

CHRISTOPHER FRAYLING Ennio, can I wish you a very happy eightieth birthday on November 10th?

ENNIO MORRICONE Who told you I am eighty? It is not true!

CHRISTOPHER FRAYLING What age are you, then?

ENNIO MORRICONE Ten years less. That's a mistake that needs to be corrected.

CHRISTOPHER FRAYLING I was never very good at math … Arrivederci.

ENNIO MORRICONE Grazie …

CHRISTOPHER FRAYLING [to Roberta as they leave] He is a very abstract thinker, isn't he – at his most comfortable when talking in abstract terms about his music.

ROBERTA RINALDI Yes – and, as you will have heard from his reaction, he enjoyed that conversation very much.

CHRISTOPHER FRAYLING The best moments, for me, were … to be singing a duet of the theme from *The Battle of Algiers* with Ennio Morricone … and to hear him confirm that 'The Ecstasy of Gold' is amongst *his* favourites as well. These were very memorable moments for me.

GERMANO BARBAN
MAURIZIO BARONI

About This Book

The book you are holding and are about to leaf through is the result of long and passionate work with the purpose of celebrating the most famous and cherished composer alive: Maestro Ennio Morricone. It is a tribute that, by way of the album covers of all the soundtracks that he has ever composed, we can bear witness to that extraordinary, amazing universe composed of shapes and colors, and of the music that for over half a century has accompanied our lives.

Throughout the complex and articulated drafting of this book, we often tried to go even further, because the material that we were covering lent itself to that possibility. However, the territory was endless and to be able to acquire all of it, we would have needed an entire theme-based encyclopedia; and we would still have run into obstacles due to the fact that, up to now, some parts of said territory have only partially been explored. Ennio Morricone has devoted his entire life to music, sharing all its creative and artistic expressions: from popular music of the years of the Italian economic miracle, to various movie genres like Comedies, Westerns, Dramas, and Thrillers. He has written songs that have become very famous, scored music for documentaries, crafted leitmotifs for advertising, written music for the theater, and for radio and TV jingles; and he has also arranged music written by other composers. And as if that weren't enough, he has alternated this work with his efforts to conduct pure sound research through experimentation and the avant-garde, chamber music, and new forms of absolute music; all within an immense, endless repertoire that has become a cornerstone of music history.

Considered one of the most prolific and versatile composers of our day and age, Maestro Morricone's work has influenced the musical tastes and the directions taken by several generations of musicians and composers who have trained in the past few decades. But perhaps what he has conveyed most incisively is the profound rigor with which a musician must approach his or her music – an attitude that has always guided and edified his genius and that meanwhile has grown to global importance.

The indexes – compiled and perused with a fine-tooth comb to ensure their accuracy – of more than five hundred soundtracks composed by Morricone for cinema and TV, also include works that were not recorded and regrettably never released. To be honest, there are very few pieces unrecorded and unreleased, but the images contained here bear witness to the most significant and important recorded releases for each soundtrack. Among them are a few cases of true, absolute rarity. This makes record collecting one of the cardinal points in Ennio Morricone's story; within the historical context of his work and of the appreciation he has been given by millions of people around the world.

It might seem superfluous to emphasize the vast number of records produced with Ennio Morricone's music. In some particularly successful instances, there can even be as many as hundreds of different releases across the world, without among other things, counting the re-issues that have been made over the course of the years. To these, we must add the hundreds of collections dedicated to him as a solo artist or together with other artists. Nonetheless, an estimate that is even just an educated guess becomes such a complex and demoralizing calculation that one could easily surrender the quest. At times, a statement that encompasses every abstract or material idea about this amazing figure can be enough. What we mean to say here is demonstrated by the anonymous music lover who, several years ago, when asked about Ennio Morricone's music, made a statement that was as enigmatic as it was revealing: "Morricone's music? It's like listening to the light."

Before going right to the heart of this book, the reader should be informed about Ennio Morricone's recording output, of which, as we all know about this 'universal' composer, has not been restricted to film music. However, it is also true that without the many collections of theme songs from film soundtracks, the enjoyment of his music by film music enthusiasts and fans in general might have waned. In fact, in the golden years, generally believed to be the 1960s and 1970s, many records with these soundtracks on them, with the exception of the most successful titles, were difficult to find.

The several reasons for this were all linked to choices made by record producers and the chronic complexity in commercially distributing records in Italy. The availability of Morricone's records, like those of many other artists, even went so far as to become like an unattainable mirage when they were compositions that were unrelated to film music; that is, records containing free compositions or background music. Much of the Maestro's background music is no longer for sale because it was produced in small numbers and destined for the radio-television circuit in documentaries and TV specials. These are recordings whose existence has practically always been unknown. They only recently entered the record collecting circuit and, owing to their rarity, often at exorbitant prices.

It is a different story with the repertoire of experimental music and sound research pursued by Morricone together with his improvisation group, *Nuova Consonanza*. The group was attended by more or less famous fellow composers such as Franco Evangelisti, Egisto Macchi, and Walter Branchi; and the aim was to create a musical ensemble devoted to contemporary experimentation that went beyond composition. In this case, seeing the experimental nature of the work and the difficulty that the ordinary listener might have in approaching it, the production of these records was very small, and they were only distributed through a tiny number of sales outlets.

The contents page contain the reproduction of some of the album covers that we describe here, which can boast, in addition to their contents and rarity, a wide range of forms and colors of remarkable graphic artistry – proof of the successful fusion between two sophisticated and exceptional art forms.

Key

TV show

Year	1965
Original title	**Agent 505 Todesfalle Beirut**
Italian title	La trappola scatta a Beirut
English title	*Agent 505: Death Trap in Beirut*
French title	Baroud à Beyrouth pour F.B.I. 505
Code	LP 33g - GDM EP 6707

ACCADEMIA MUSICALE CHIGIANA
SIENA 199
GIULIANO GHIRARDI
FRANCO DONATONI
ENNIO MORRICONE
Gruppo Octandre
"FESTA DELLA DONNA"
CONCERTO
STRAORDINARIO
VENERDI 8 MARZO 1996 - ORE 21,00
PARADISO

IL FABBRO ARMONIOSO
ORCHESTRA GIOVANILE DELLA MARSICA
BANCA POPOLARE DELLA MARSICA
coin
FRANCESCO
PAPA

QUANDO LE DONNE AVEVANO
Colonna sonora originale
Album originale
1. Quando le donne avevano la coda
2. Nascita di Filly 2:51
3. Can can delle 'Filly' 5:33
4. Marcetta dei sette 2:09
5. I civettoni 4:20
6. Ulli, Grr, Maluc, Put, Uto, Zog, Kao
7. Balletto dell'uova 1:40
8. Can can delle 'Filly' 4:02
9. Pantomima della caverna 3:04
10. Introduzione all'introduzione di un
11. Preludio alla gioia 1:59
Nuovo Cinema Paradiso - bozza
The FabMax Company
presenta
NUOVO
CINEMA
PARADISO
dall'omonimo film di Giuseppe Tornatore
musiche di
Ennio e Andrea Morricone
adattamento di
Jaja Fiastri e Stefano Genovese
Regia di
Bozza di una

ORIA
NITA
ael Ende
tazione teatrale
bert Henning

ENTE DAVID DI DONATELLO
DEL PRESIDENTE DELLA REPUBBLICA
ACCADEMIA DEL CINEMA ITALIANO
PREMI DAVID DI DONATELLO
SOTTO L'ALTO PATRONATO
DEL PRESIDENTE DELLA REPUBBLICA
MIGLIORE MUSICISTA
Roma, 2013

TO
IN RECOGNITION OF
AND MULTIFACETED
THE ART OF FILM MUSIC
2006
PARDO D'ON
AL COMPOSITO
ENNIO MORRI
PER LA CARRIE
FESTIVAL INTERNAZIONAL
LOCARNO

OPERA
Richard III
Ennio Morricone
TEATRO ALLA SCALA
FILARMONICA DELLA SCALA
CORO FILARMONICO DELLA SCALA
ENNIO MORRICONE
ANABOX 7 GIORNI
MSC

La Musica e la Bibbia
MUSICA PRIMA
OPERE IN DISCO
50 anni di musica
TOSCA

TEATRO
SCALA

Auditorio
di via della Conciliazione
Daniele Gatti
Roberto Fabbriciani
Rocco Filippini
Berlioz
Morricone
Stravinsky
Strauss
Auditorio
di via della Conciliazione
Ennio Morricone
CASIO
TV-470
Carlsen

ARLP 2002 A

Colonna sonora origir

1. TEOR
2. FRAMM
3. FRUSCIO DI FOGLI
4. L'ULTIMA
5. BEAT

Musica composta
Diretta da
Brani n
« I CANTORI MODER
Brano n. 3 «
* Testo

1961—1969

Lunga Durata
33 ⅓ giri

Facciata 1

del film "Teorema"
4'15"
I 2'30"
RDI (cantato) 2'25" •
RIDA 2'40"
2'47"
E. MORRICONE
NICOLAI
-4 con
I ALESSANDRONI »
O JUNIOR »
Nhora

Discography

1961 — 1969

1961
Piccolo concerto, Enzo Trapani
The Fascist, Luciano Salce
Ventimila leghe sotto i mari, Francesco Ghedini

1962
A Girl... and A Million, Luciano Salce
Caccia ai corvi (TV), Anton Giulio Majano
Crazy Desire, Luciano Salce
Eighteen in the Sun, Camillo Mastrocinque
I drammi marini (TV), Mario Landi
I motorizzati, Camillo Mastrocinque

1963
Beautiful Eyes, Lucio Fulci
Gli italiani e le vacanze, Filippo Ratti
La fidanzata del bersagliere, Paolo Ferrero
Musica Hotel, Enzo Trapani
Ndriringhete'ndrà, Enzo Trapani
Smash, Enzo Trapani
The Basilisks, Lina Wertmüller
The Little Nuns, Luciano Salce
The Success, Mauro Morassi
Tutto è musica, Domenico Modugno

1964
A Fistful of Dollars, Sergio Leone
Before the Revolution, Bernardo Bertolucci
Biblioteca di Studio Uno, Antonello Falqui
Centrale elettronucleare del Garigliano, Daniele G. Luisi
Full Hearts and Empty Pockets, Camillo Mastrocinque
Gunfight in the Red Sands, Riccardo Blasco
In ginocchio da te, Ettore Maria Fizzarotti
Two Escape from Sing Sing, Lucio Fulci
Ma l'amore no, Romolo Siena
Malamondo, Paolo Cavara
Multmir 1 – Mondo animato n. 1, Autori vari
Pistols Don't Argue, Mario Caiano
The Twelve-Handed Men of Mars, Franco Castellano e Giuseppe Moccia

1965
A Pistol for Ringo, Duccio Tessari
Agent 505: Death Trap in Beirut, Manfred R. Kohler
Fists in the Pocket, Marco Bellocchio
For a Few Dollars More, Sergio Leone
Half a Man, Vittorio De Seta
Highest Pressure, Enzo Trapani
Idoli controluce, Enzo Battaglia
Mare contro mare, Romolo Siena e Lino Procacci
Menage Italian Style, Franco Indovina
Mi vedrai tornare, Ettore Maria Fizzarotti
Mission Bloody Mary, Sergio Grieco
Nightmare Castle, Mario Caiano
Non son degno di te, Ettore Maria Fizzarotti
Rotocalco, Mario Landi
Se non avessi più te, Ettore Maria Fizzarotti
Senza fine, Vito Molinari
Snow Job, Luciano Salce
Stasera Rita, Antonello Falqui
The Return of Ringo, Duccio Tessari
Thrilling, Carlo Lizzani, Gian Luigi Polidoro, Ettore Scola

1966
El Greco, Luciano Salce
For a Few Extra Dollars, Giorgio Ferroni
How I Learned to Love Women, Luciano Salce
Lo squarciagola, Luigi Squarzina
Navajo Joe, Sergio Corbucci
Seven Guns for the MacGregor, Franco Giraldi
The Battle of Algiers, Gillo Pontecorvo
The Big Gundown, Sergio Sollima
The Good, the Bad and the Ugly, Sergio Leone
The Hawks and the Sparrows, Pier Paolo Pasolini
The Hellbenders, Sergio Corbucci
The Hills Run Red, Carlo Lizzani
The Witches (Segment: *La terra vista dalla luna*), Pier Paolo Pasolini
Wake Up and Die, Carlo Lizzani

1967

Arabella, Mauro Bolognini
China is near, Marco Bellocchio
Death Rides a Horse, Giulio Petroni
Dirty Heroes, Alberto De Martino
Face to Face, Sergio Sollima
Garden of Delights, Silvano Agosti
Grand Slam, Giuliano Montaldo
Her Harem, Marco Ferreri
Listen, Let's Make Love, Vittorio Caprioli
Mission Top Secret, Alberto Lattuada
Musica da sera, Enzo Trapani
Operation Kid Brother, Alberto De Martino
The Girl and the General, Pasquale Festa Campanile
The Rover, Terence Young
Up the MacGregor, Franco Giraldi

1968

A Fine Pair, Francesco Maselli
A Quiet Place in the Country, Elio Petri
A Sky Full of Stars for a Roof, Giulio Petroni
Comandamenti per un gangster, Alfio Caltabiano
Danger: Diabolik, Mario Bava
Eat it, Francesco Casaretti
Escalation, Roberto Faenza
Fräulein Doktor, Alberto Lattuada
Galileo, Liliana Cavani
Guns for San Sebastian, Henri Verneuil
Machine Gun McCain, Giuliano Montaldo
Once Upon a Time in the West, Sergio Leone
Partner, Bernardo Bertolucci
Tepepa, Giulio Petroni
Thank You, Aunt, Salvatore Samperi
The Great Silence, Sergio Corbucci
The Mercenary, Sergio Corbucci
Theorem, Pier Paolo Pasolini

1969

A Brief Season, Renato Castellani
Alibi, Adolfo Celi, Vittorio Gassman, Luciano Lucignani
Bandits in Rome, Alberto De Martino
Behold Man. The Survivors, Bruno Alberto Gaburro
Burn!, Gillo Pontecorvo
Dirty Angels, Mauro Severino
Geminus (Series), Luciano Emmer
Giovanni ed Elviruccia (Series), Paolo Panelli
H 2 S, Roberto Faenza
Il libro dell'arte: Giotto, Luciano Emmer
Kill the Fatted Calf and Roast It, Salvatore Samperi
Love Circle, Giuseppe Patroni Griffi
Mother's Heart, Salvatore Samperi
Season of the Senses, Massimo Franciosa
Senza sapere niente di lei, Luigi Comencini
She and He, Mauro Bolognini
That Splendid November, Mauro Bolognini
The 5-Man Army, Italo Zingarelli
The Fifth Day of Peace, Giuliano Montaldo
The Invisible Woman, Paolo Spinola
The Lady of Monza, Eriprando Visconti
The Red Tent, Mikhail Kalatozov
The Sicilian Clan, Henri Verneuil
What Did Stalin Do to Women?, Maurizio Liverani

1961
Piccolo concerto
45 rpm - RCA PM45 - 3038

In 1961, Ennio Morricone was already very active in the light music sector as an arranger and an orchestra conductor for some of Italy's most famous singers. This allowed him to work consistently in the context of RCA and Radio Televisione Italiana, which often commissioned him to write singles. A case in point is the *Piccolo concerto*, a six-part musical performance directed by Enzo Trapani. The foundations that would lead the composer to increasingly work for the cinema were reinforced with this project. Naturally, because so much time has passed, much of the information that concerns Morricone's work during those first years is often difficult to track down, and in some cases the facts are inaccurate, such as for the short *Verrò* e *Vicino al ciel*, whose theme songs, sung by Milva, are attributed by many sources to Ennio Morricone, misled by the name "Morrione" that appears on the records and is understood to be a printing error. In actual fact, the two songs were written by the composer Mario Marletta with lyrics by Paolina Morrione, and therefore have nothing to do with Maestro Ennio Morricone.

IL CANTASTORIE

EDIZIONI LETTERARIE RCA

VENTIMILA LEGHE SOTTO I MARI

30-C-8/9

1961

Ventimila leghe sotto i mari

LP 33 rpm - RCA 30-C 8/9
45 rpm - RCA 7DP 200

Il federale - M° E. Morricone 6

I5 ocir mono - Rg International I9.I0.I96I

I°sostola

M I5(canto)/I°	cori (stranieri); cantato in inglese da coro maschile sul tema di "Rosamunda"; come di soldati stanchi e un po' ubriachi	0,50
M I5(canto)/2°	id.	0,48
I5(canto)/3°	id.	0,48
I5(canto)/4°	id.	0,49
I5(Canto)/5°	id.	0,52
I5(canto)/6°	id. con vitalità come di soldati in marcia	0,55
I6/I°	? [effetti vari; parlato in americano da un gruppo con battute di scherno ai fascisti	0,39
I6/2°	[id.	0,39
4(canto/I°	scarto	0,I0
4(canto)/2°	scarto	0?II
4(canto)/3°	scarto	0,59
4(canto)/4°	scarto	0,38
4(canto)/5°	scarto	I,00
4(canto)/6°	cori; canto battagliero di marinai italiani dell'epoca fascista; marcia ITALIANO	I,02
4(canto)/7°	scarto	0,48
32	paesaggi/campagne; per piccolo organico con canto per oboe e flauto	0,35
9	stacchi/giallo rosa; moderato per piccola orchestra; in prevalenza effetti con fiati evidenziati; finalino a salire con pieno di strumenti	0,27
I5	grottesco/giallo rosa; dapprima lento, poi piu' mosso (0,33) per piccola orchestra: legni, tromba con sordina, basso tuba e archi; dapprima solo effetti poi accenni a melodia per archi 51	I,03

CAM - DET T 5

NO M15 CANTO 5° 3 TEMPO 0'48" CANTATO

1961

Il federale

The Fascist

Mission ultra-secrète

EP 45 rpm - RCA PME 30-477

LP 33 rpm - DOXI CINEMATIC DOC 143

The Fascist was the first cinema score written and orchestrated by Ennio Morricone and was directed by Pierluigi Urbini. This is a pioneering work, in which we can already hear many of those elements that would characterize future compositions by the Maestro. A kaleidoscope of sonorities, where irony, drama, sentiment, and the search for sounds, at the same time strange and irreverent, are combined to bring the entire soundtrack to life, and greatly contribute to the quality of the film.

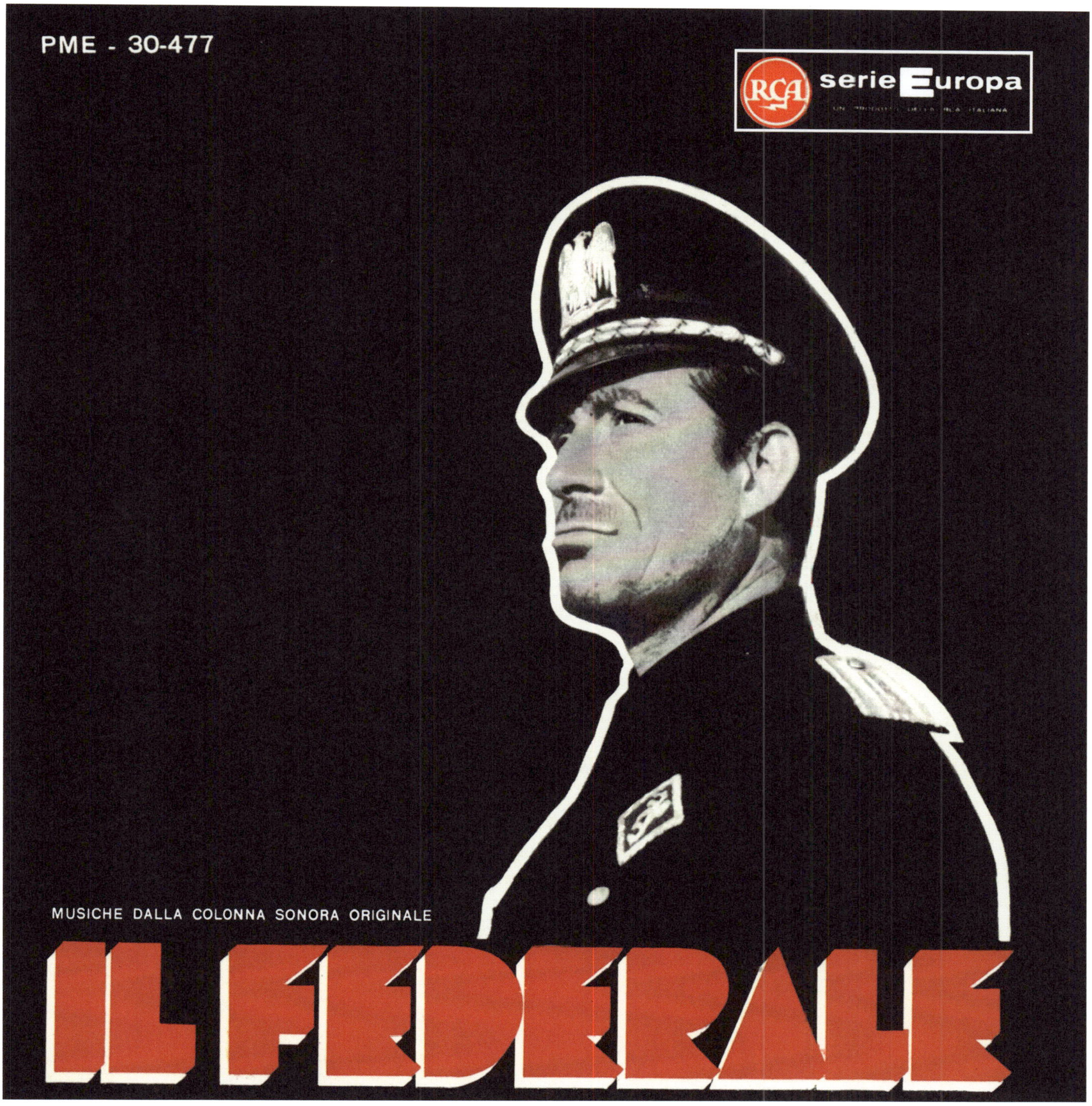
PME - 30-477
RCA serie Europa
MUSICHE DALLA COLONNA SONORA ORIGINALE
IL FEDERALE

COLONNA SONORA ORIGINALE
IL FEDERALE
MUSICHE DI ENNIO MORRICONE

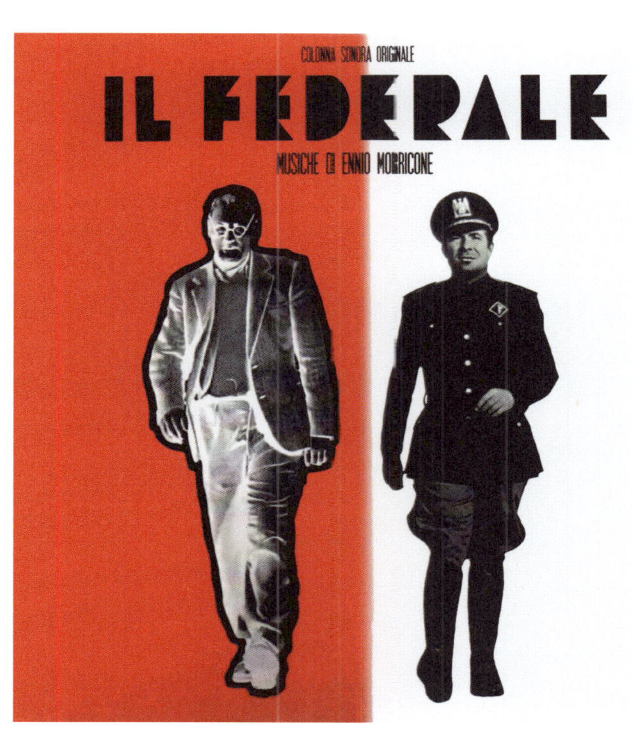

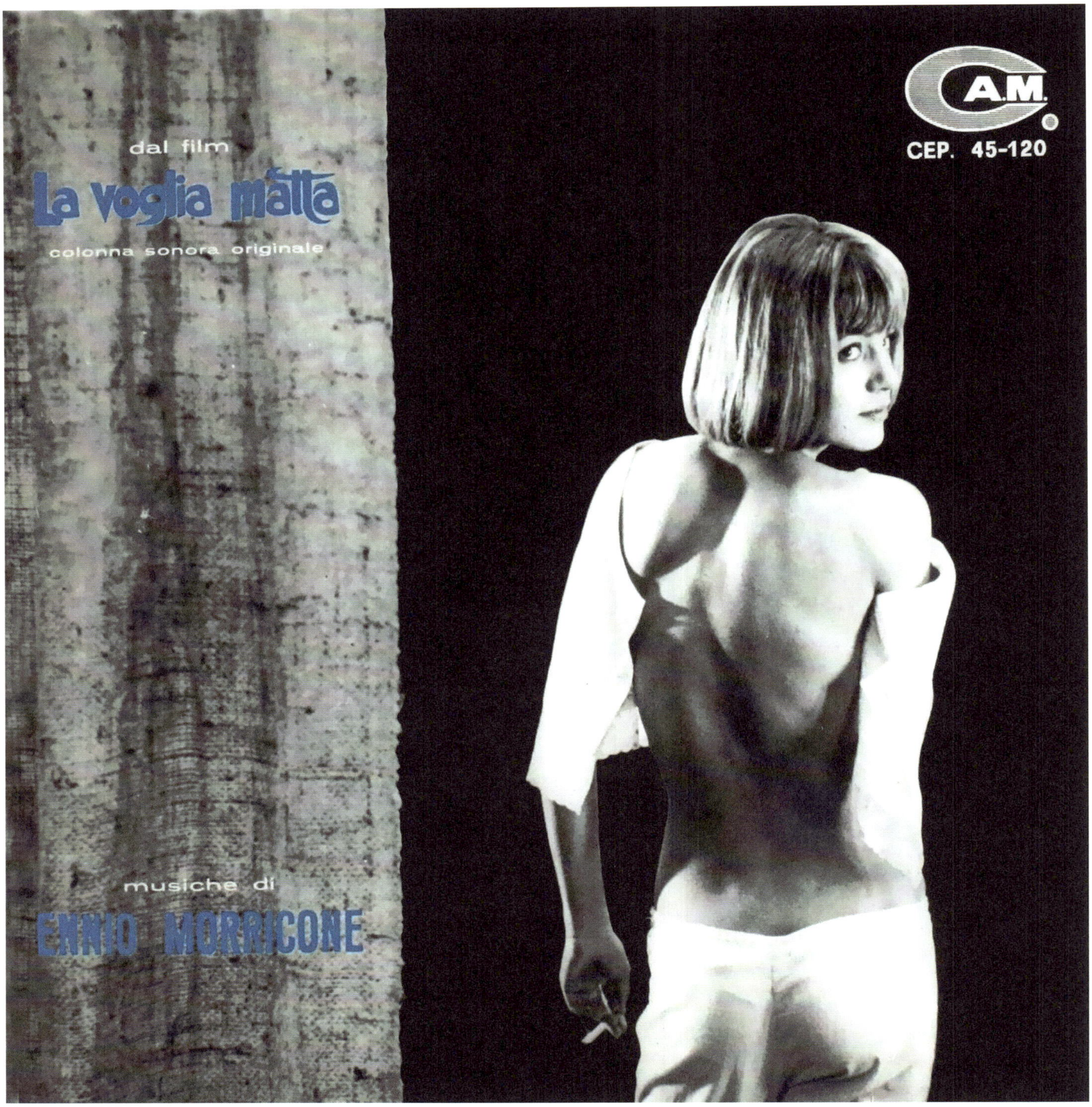
dal film
La voglia matta
colonna sonora originale
musiche di
ENNIO MORRICONE
C.A.M.
CEP. 45-120

SASSI
SRL 10-161
RICORDI
DI GINO PAOLI
dalla colonna sonora
del film
La voglia
matta

RCA VICTOR
DALLA COLONNA SONORA
ORIGINALE DEL FILM
LA VOGLIA
MATTA
LA TUA
STAGIONE
TONY
DEL MONACO
VIVA
IL JUMP UP
I FLIPPERS
PM 45 3085 serie europa

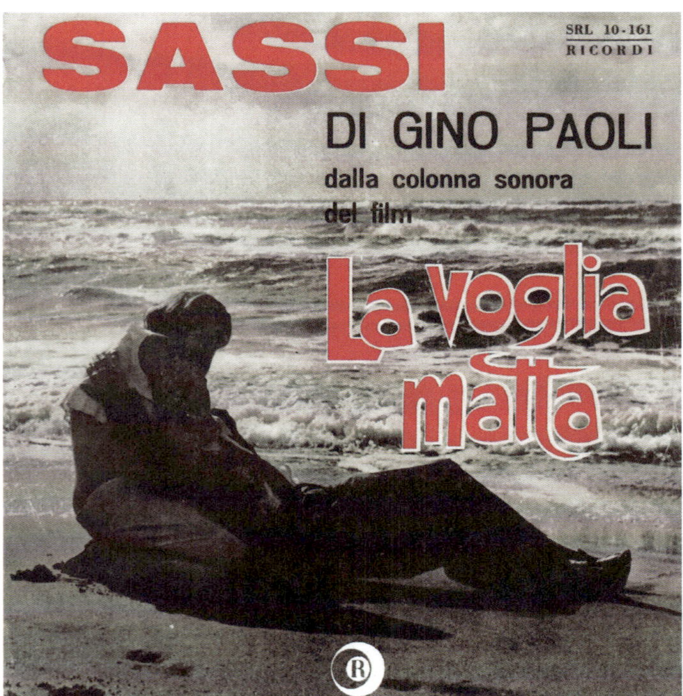

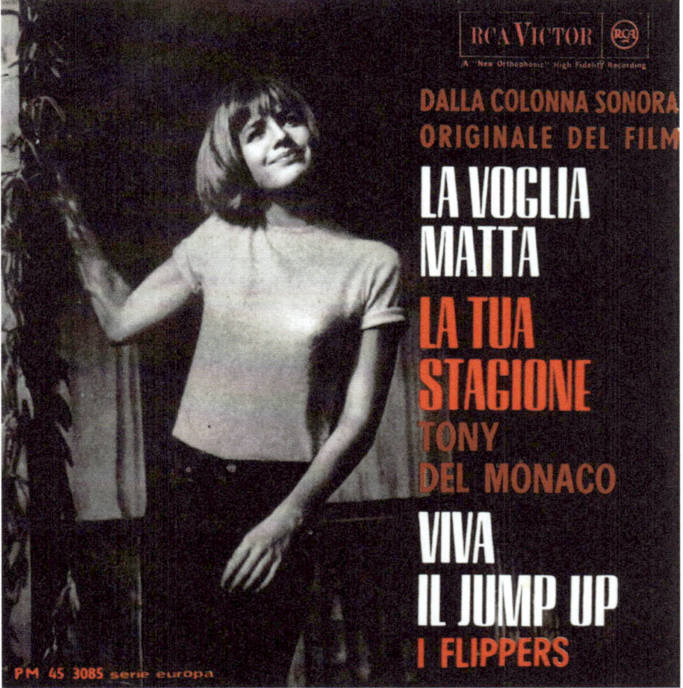

1.

La voglia matta - M° E.Morricone
15 ocir mono - Rg. Fono Roma 30/1/1962

55

1^ scatola

40 frammentario: introspettivo, lento per flauto, arpa, archi (con accordi dissonanti), celeste, spinetta e batteria (leggerissimo accompagnamento a slow delle spazzole sul piatto) fino a 1,02; quindi romantico/introspettivo, dapprima a slow per arpa (canto), archi e batteria (sempre leggerissimo accompagnamento delle spazzole sul piatto) fino a 1,48, poi lento per flauto, archi, voce femminile (che entra a 2,18 a condurre) arpa, spinetta e celeste 3,32

38 frammentario: tensivo/introspettivo, dapprima ritmico moderato per clarino, flauto, arpa, spinetta, oboe e timpani (0,53), poi mod. lento per archi, arpa, spinetta, flauto, vibrafono, clarino, timpani, batteria (interventi); a partire da 2,04 diventa giallo rosa con frasi briose per legni e spinetta con archi in sottofondo; infine, da 2,26, di nuovo tensivo/introspettivo, sostenuto, per spinetta, archi e timpani 2,40

42 frammentario: ~~tensivo/in~~ canzoni, cantata da voce maschile in italiano, con parole romantiche vecchio stile (A. Togliani)(?), accompagnata da piccolo; il brano è in playback e si sente l'attacco e l'effetto della interruzione del brano tipo radio; a partire da 0,22, registrazione orchestra in diretta, romantico, a duine, per archi (canto), organo e ritmica (con timpani) 0,50

6 tensivo (drammatico); praticamente per sole percussioni, anche ritmiche (timpani e tom) fino a 0,24; poi accordo di chiusura, dissonante, di archi, introdotti dal pforte e sempre con percussioni in sottofondo 0,33

7 stacchi/vari (brillante); lieto e scherzoso per metallofono, legni, archi, xilofono, organo e arpa 0,25

3 stacchi/vari (brillante ?); lento per flauti, arpa e archi con interventi rapidi e scherzosi dei clarinetti; la base di flauti, arpa e archi è tuttavia discorsiva e poco tensiva 0,25

... segue retro...

CAM - DET T 5

1962

La voglia matta

Crazy Desire

Elle est terrible

EP 45 rpm - CAM CEP. 45-120
45 rpm - RICORDI SRL 10 - 161
45 rpm - RCA PM 45 3085

On this occasion for a comedy film, Ennio Morricone expands the musical space and broadly overcomes the limits of songs for easy listening that were popular in those days. He adds dissonant sounds and airy sonorities, with the contribution of the hearty soprano voice of Maria Rigel Tonini. The result is a film whose rich discography includes two rare records released by CAM (Creazioni Artistiche Musicali) Records with compositions by the Maestro, and a variety of singles.

1962
La cuccagna
A Girl… and A Million
45 rpm - RCA VICTOR PM45 3129

▸

1962
Diciottenni al sole
Eighteen in the Sun
45 rpm - VICTOR SS - 1334
45 rpm - RCA VICTOR PM45 - 3124
45 rpm - RCA VICTOR PM45 - 3125

Eighteen in the Sun was also distributed in Japan where it achieved remarkable success, becoming a true cult phenomenon. This appreciation is especially proven by the vast number of local recordings, containing the five songs composed by Morricone for this film to lyrics by Pilantra (Luciano Salce); production included at least 20 notable releases, including 45s, extended plays, LPs, and CDs.

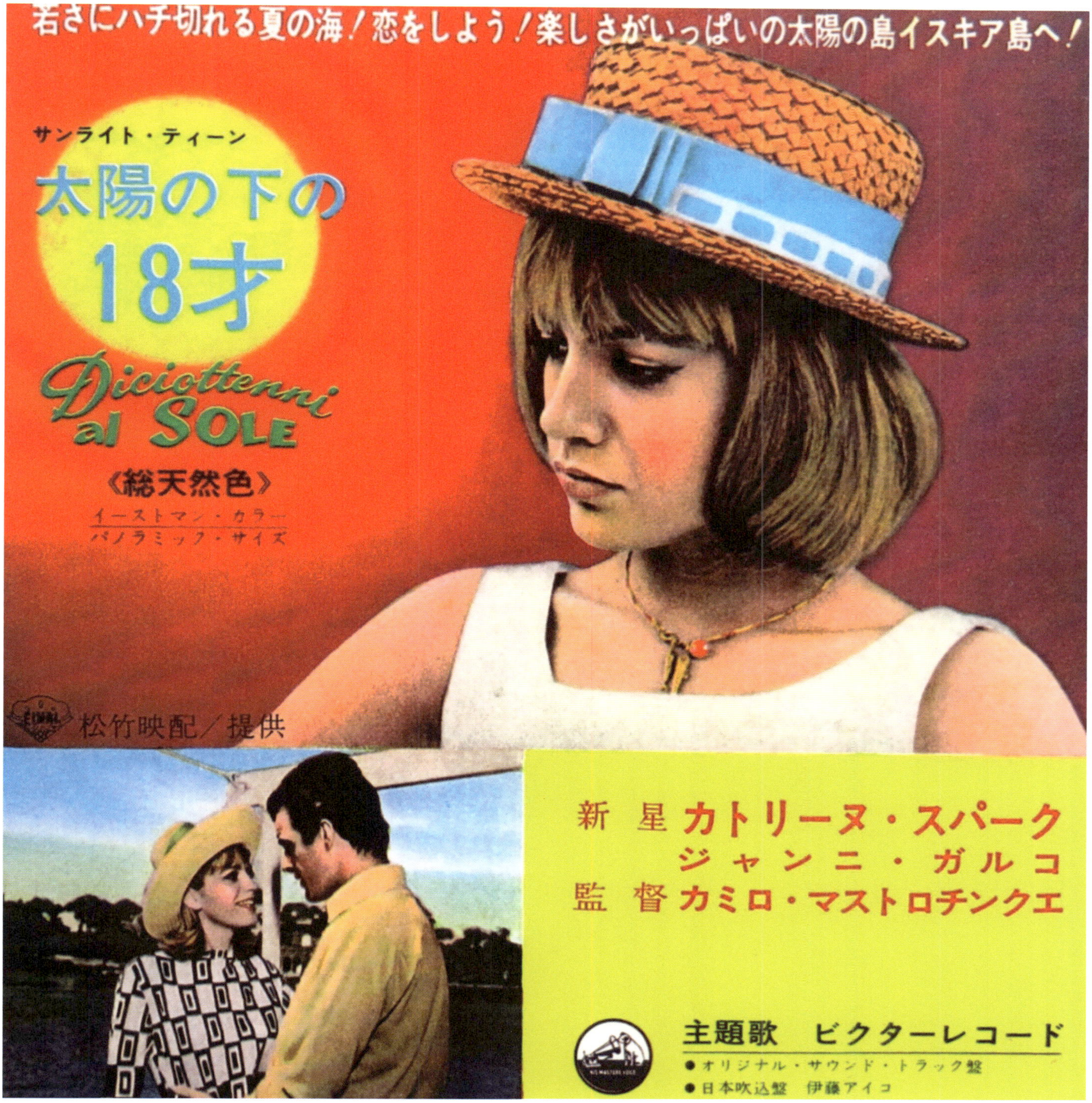
若さにハチ切れる夏の海！恋をしよう！楽しさがいっぱいの太陽の島イスキア島へ！
サンライト・ティーン
太陽の下の
18才
Diciottenni al SOLE
《総天然色》
イーストマン・カラー
パノラミック・サイズ
松竹映配／提供
新　星　カトリーヌ・スパーク
ジャンニ・ガルコ
監　督　カミロ・マストロチンクエ
主題歌　ビクターレコード
●オリジナル・サウンド・トラック盤
●日本吹込盤　伊藤アイコ

PM45 - 3124 serie europa
RCA VICTOR
DALLA COLONNA SONORA ORIGINALE DEL FILM
DICIOTTENNI AL SOLE
GO-KART TWIST • DONNA DA MORIRE
GIANNI MORANDI • TONY DEL MONACO

PM45 - 3125 serie europa
RCA VICTOR
DALLA COLONNA SONORA ORIGINALE DEL FILM
DICIOTTENNI AL SOLE
NICOLE
TWIST N.9
GIANNI MECCIA
JIMMY FONTANA

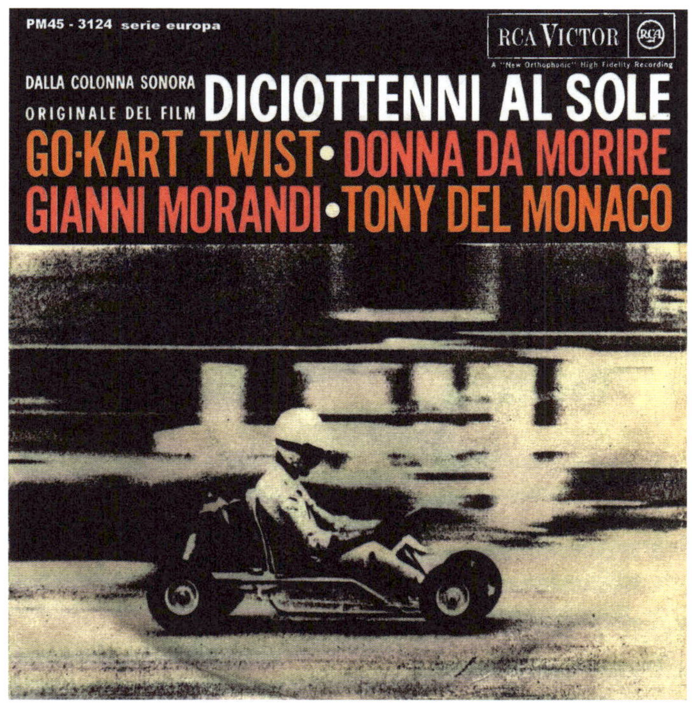

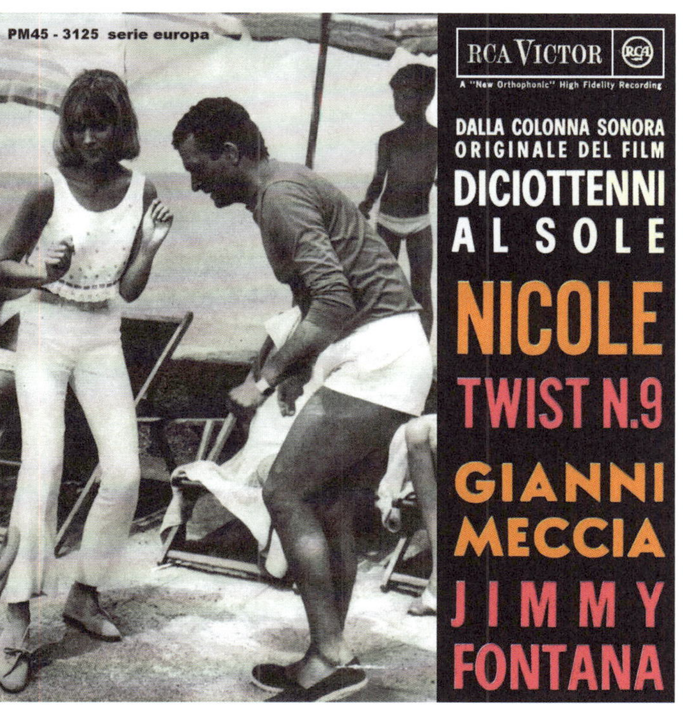

1962
I motorizzati
45 rpm - RCA PM45 - 3162

In addition to its two most famous songs, Morricone composed an instrumental theme for this film entitled, *Ballata dei motori*, whose only recording can be heard on a rare record of background music that has been off the market since 1968: Industrial development, Sermi Records SR 03.

PM45-3162
TWIST DEI VIGILI/CORRI CORRI
EDOARDO VIANELLO - GIANNI MORANDI
DAL FILM
"I MOTORIZZATI"
CON NINO MANFREDI - UGO TOGNAZZI - FRANCA VALERI
WALTER CHIARI
REGIA DI CAMILLO MASTROCINQUE MUSICHE DI ENNIO MORRICONE

▸

1963
Il successo
The Success
EP 45 rpm - RCA VICTOR MKE-650

1963
Gli italiani e le vacanze
45 rpm - VICTOR SS-1383

1963
Tutto è musica
with Luis Enríquez Bacalov and Nello Cingherotti
LP 33 rpm - FONIT LPR. 20024

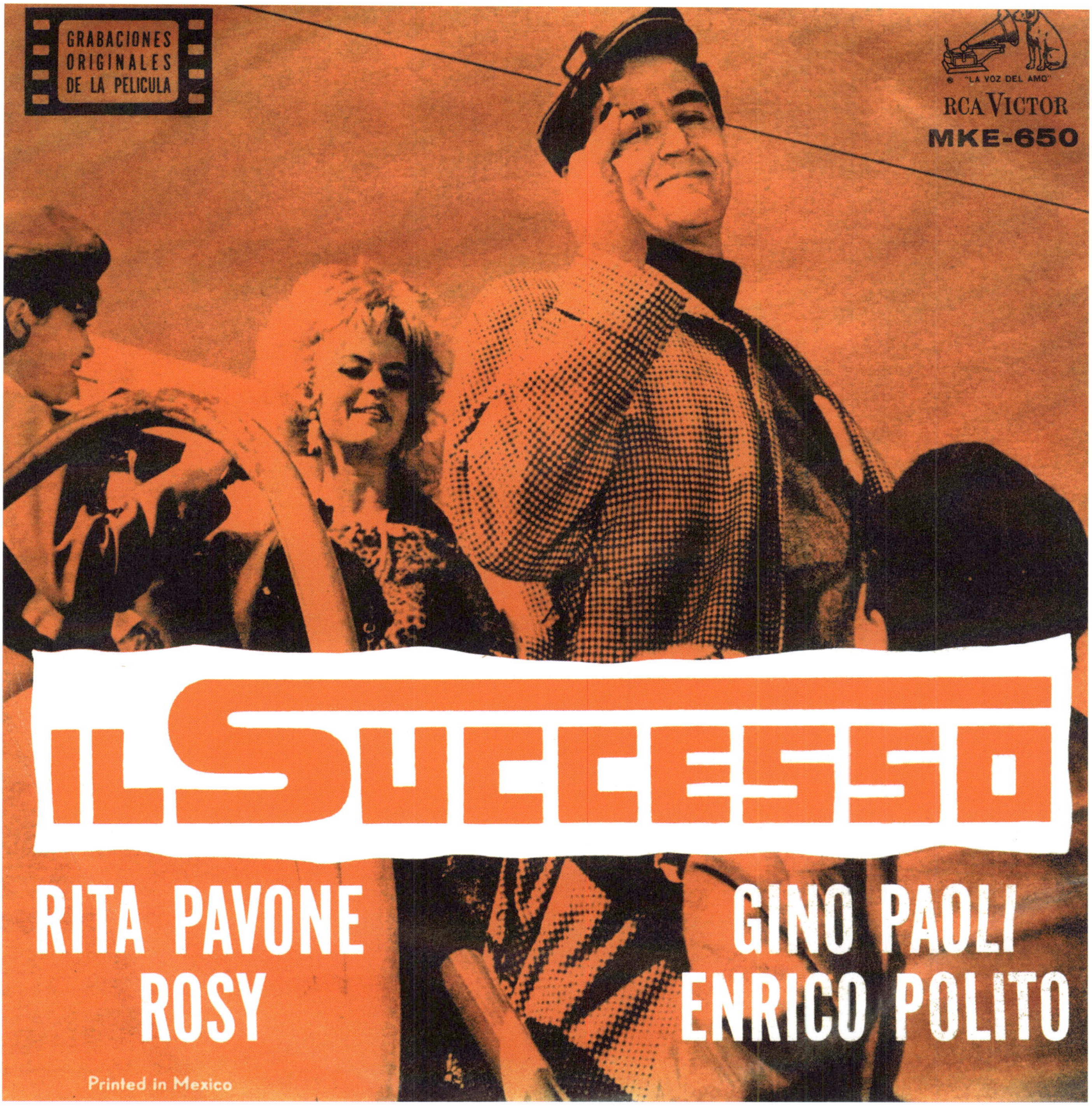
GRABACIONES
ORIGINALES
DE LA PELICULA
"LA VOZ DEL AMO"
RCA VICTOR
MKE-650
IL SUCCESSO
RITA PAVONE
ROSY
GINO PAOLI
ENRICO POLITO
Printed in Mexico

強烈なビキニ・スタイルと音楽で招く
イタリアンバカンス！
45 RPM
VICTOR
SS-1383
撮影■マルセロ・ミディ
音楽■マリオ・カンティーニ
総天然色■イーストマン カラー 〈イタリア映画〉
太陽のバカンス
gli ITALIANI e le VACANZE
日本語版（台本・解説）前田武彦
ビクターレコード

LPR. 20024
DOMENICO MODUGNO
IN
TUTTO È MUSICA
FONIT

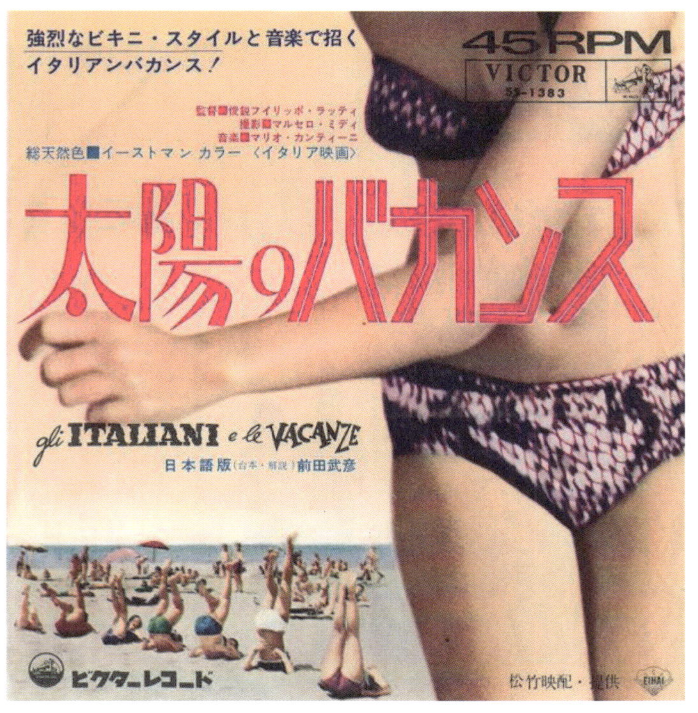

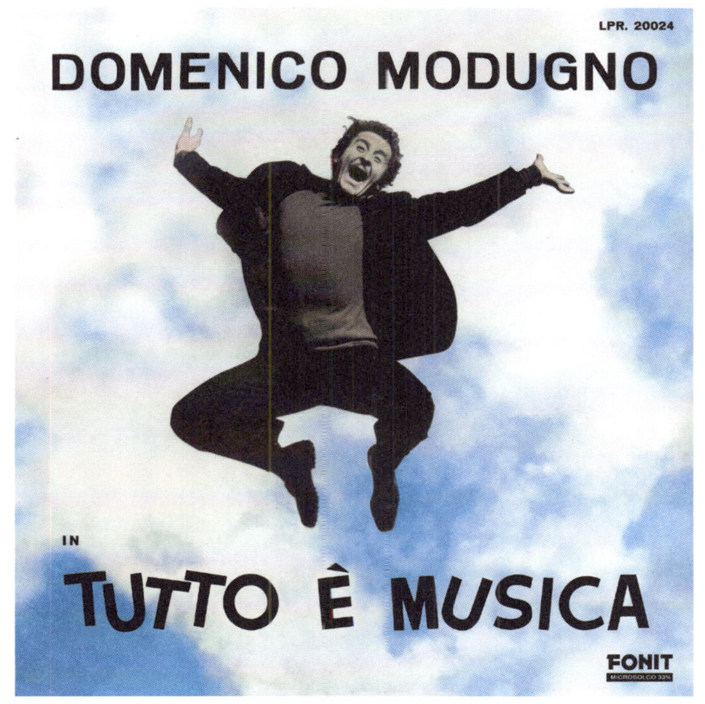

1963
Le monachine
The Little Nuns
EP 45 rpm - CAM CEP 45 -108

Given the musical nature of this movie, some of the pieces were chosen to be added to a 10-inch LP album of background music, released off-market by CAM, and entitled *Natalizio* (CAM Cmt 001). Subsequently, while the original extended play released by CAM became almost impossible to find, the American company, Cerberus Records, published a part of this soundtrack in tandem with the music for the movie *The Meadow* (Cerberus CEM-S 0115).

LA FIDANZATA DEL BERSAGLIERE

Musiche di ENNIO MORRICONE

1963

La fidanzata del bersagliere

LP 33 rpm - COMETA CMT 1004/12
45 rpm - RICORDI SRL 10-334

The comedy, *La fidanzata del bersaglier*, was staged for the first time at the Odeon theater in Milan on March 29, 1963 and starred Ornella Vanoni who earned the San Genesio Award for her role. That same year, Dischi Ricordi released the single containing the eponymous song on the B-side with two different covers.

1963
I maniaci
Beautiful Eyes
45 rpm - RCA PM45 - 3267

1963
I basilischi
The Basilisks
45 rpm - RCA PM45 - 3219

1963
Smash
45 rpm - PRIMARY CRA 91920

1964
I marziani hanno 12 mani
The Twelve-Handed Men of Mars
45 rpm - RCA PM45 -3270

1964
Duello nel Texas
Gunfight in the Red Sands
Duel au Texas
LP 33 rpm - DIGITMOVIES LPDM 005

1964
Le pistole non discutono
Pistols Don't Argue
Mon colt fait la loi
45 rpm - SEVEN SEAS HIT - 1414

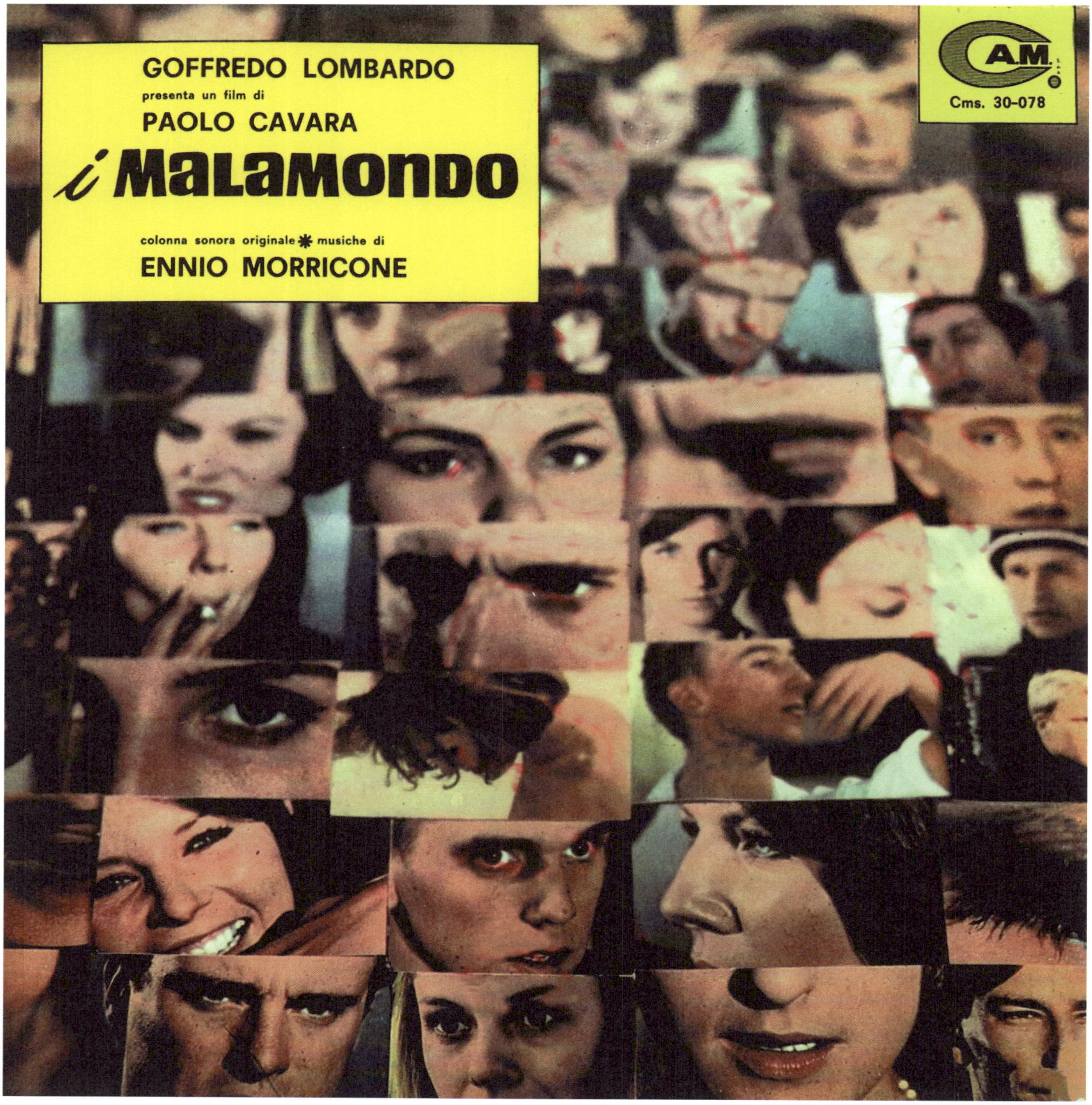

GOFFREDO LOMBARDO
presenta un film di
PAOLO CAVARA
i MALAMONDO
colonna sonora originale ✻ musiche di
ENNIO MORRICONE

CAM
Cms. 30-078

◄

1964
I malamondo
Malamondo
LP 33 rpm - CAM CMS 30-078
45 rpm - RICORDI SRL 10-340
45 rpm - CAM CA. 2547

1964
Prima della rivoluzione
Before the Revolution
with Gino Paoli
45 rpm - RCA PM45 - 3274

The music for *Before the Revolution* is generally attributed to Gino Paoli and Ennio Morricone. But the songs were actually written by Paoli and arranged and directed by Maestro Morricone, who exclusively composed the instrumental score, which was then conducted by Franco Ferrara.

1964

Per un pugno di dollari

A Fistful of Dollars

Pour une poignée de dollars

LP 33 rpm - RCA PML 10414
45 rpm - VICTOR SS -1514
45 rpm - RCA PM45 - 3285

The original version of the opening credits dates to 1962 for the song by Woody Guthrie entitled, *Pastures of Plenty,* and sung by Peter Tevis. This was the version without the famous whistling sound by Alessandro Alessandroni that distinguished it. For the trumpet sound, which is crucial to the score, Sergio Leone wanted to hire Nini Rosso, who was already famous. Morricone said no however, preferring the excellent but less well-known Michele Lacerenza. In the end, the composer had everyone's blessing, including the musician's friend, director Sergio Leone.

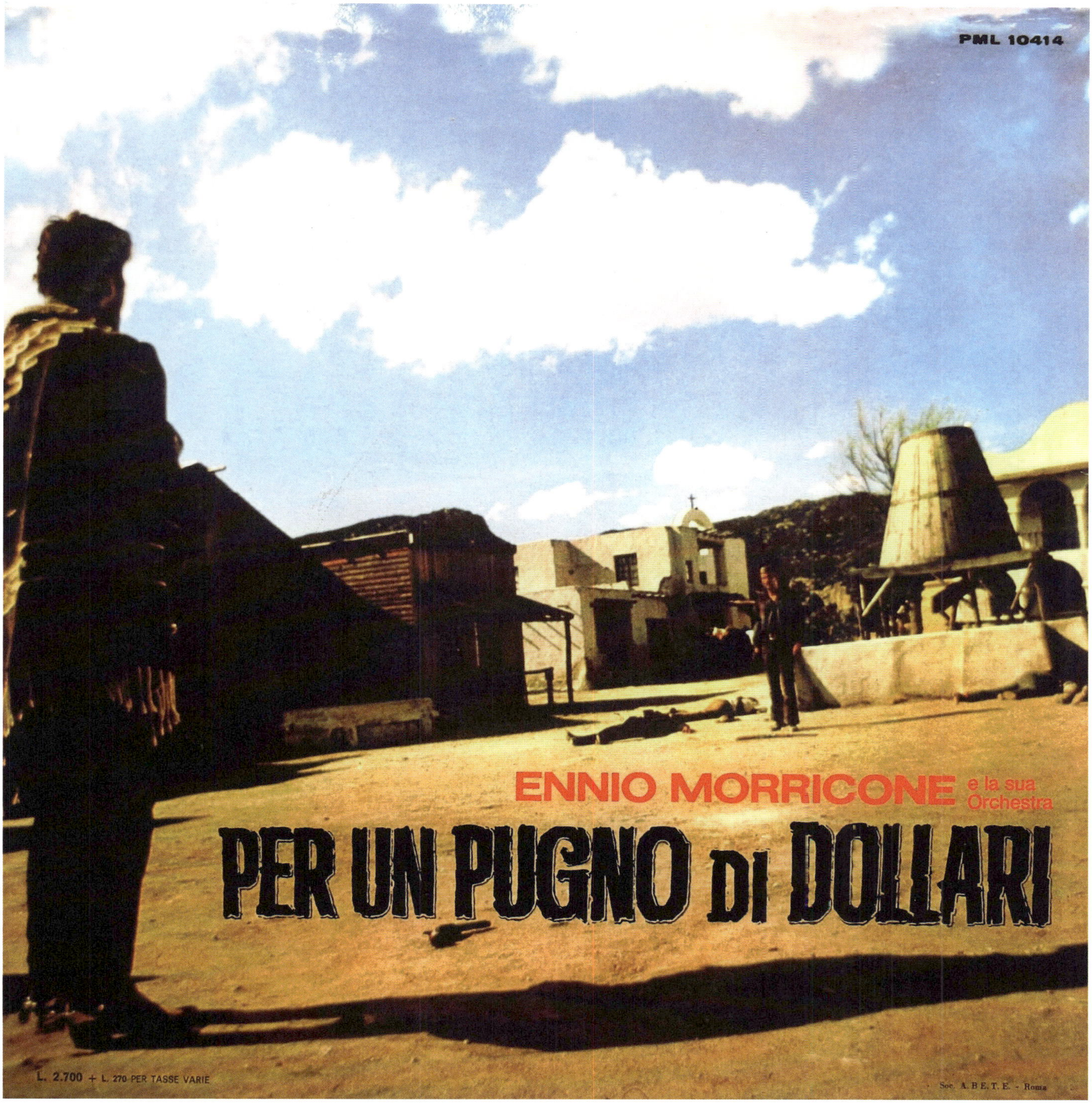
PML 10414
ENNIO MORRICONE e la sua Orchestra
PER UN PUGNO DI DOLLARI
L. 2.700 + L. 270 PER TASSE VARIE
Soc. A.B.E.T.E. - Roma

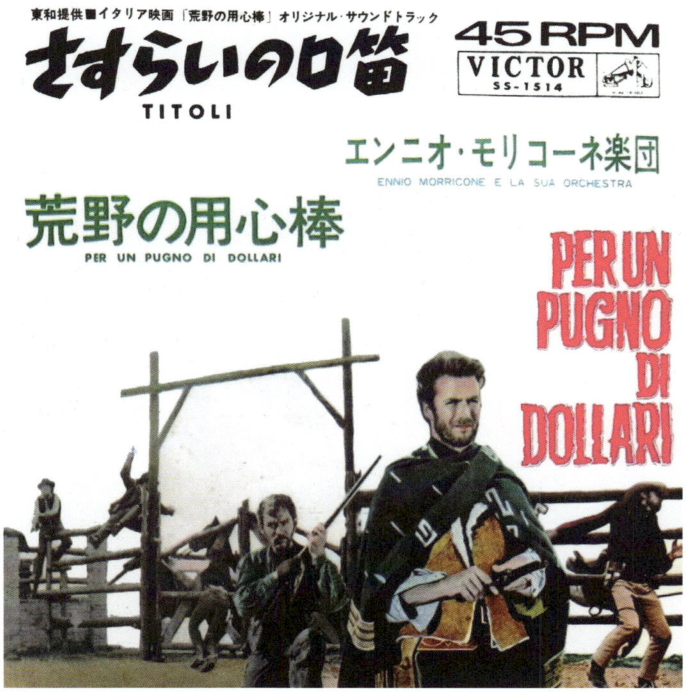

東和提供■イタリア映画「荒野の用心棒」オリジナル・サウンドトラック
さすらいの口笛
TITOLI
45 RPM
VICTOR
SS-1514
エンニオ・モリコーネ楽団
ENNIO MORRICONE E LA SUA ORCHESTRA
荒野の用心棒
PER UN PUGNO DI DOLLARI
PER UN PUGNO DI DOLLARI

RCA ITALIANA
musiche di ENNIO MORRICONE
DALLA COLONNA SONORA ORIGINALE DEL FILM OMONIMO
PER UN PUGNO DI DOLLARI

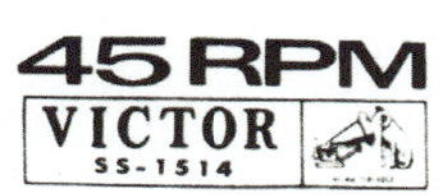

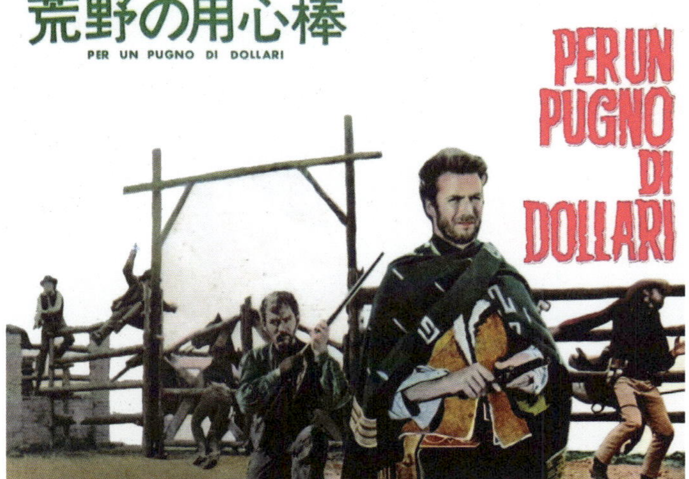

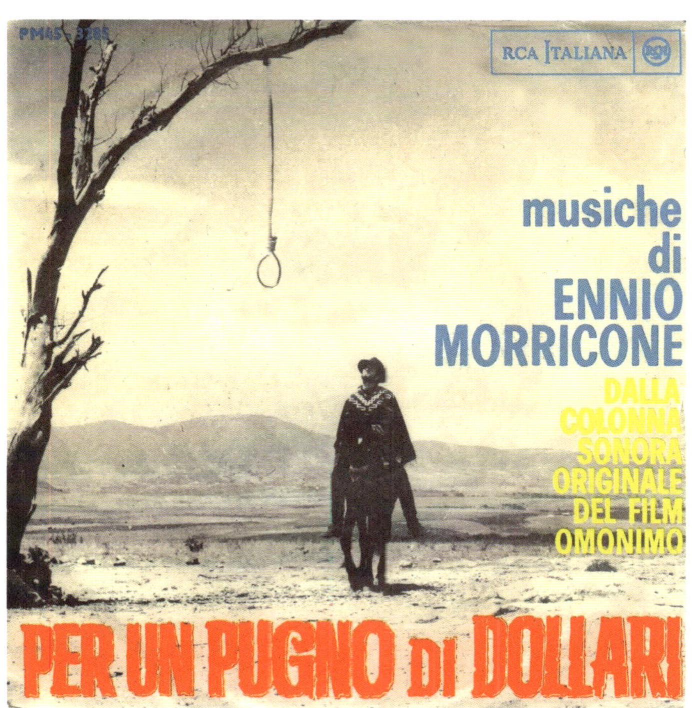

1964
I due evasi di Sing Sing
Two Escape from Sing Sing
Centrale elettronucleare del Garigliano
CD - RECORDING ARTS SA - 2X903

1964
In ginocchio da te
45 rpm - RCA PM45 - 3263

1964
E la donna creò l'uomo
Full Hearts and Empty Pockets
Un coeur plein et les poches vides
CD - GDM 2058

1965
Idoli controluce
45 rpm - RCA PM45 - 3336

1965
Non son degno di te
45 rpm - RCA PM45 - 3325

1965
Mi vedrai tornare
45 rpm - RCA PM45 - 3346

1965
Se non avessi più te
45 rpm - RCA PM45 - 3322

1965
Altissima pressione
Highest Pressure
with Luis Enríquez Bacalov
45 rpm - ARC AN 4060

The successful season of the "musicarelli" interpreted and sung by Gianni Morandi witnessed a notable commitment by Ennio Morricone. The Maestro did not limit himself to arranging songs written by other composers, but actually composed and directed all of the musical commentary in these light-hearted movies that were box office hits.

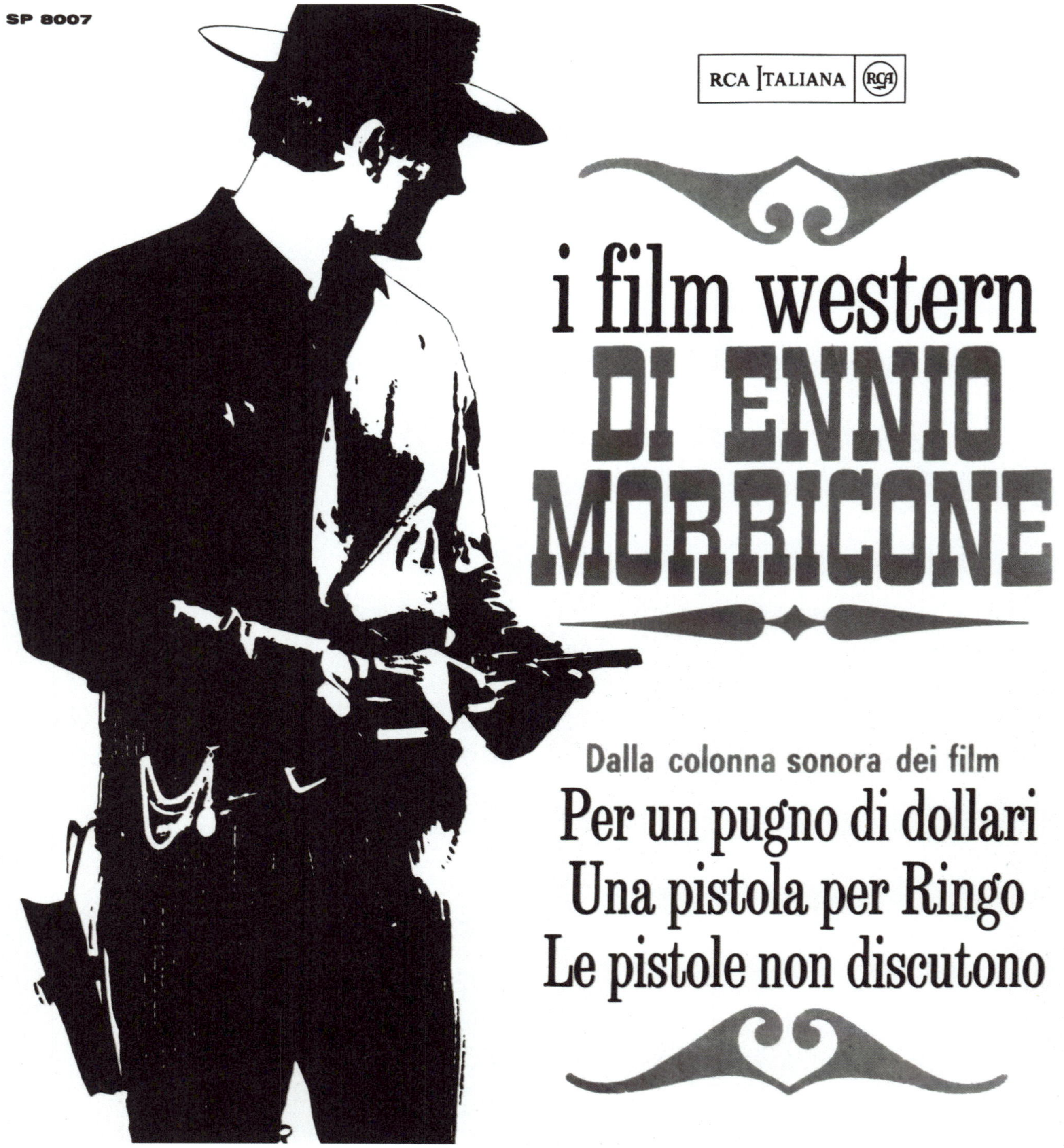
SP 8007
RCA ITALIANA
RCA
i film western
DI ENNIO
MORRICONE
Dalla colonna sonora dei film
Per un pugno di dollari
Una pistola per Ringo
Le pistole non discutono

AN 4052
ANGEL FACE
DALLA COLONNA SONORA
DEL FILM OMONIMO
UNA
PISTOLA
PER
RINGO
arc
MUSICHE
DI
ENNIO MORRICONE

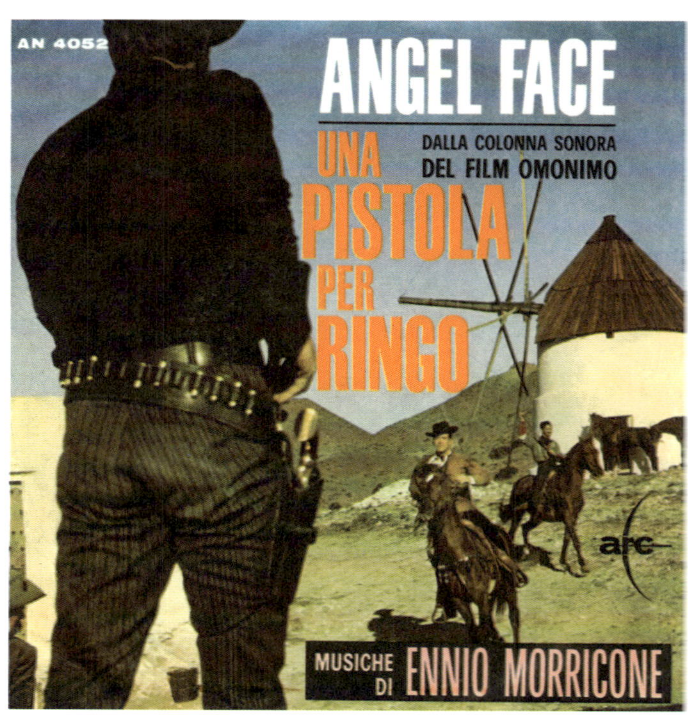

1965

Una pistola per Ringo

A Pistol for Ringo

Un pistolet pour Ringo

LP 33 rpm - RCA SP 8007

45 rpm - ARC AN 4052

Maurizio Graf (real name Maurizio Attanasio) was the vocal interpreter of the two films directed by Duccio Tessari: *A Pistol for Ringo*, in which he sang *Angel Face*, written by Gino Paoli, and the following *The Return of Ringo*, for which he wrote the lyrics of the eponymous song heard during the opening credits. There is also a splendid, recent version of *Angel Face* for whistle and guitar, performed live by Alessandro Alessandroni, and taped for the CD-book, *Morricone Western,* released in 2006 by Cinedelic Records.

SP 8013

MENAGE ALL'ITALIANA

musiche di

ENNIO MORRICONE

dalla colonna sonora originale del film

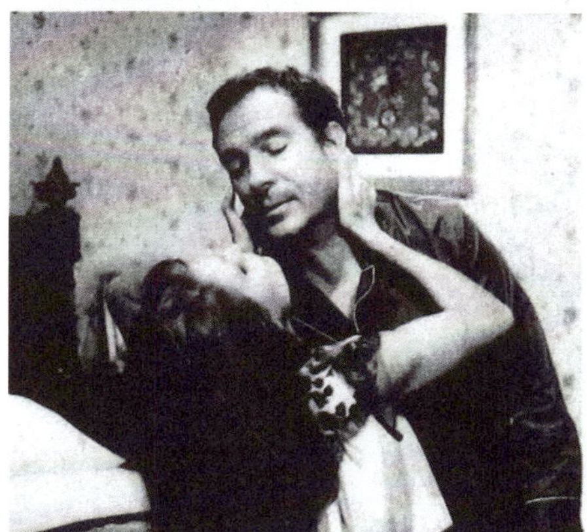
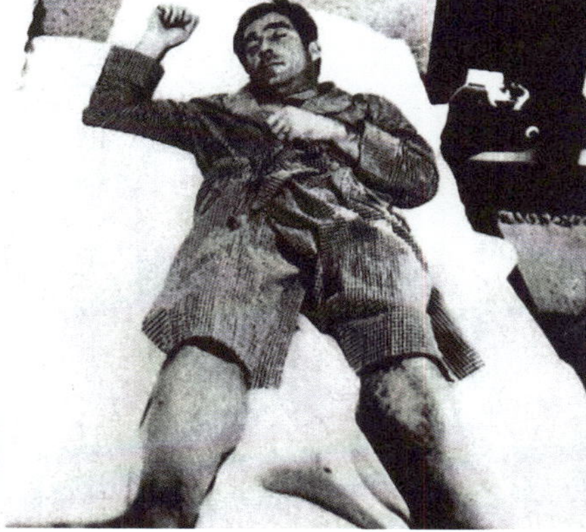

1965
Ménage all'italiana
Menage Italian Style
LP 33 rpm - RCA SP 8013
45 rpm - RCA 45N 1468

The film, *Menage Italian Style,* includes a song entitled, *Un fiore è nato,* written by Sergio Bardotti and Gino Paoli with the arrangement by and musical direction of Morricone. The American soprano, Anna Moffo, who was a cast member and sang the song, decided to also use it as the theme song for the *Anna Moffo Show* which she hosted on Italian television.

1965
Per qualche dollaro in più
For a Few Dollars More
Pour quelques dollars de plus
LP 33 rpm - RCA PML 10414
EP 45 rpm - RCA VICTOR 3-20997
45 rpm - VICTOR SS-1696
45 rpm - RCA PM45 3342

When *A Fistful of Dollars* was released, RCA limited itself to publishing only a single 45 rpm, but because of the movie's amazing success which generated the second part of the famous "dollar trilogy," an album, *For a Few Dollars More*, was made containing a portion of both soundtracks. Later, it was re-released and co-edited around the world. The use of a carillon in the final scene of the duel called, *La resa dei conti* is ingenious, disturbing, and memorable.

RCA VICTOR
3-20997
LA MUERTE TENIA UN PRECIO
banda sonora original de la película
música de
ENNIO MORRICONE

ユナイト映画「夕陽のガンマン」
オリジナル・サウンド・トラック
45RPM
VICTOR
SS-1696
夕陽のガンマン
PER QUALCHE DOLLARO IN PIU'
ガンマンの祈り
LA RESA DEI CONTI
エンニオ・モリコーネ楽団
定価 ¥370

PM45 3342
RCA ITALIANA
LA RESA DEI CONTI
PER QUALCHE DOLLARO IN PIU'
MUSICHE DI
ENNIO MORRICONE
DAL FILM
PER QUALCHE DOLLARO IN PIU'
con
CLINT EASTWOOD
LEE VAN CLEEF - GIAN MARIA VOLONTE'
MARA KRUP - LUIGI PISTILLI - KLAUS KINSKI - JOSEF EGGER - PANOS PAPADOPULOS -
BENITO STEFANELLI - ROBERT CAMARDIEL - ALDO SAMERELL - LUIS RODRIGUEZ e MARIO BREGA
UN FILM DI SERGIO LEONE
PRESENTATO DALLA PEA

1965
Amanti d'oltretomba
Nightmare Castle
Les amants d'outre-tombe
LP 33 rpm - OVERDRIVE GDM 6611

The year is 1965. Ennio Morricone, who has been working in film music for just four years, has recently become known to the public thanks to the success of the music score of *A Fistful of Dollars*. And yet, the production of *Nightmare Castle*, a quality horror movie, adds to the opening credits the attribution of "Maestro" to Ennio Morricone's name; more specifically, it reads "original music by Maestro Ennio Morricone performed by the author." It was a rare instance back then to have this acknowledgement, but definitely something Morricone deserved due to the impactful score that he had composed. It was dominated by the gloomy sound of a brass pipe organ, which the composer offset with a romantic love theme for piano and orchestra. Unfortunately, the only four pieces from this soundtrack that were available at the time were included in rare albums that are now off-market and used as background music (released by RCA in 1970 in the series SP 10.000).

1965
I pugni in tasca
Fists in the Pocket
Les poings dans les poches
LP 33 rpm - DAGORED RED221 C

An angry film, a film maudit – it isn't easy to classify the first controversial movie made by Marco Bellocchio even now that many years have gone by. Ennio Morricone, who was asked to write the score for the movie, found himself faced with a real challenge, and wisely decided not to overpower the work with his music.

MUSICHE DI ENNIO MORRICONE
dirette da Bruno Nicolai
dalla colonna sonora originale del film
SLALOM

1965
Slalom
Snow Job
45 rpm - RICORDI SRL 10-397

This film has carefree, almost cartoonish tunes and lots of tongue-in-cheek moments for the incredible adventures of the reluctant would-be (in spite of himself) special agent played by Vittorio Gassman. Morricone does not disappoint with his sparkling allegro con brio music, and Alessandro Alessandroni, although absent from the credits, supports him with a highly original "whipped up" whistle.

1965
Un uomo a metà
Half a Man
45 rpm - RCA PM45 3350

1965
Agent 505 Todesfalle Beirut
La trappola scatta a Beirut
Agent 505: Death Trap in Beirut
Baroud à Beyrouth pour F.B.I. 505
LP 33 rpm - GDM EP 6707

1965
Thrilling
45 rpm - ARC AN 4068

1965
Agente 077 missione Bloody Mary
Mission Bloody Mary
Operation lotus bleu
with Angelo Francesco Lavagnino
45 rpm - ODEON - OR 1627

Belonging to the same spy movie genre as *Agent 505: Death Trap in Beirut* is the movie *Mission Bloody Mary* that was made the same year and set to music by Angelo Francesco Lavagnino. The main theme was written by Maurizio Graf (Attanasio) and Maestro Morricone who are both credited; and Mr. Graf also sang the opening song of the soundtrack.

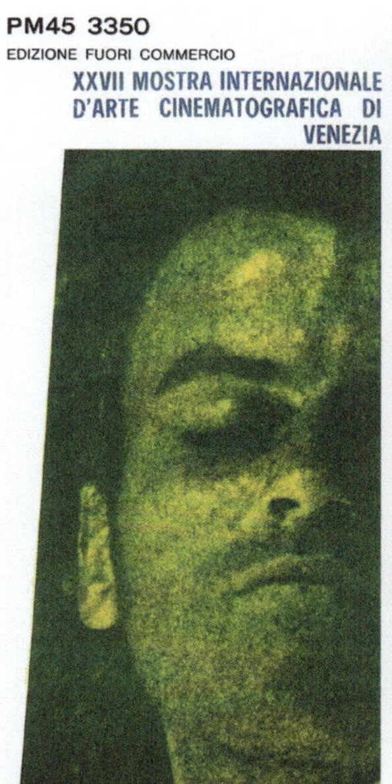

1965

Il ritorno di Ringo

The Return of Ringo

Le retour de Ringo

LP 33 rpm - ARC SA 7

45 rpm - VICTOR SS-1742

This soundtrack includes the tune, *L'incontro con la figlia*, originally composed by Morricone for the musical screen test for the movie *La Bibbia* in 1964 and corresponding to the moment of the "Creation." This screen test, conducted by Franco Ferrara, was not approved by director John Huston, who later commissioned the film score from the Japanese composer, Toshiro Mayuzumi.

1966
Un fiume di dollari
The Hills Run Red
Du sang dans la montagne
45 rpm - RICORDI SIR 20-029

1966
7 pistole per i MacGregor
Seven Guns for the MacGregor
Sept écossais au Texas
45 rpm - RCA PM45 3301

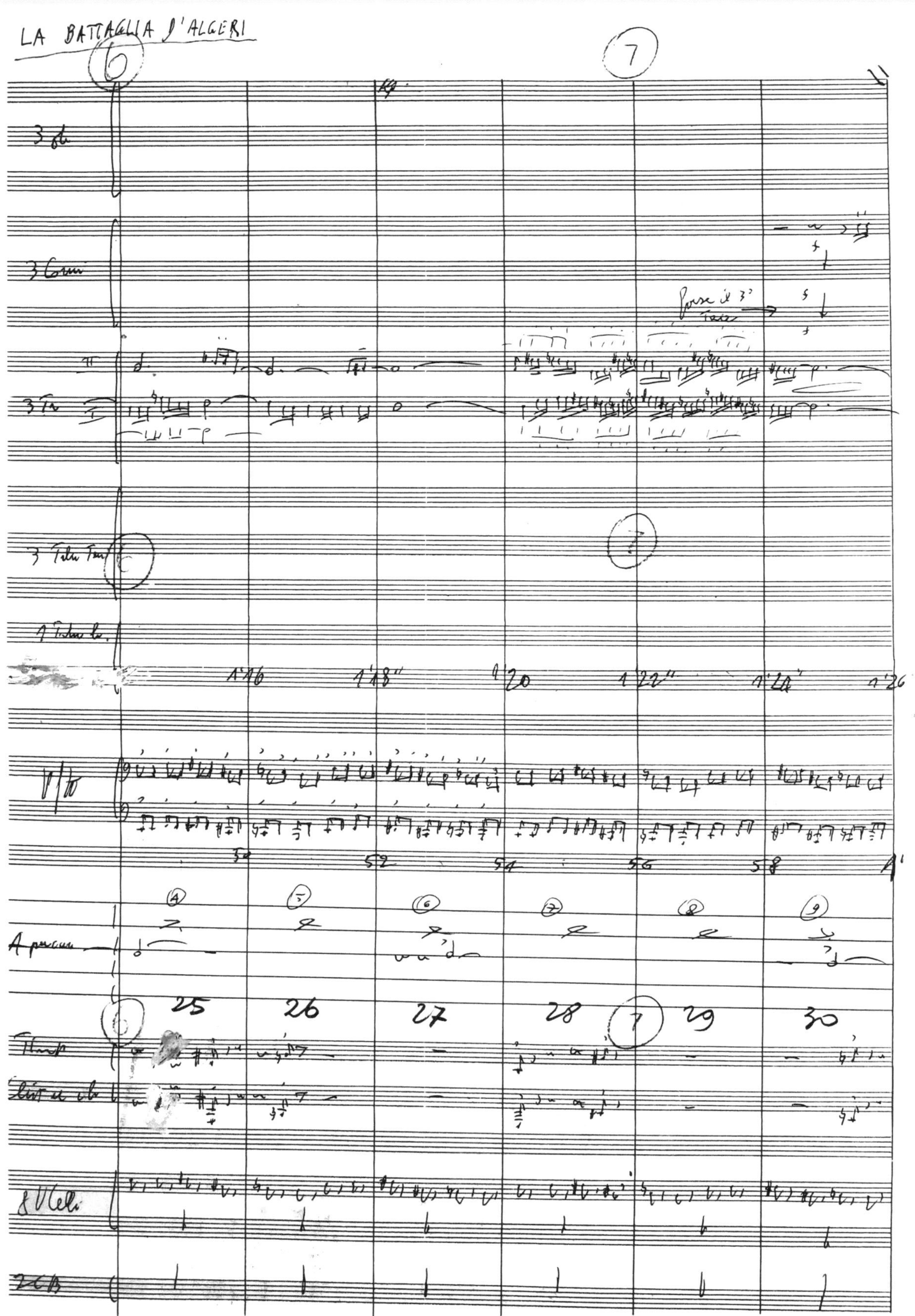

1966
La battaglia di Algeri
The Battle of Algiers
La bataille d'Alger
with Gillo Pontecorvo
LP 33 rpm - RCA SP 8019
45 rpm - RCA PM45 3350
LP 33 rpm - UNITED ARTISTS UAS 5171

The entire soundtrack was composed by Morricone, with the participation of and suggestions by the director/ producer himself, Gillo Pontecorvo; and was conducted by Bruno Nicolai. It is distinguished by a hammering and ever-present drum sound played by the great unknown Pierino Munari, a percussionist who was very active in film music both in Italy and abroad between the 1950s and '70s.

SP 8019

COLONNA SONORA ORIGINALE DEL FILM

LA BATTAGLIA DI ALGERI

Musiche di

ENNIO MORRICONE

e

GILLO PONTECORVO

Dirette da

BRUNO NICOLAI

LEONE D'ORO ALLA MOSTRA D'ARTE CINEMATOGRAFICA DI VENEZIA

SP 8020

come imparai ad amare le donne

COLONNA SONORA ORIGINALE DEL FILM

MUSICHE DI

ENNIO MORRICONE

DIRETTE DA

BRUNO NICOLAI

1966
Come imparai ad amare le donne
How I Learned to Love Women
Comment j'ai appris à aimer les femmes
LP33 rpm - RCA SP 8020

Performing in this movie is the English group, *The Sorrows*, who sing two songs: *Pioggia sul tuo viso* written by Nistri/Pilantra with music by Morricone; and *La diva*, which was used again for the soundtrack of *Spasmo* in 1974.

▶

1966
Svegliati e uccidi
Wake Up and Die
Lutring... réveille-toi et meurs
LP33 rpm - RCA SP 8018
45 rpm - ARC AN 4080

The theme song performed by Lisa Gastoni entitled, *Una stanza vuota,* in the edited version of a single differs in execution and length from the same song on the RCA album (SP 8018). The tune, *Una tromba nella note,* was released again on the B-side of the single, *La ballata dei berretti verdi*, Morricone's version for the Italian edition of *Green Berets*.

SP 8018

SVEGLIATI E UCCIDI

DALLA COLONNA SONORA ORIGINALE DEL FILM: SVEGLIATI E UCCIDI

MUSICHE DI
ENNIO MORRICONE
DIRETTE DA
BRUNO NICOLAI

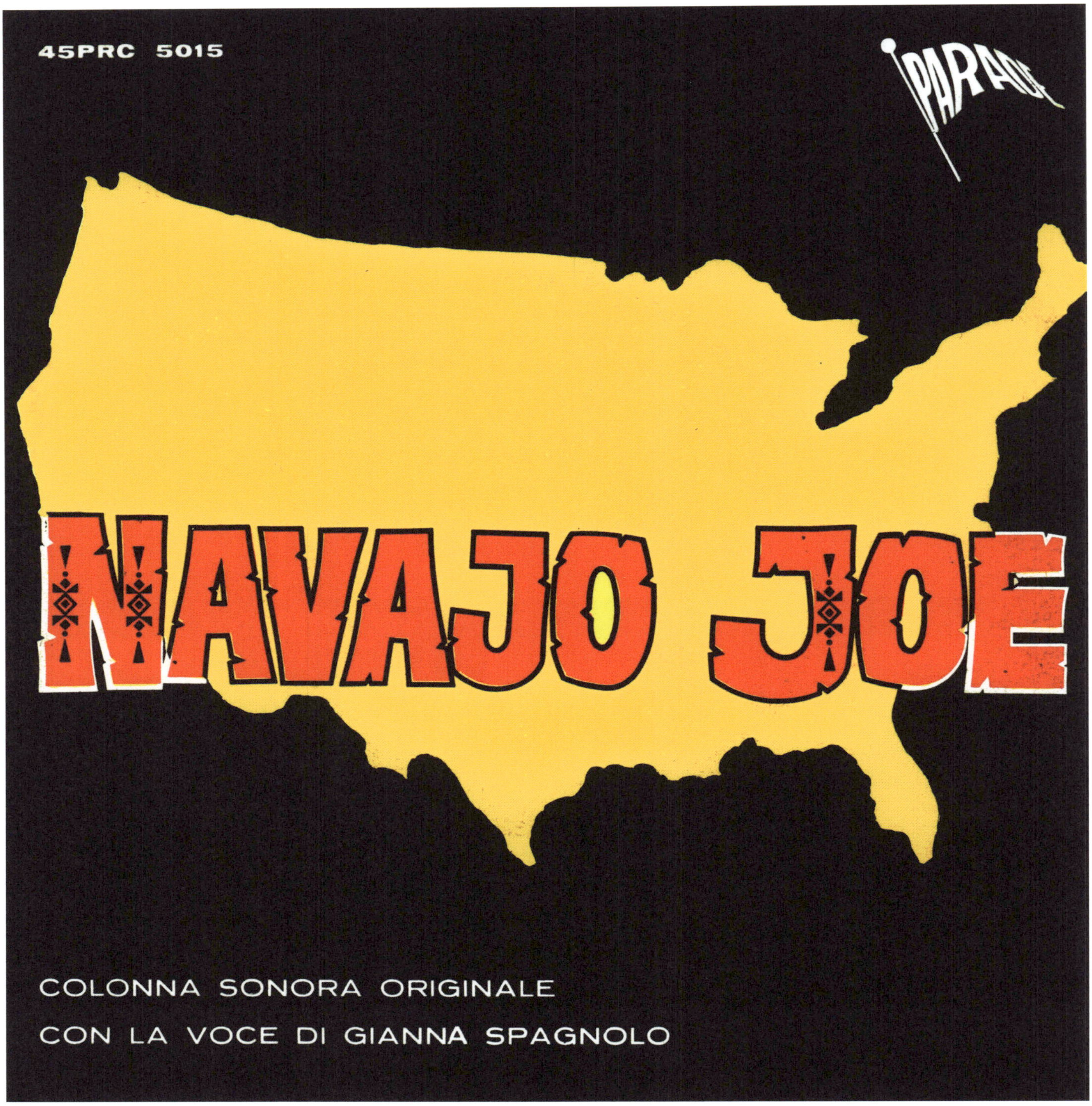

45PRC 5015

PARADE

NAVAJO JOE

COLONNA SONORA ORIGINALE

CON LA VOCE DI GIANNA SPAGNOLO

1966

Navajo Joe

45 rpm - PARADE 45PRC 5015

LP 33 rpm - UNITED ARTISTS UA-LA292-G

This is one of the rare known cases of Maestro Morricone's use of the pseudonym, Leo Nichols, a credit inserted into the American edition of the soundtrack; while in the single released in *Italia dalla Parade*, the composer's name is not even on the cover, only on the record label. The latter was issued in two different versions, one of which introduces the vocal group, *I Cantori Moderni di Alessandroni*, including a group shot.

1966

La resa dei conti

The Big Gundown Colorado

LP 33 rpm - PARADE EPL 2891 (S)
45 rpm - PARADE EPC 1801

This is no doubt one of the least famous film tunes for an Italian Western composed by Ennio Morricone. Nonetheless, the richness of the timbre, the inventiveness of the sound, the powerful vocals of Christy, and above all, the fast rhythm accompanying the huge manhunt that is the core of the movie, make it one of the most impressive soundtracks in the universe of Morricone's music.

Il buono, il brutto, il cattivo
Ottavini
Campane
Sul magnete (in SP)
Sulla cassa

1966
Il buono, il brutto, il cattivo
The Good, the Bad and the Ugly
Le bon, la brute et le truand
LP 33 rpm - PARADE EPL 2890(s)
45 rpm - UNITED ARTISTS UP 35240

To have some understanding of the international success of this soundtrack, consider that to date there have been at least 200 recording releases around the world, including LPs, singles, tapes, and CDs, without counting the re-editions, compilations, covers, versions that can be downloaded on mp3, and ringtones on cell phones with the famous strangled cry of the opening credits.

a film directed by Pier Paolo PASOLINI

UCCELLACCI E uccellini

music by Ennio MORRICONE

1966
Uccellacci e uccellini
The Hawks and the Sparrows
Des oiseaux, petits et gros
LP 33 rpm - GDM EP 6712

1966
I crudeli
The Hellbenders
Les cruels
LP 33 rpm - BELLA CASA 15LP

This soundtrack was recorded many years after the film came out, and it is not listed among the best Western music by Ennio Morricone, who used the pseudonym Leo Nichols for the second and last time here.

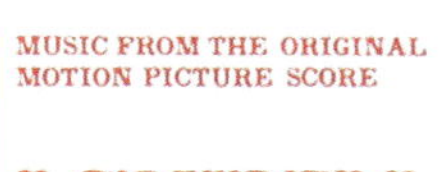

CHOIR I CANTORI MODERNI DI ALESSANDRONI

1966
El Greco
Le Greco
LP 33 rpm - RCA/INTERMEZZO SP 8061

1966
Le streghe
The Witches
Les sorcières
45 rpm - UNITED ARTISTS UA 3113

1966
Lo squarciagola
45 rpm - ARISTON AR 0153

1966
Per pochi dollari ancora
For a Few Extra Dollars
Trois cavaliers pour fort Yuma
with Gianni Ferrio
45 rpm - CAM AMP 11

Owing to its musical structure, which sounded very Spaghetti Western-like, the film used four different orchestra arrangements for the tune, *Penso a te*, from the soundtrack of *Malamondo* where it is sung by Catherine Spaak. These versions could only be heard in the movie until the publication of the "complete score" CD, released by GDM Music in 2007.

1967
Il giardino delle delizie
Garden of Delights
Le jardin des délices
LP 33 rpm - GENERAL MUSIC GM 33/01-1 33/02-2

1967
La Cina è vicina
China is near
La Chine est proche
45 rpm - CAM AMP 24

1967

Faccia a faccia

Face to Face

Il était une fois en Arizona

45 rpm - PARADE EPC 1803

LP 33 rpm - INTERMEZZO IM 004

The album released by Intermezzo in 1985, containing the soundtrack of the movie of which just one single was released in 1967, features a change in the title of the song, *Faccia a faccia (Intermezzo)* instead of *Quelli del branco selvaggio*. Moreover, the introductory excerpt from the original tune is missing. Were these recording quirks or mistakes? No one knows for sure. If it is a mistake, then the original single also contains a big one. On the back of the record, the director's name is spelled "Solima" instead of "Sollima." Luckily, it's spelled correctly on the front cover.

SP 8021

COLONNA SONORA ORIGINALE DEL FILM

AD OGNI COSTO

Musiche di
ENNIO MORRICONE

Dirette da
BRUNO NICOLAI

1967
Ad ogni costo
Grand Slam
Le carnaval des truands
LP 33 rpm - RCA SP 8021
45 rpm - RCA PM 3423

Bruno Nicolai conducted the orchestral parts of this soundtrack, while the Brazilian dance music, written by Morricone, Pilantra (Luciano Salce), and Brazilian singer/songwriter Getúlio Prates were performed by the group, La Brasiliana. Excerpts of these sambas and bossa novas were added to the movies *Almost Human* and *Spasmo*, both made in 1974.

SP 8022

COLONNA SONORA ORIGINALE DEL FILM

L'AVVENTURIERO

THE ROVER

Musiche di
ENNIO MORRICONE
Dirette da
BRUNO NICOLAI

1967
L'avventuriero
The Rover
Peyrol le boucanier
LP 33 rpm - RCA SP 8022

1967
Da uomo a uomo
Death Rides a Horse
La mort était au rendez-vous
45 rpm - RCA PM 3423

1967
La ragazza e il generale
The Girl and the General
La fille et le général
CD - Bootleg

1967
O.K. Connery
Operation Kid Brother
Opération frère Cadet
with Bruno Nicolai
45 rpm - PARADE PRC 5035

1967
7 donne per i MacGregor
Up the MacGregor
Les sept écossais explosent
45 rpm - RCA PM45 3301

1967
Dalle Ardenne all'inferno
Dirty Heroes
La gloire des canailles
with Bruno Nicolai
LP 33 rpm - BEAT LP 001

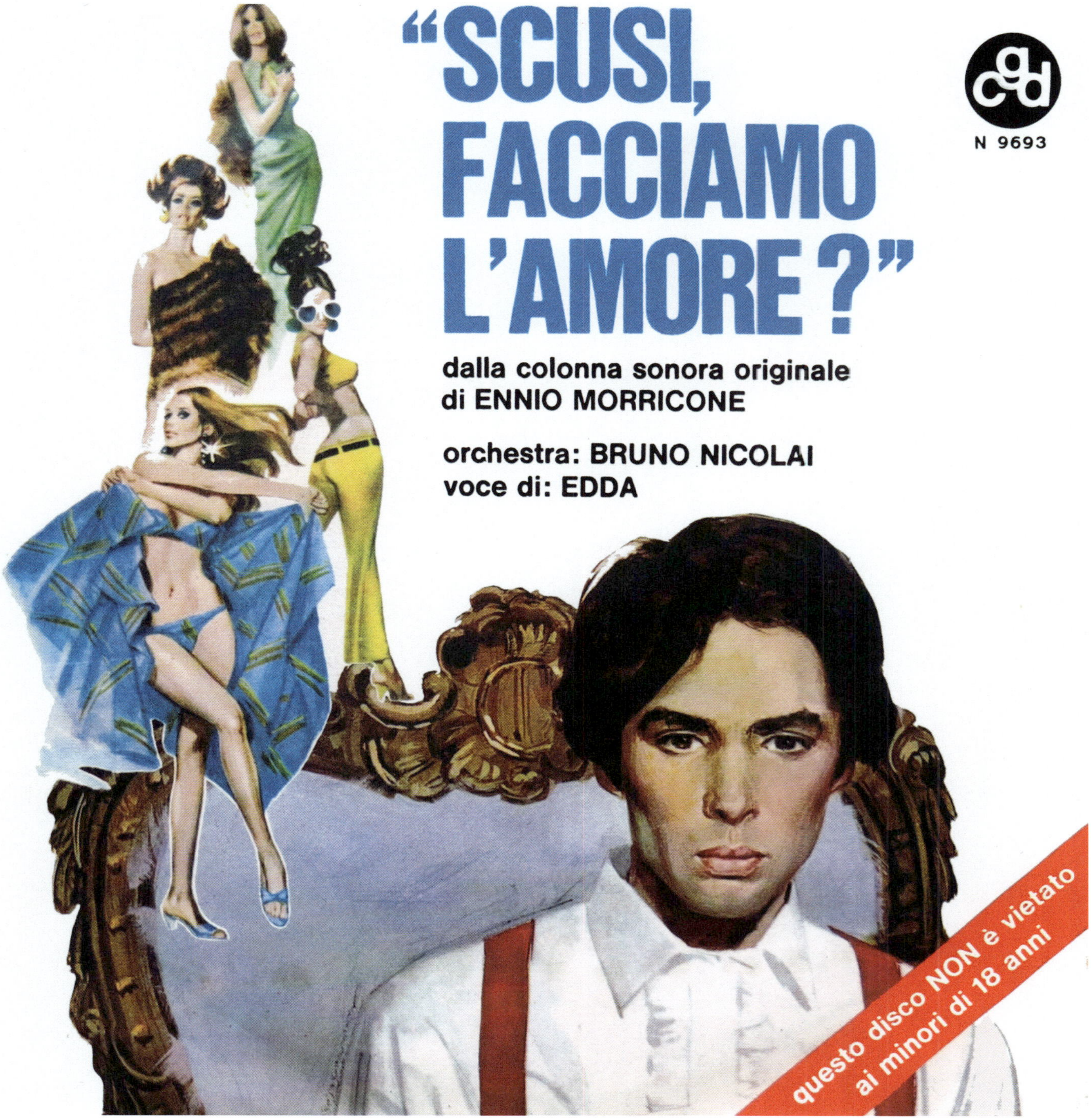
"SCUSI,
FACCIAMO
L'AMORE ?"
dalla colonna sonora originale
di ENNIO MORRICONE
orchestra: BRUNO NICOLAI
voce di: EDDA
cgd
N 9693
questo disco NON è vietato
ai minori di 18 anni

"listen,
let's make love"
"SCUSI,
FACCIAMO
L'AMORE ?"
dalla colonna sonora originale
di ENNIO MORRICONE
orchestra: BRUNO NICOLAI
voce di: EDDA
questo disco NON è vietato
ai minori di 18 anni

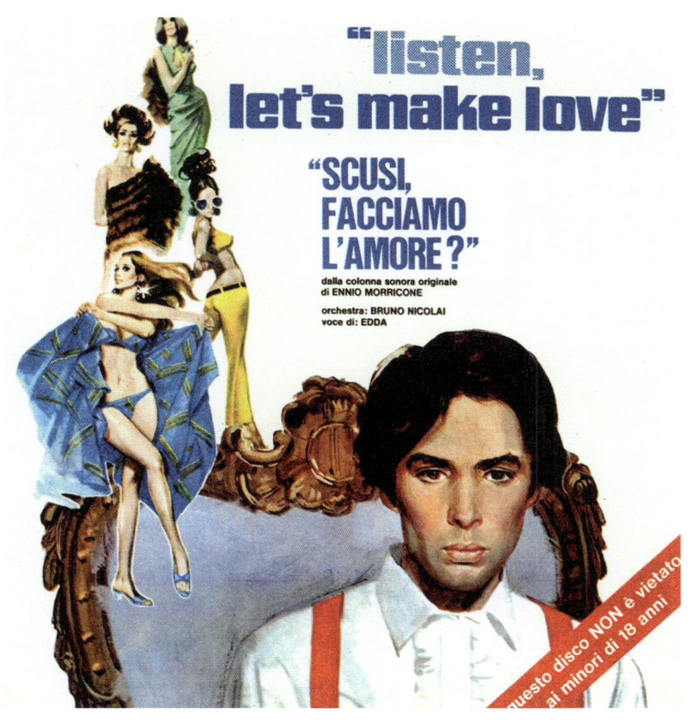

1967

Scusi, facciamo l'amore?

Listen, Let's Make Love

Et si on faisait l'amour

45 rpm - CGD N 9693

LP 33 rpm - Bootleg - GSF RECORDS GSF 1003

In 1978, an FBI raid led to the impounding of a huge quantity of records produced illegally by the label *Poo Records*, which was later shut down. Among the records that were confiscated, there were about 1,000 copies of this soundtrack, which up until then was represented by a single, released in Italy by CGD in 1969. More importantly, this discovery speaks volumes about the interest in Ennio Morricone's music across the ocean, even before he became famous.

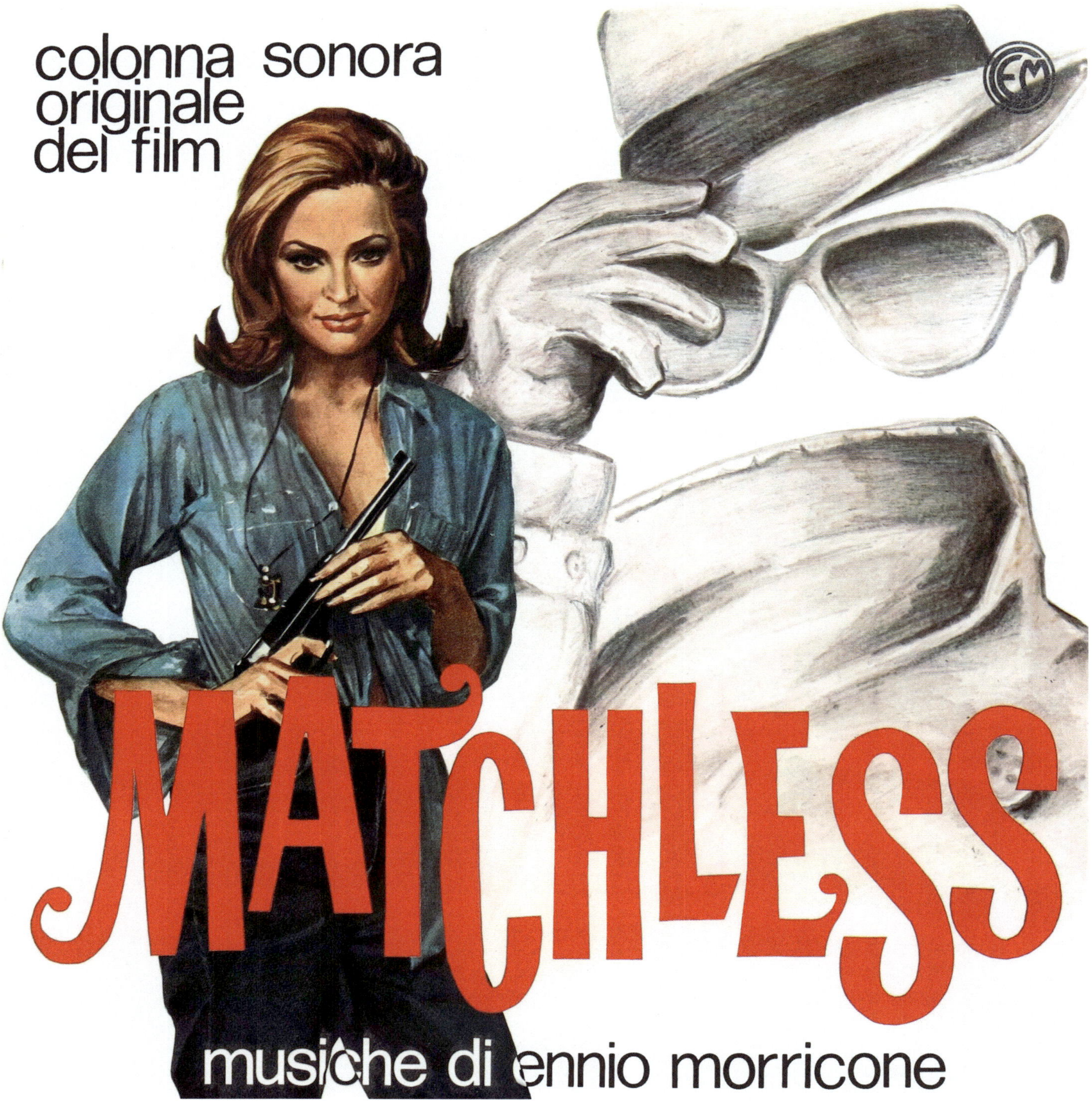
colonna sonora
originale
del film
MATCHLESS
musiche di ennio morricone

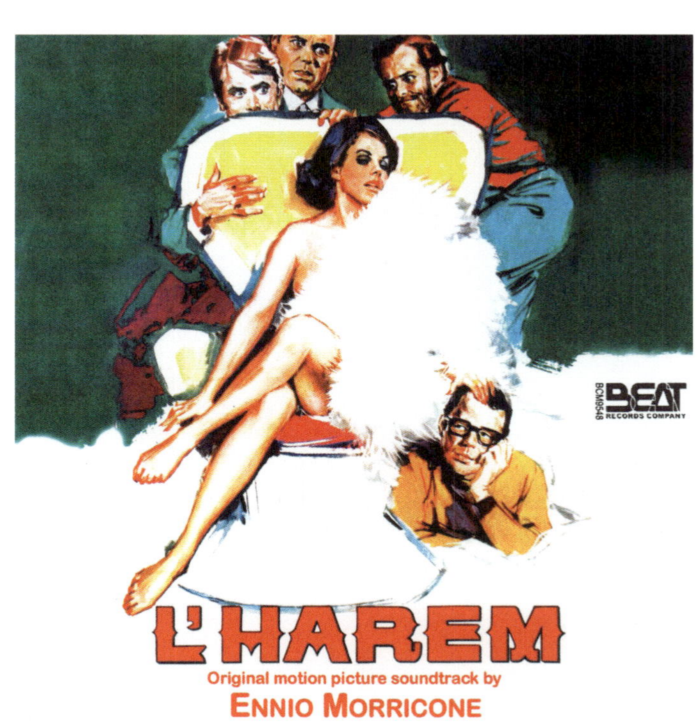

1967
Matchless
Mission Top Secret
Mission T.S.
LP 33 rpm - COMETA CMT 1015/29

1967
L'harem
Her Harem
Le harem
CD - BEAT BCM 9548

This soundtrack was woven by Morricone into a mysterious fabric, embellished with arabesques of sound improvised on the sax by Gato Barbieri.

BEAT
L'HAREM
Original motion picture soundtrack by
ENNIO MORRICONE

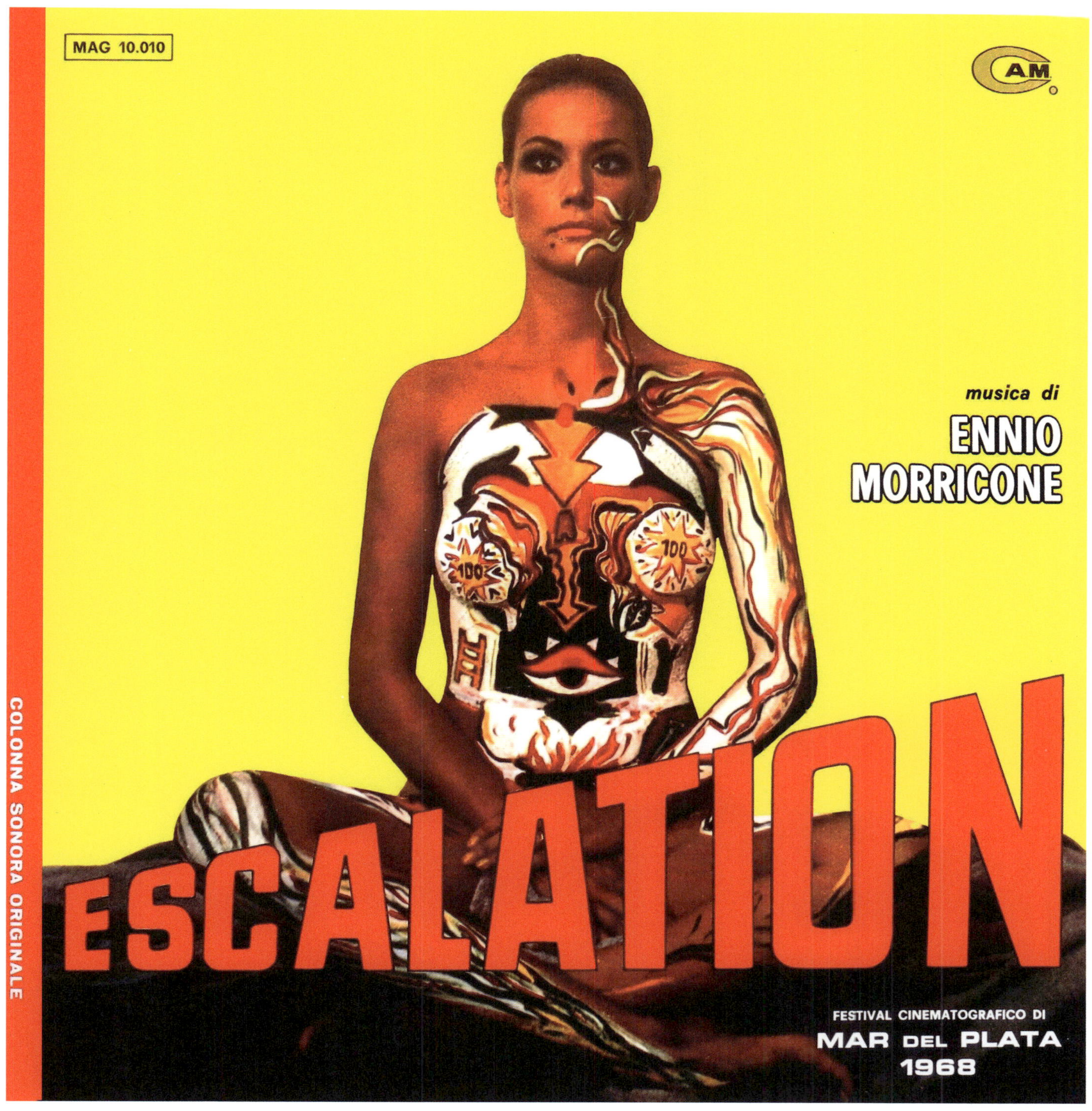

1968
Escalation
LP 33 rpm - CAM MAG 10.010

Peaceful music, which can also be disconcerting and deceptive at times, accompanies the grotesque story told in Roberto Faenza's movie. Morricone lets his imagination run wild amidst light sonorities that seem to accentuate the underlying sense of false tranquility, which hides the ferocious contrast with the developments in the plot. Published in the series known as *Mag*, recorded and cut in mono by CAM, the album with this soundtrack instantly became an item you had to have because of its magnetic cover, whose bright colors recall the pop psychedelia of that period.

1968

Grazie zia

Thank You, Aunt

Merci Lea

45 rpm - CAM AMP 40

45 rpm - AZ EP 1259

Notwithstanding the presence of a boys' choir, *I bambini di Renata Cortiglione*, the theme song of *Thank You, Aunt*, ironically titled, *Guerra e pace, pollo e brace*, is as grotesque and problematic as the film posters, designed by Sandro Symeoni in his unmistakable style.

1968
Gli intoccabili
Machine Gun McCain
Les intouchables
LP 33 rpm - JOLLY LPJ 5094
45 rpm - JOKER M 7023

1968
Teorema
Theorem
Théorème
LP 33 rpm - ARIETE AR/LP 2002
45 rpm - ARIETE AR 8005

For this much-debated film by Pier Paolo Pasolini, Ennio Morricone shares the musical scene with Mozart's *Requiem Mass.* The director made this request and the Maestro boldly offset it with upbeat vocals, dissonances, and arias featuring a vaguely Western flavor.

5 (nastri mono ricavati colonna sonora del film)

Buste Magica

N° DISCO ARLP 2002 LP 33 1/3

Fabbrica AMBROSIO

Pubblicato il 30/11/68

N. Matrice	1° FACCIATA	2° FACCIATA
	ARLP 2002 A	ARLP 2002 B
	Colonna sonora originale del film "Teorema"	
	1. TEOREMA	1. REQUIEM
	2. FRAMMENTI	2. KYRIE ELEISON
	3. FRUSCIO DI FOGLIE VERDI (cantato	3. REX TREMENDAE MAJESTATIS
	4. L'ULTIMA CORRIDA	4. CONFUTATIS MALEDICTIS
	5. BEAT N° 3	5. LACRIMOSA DIES ILLA
		6. AGNUS DEI
	Musica composta da E. Morricone	MESSA DA REQUIEM – W. A. MOZART
	Diretta da B. Nicolai	Solisti E. Egorova – G. Kozlova –
	Brani 1-2-4 con "I cantori moderni	A. Maslennikov – M. Rescentin
	di Alessandroni Brano 3 "Trio Jinior"	
	Testo di A. Nhora	
	1)	
	2) "	"
	3) "	"
	4) "	"
	5 "	"

1968
Galileo
LP 33 rpm - CAM SAG 9010

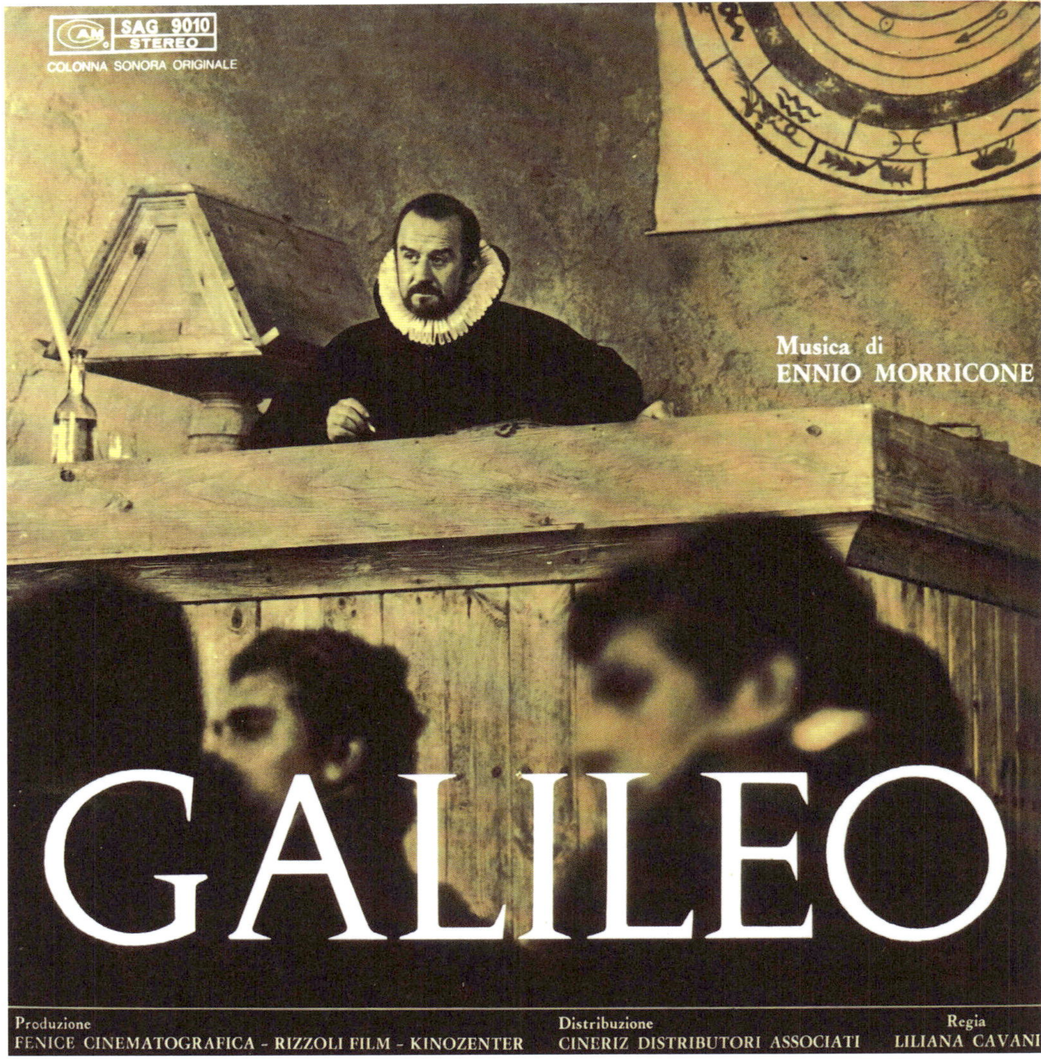

1968
Fräulein Doktor
CD - LEGEND CD 34 DLX

It is truly impossible to understand how such a beautiful soundtrack, dominated by a main theme of great intensity and inspired romanticism, was relegated for so many years to minor and obscure recordings for background music and compilations; and contained just two themes. The fictionalized events in the life of the mysterious German spy, code name Fräulein Doktor, scored by Ennio Morricone, certainly deserved greater appreciation at the time of release, instead of waiting nearly four decades to be acknowledged.

1968
Partner
LP 33 rpm - CAM SAG 9010

CAM SAG 9010 STEREO

COLONNA SONORA ORIGINALE

PARTNER.

PARTNER.

DISTRIBUZIONE CA.DI Via Virgilio, 8 - ROMA

Produzione RED FILM

Distribuzione ITALNOLEGGIO CINEMATOGRAFICO

Regia BERNARDO BERTOLUCCI

Musica ENNIO MORRICONE

1968
Eat It
45 rpm - CAM AMP 50

1968

C'era una volta il West

Once Upon a Time in the West

Il était une fois dans l'Ouest

LP 33 rpm - RCA OLS 3
45 rpm - RCA OC 7
45 rpm - RCA OC 11

The main theme of this soundtrack, which has become a tune familiar to almost everyone, is no doubt one of the most famous arias composed by Ennio Morricone for the cinema. The composition is marked by the fluid musicality with which the lyricism, accentuated by the astonishing voice of Edda Dell'Orso, caresses its listeners, sometimes ushering them into a dreamlike state. It is perhaps the pinnacle of music in the Italian Western genre, although its intense romanticism would have lent itself to any story. The excellent musical cast includes, besides Dell'Orso, Franco De Gemini on the harmonica and the *Cantori Moderni di Alessandroni*, under the impeccable conducting of Maestro Ennio Morricone.

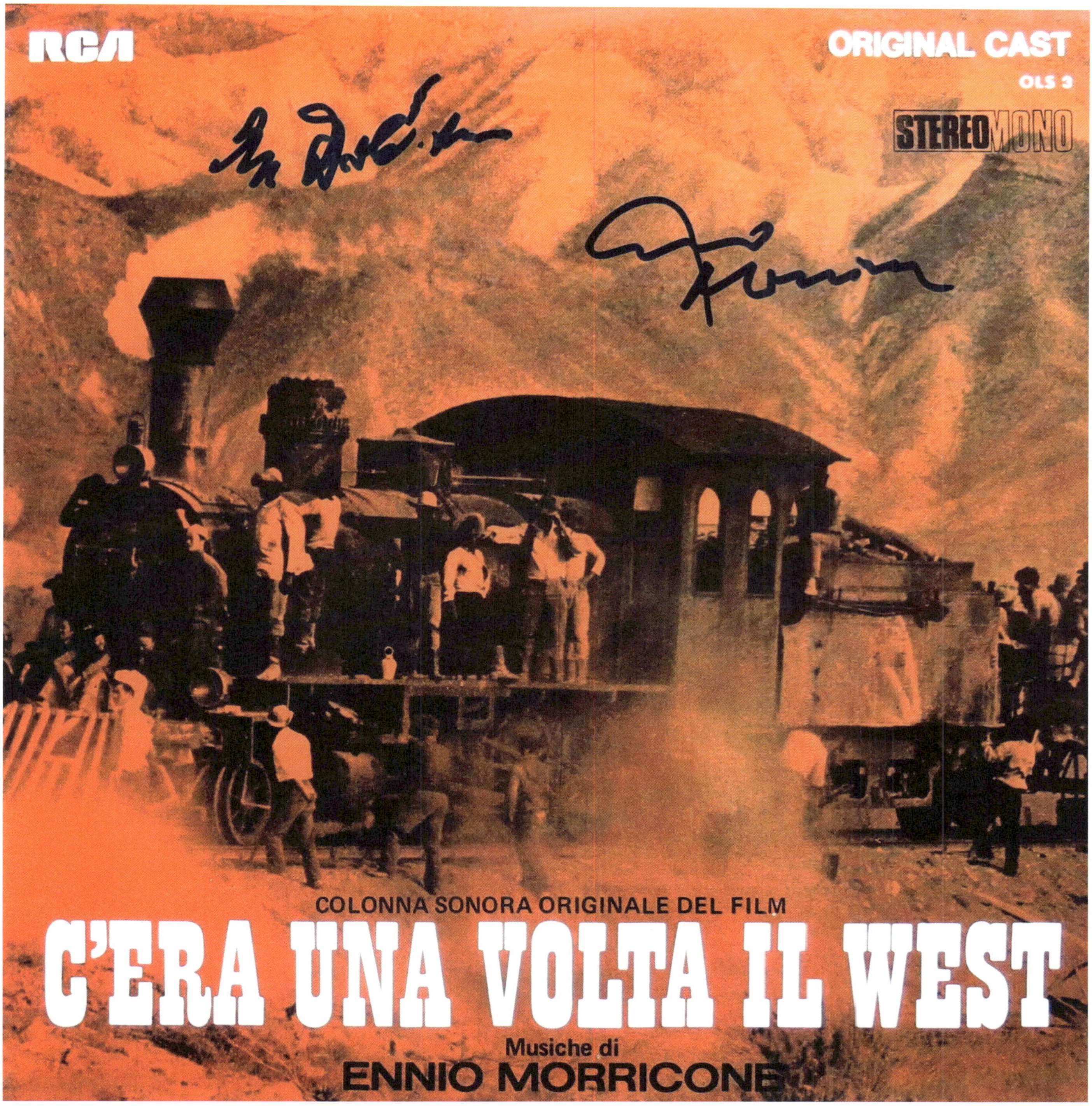
RCA
ORIGINAL CAST
OLS 3
STEREO MONO
COLONNA SONORA ORIGINALE DEL FILM
C'ERA UNA VOLTA IL WEST
Musiche di
ENNIO MORRICONE

RCA
ORIGINAL CAST
OC 7
dalla colonna sonora originale del film omonimo
C'ERA UNA VOLTA IL WEST
L'UOMO DELL'ARMONICA
MUSICHE DI ENNIO MORRICONE

RCA
ORIGINAL CAST
OC 11
dalla colonna sonora originale del film
C'ERA UNA VOLTA IL WEST
ADDIO A CHEYENNE
COME UNA SENTENZA
Musiche di ENNIO MORRICONE

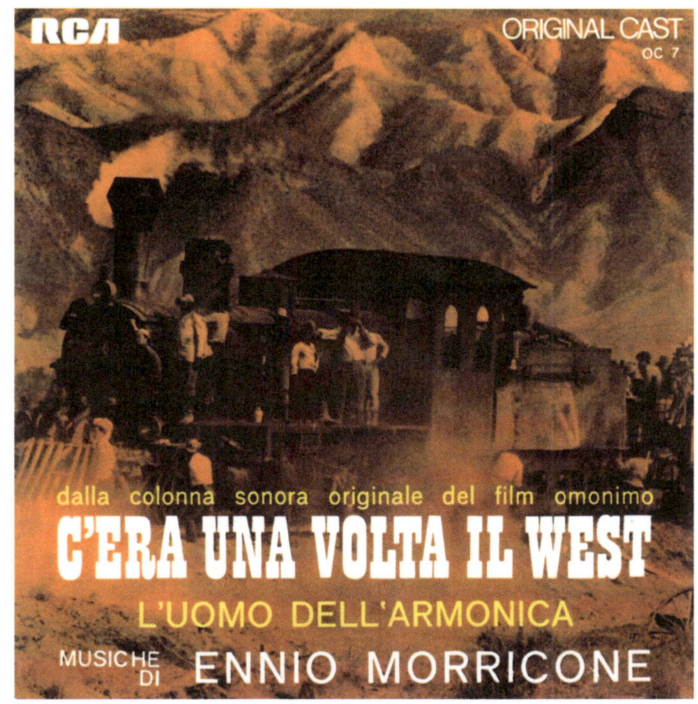

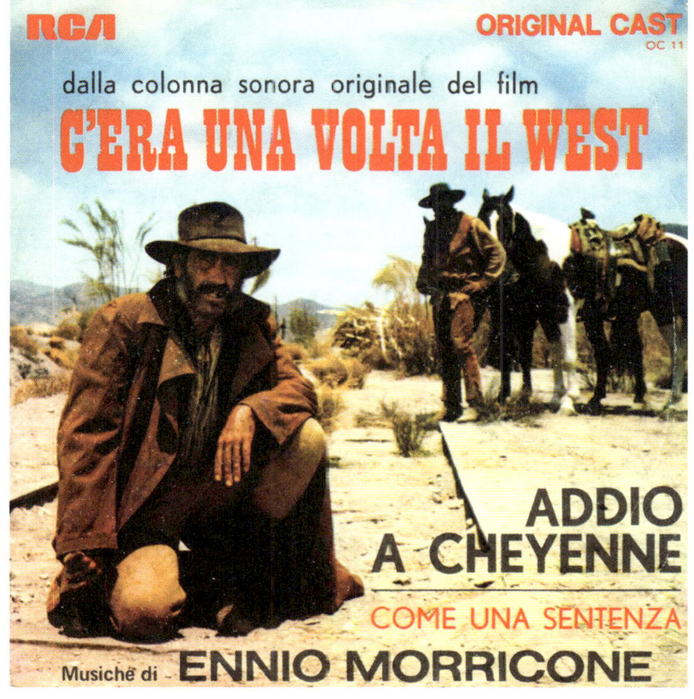

1968

Tepepa

Trois pour un massacre

45 rpm - RCA PM 3485
LP 33 rpm - CERBERUS CEM-S 0106

We have yet another excellent example of the work of the vocalist Christy (real name Maria Cristina Brancucci) in this Western with an underlying social theme, featuring the song *Al Messico che vorrei*.

1968
La bataille de San Sebastian
I cannoni di San Sebastian
Guns for San Sebastian
LP 33 rpm - MGM SE-4565 ST

1968
Ruba al prossimo tuo
A Fine Pair
Un couple pas ordinaire
CD - DIGITMOVIES CDDM 109

1968

Il grande silenzio

The Great Silence

Le grand silence

LP 33 rpm - PARADE FPR 317
LP 33 rpm - BEAT CR 1 Serie Blu

Musically as well as for other reasons, *The Great Silence* is perhaps the most peculiar of all the "Spaghetti Westerns," in which we find a Morricone who is definitely off the beaten path but with clear ideas about the winter setting amidst the snowy landscape of Cortina D'Ampezzo, while simulating the frontier in Utah. Both the film and the soundtrack inspired Quentin Tarantino for *The Hateful Eight*. Curiously, Beat Records' re-release inaugurating the Serie Blu was produced with three different album sleeves.

1968
Un tranquillo posto di campagna
A Quiet Place in the Country
Un coin tranquille à la campagne
LP 33 rpm - ROUNDTABLE ROMA 101 LP

Distanze per undici violini, voce di donna e percussioni is the title of the only composition known for Elio Petri's *A Quiet Place in the Country*. The remainder of the musical commentary is developed through the instrumental arbitrariness of the *Gruppo d'Improvvisazione Nuova Consonanza*. Morricone himself was a member of the group, and at the time his interest was also in more unconventional music with purely experimental aims and an eye toward musical research.

1968
E per tetto un cielo di stelle
A Sky Full of Stars for a Roof
Ciel de plomb
LP 33 rpm - COMETA CMT 1003.11

This is another soundtrack for a Western genre, where Morricone applies more of his style, but ultimately is unconvincing. The music's main structure is based on guitar chords and whistling by Alessandro Alessandroni. The album, whose cover is rather naïf, was not released by Cometa (Comet Records) until ten years after the movie release.

1968

Il mercenario

The Mercenary

45 rpm - UNITED ARTISTS UA 3153
LP 33 rpm - UNITED ARTISTS 2 C 062 90891

Versatility seems to be the gift that a composer like Ennio Morricone has in common with an actor of the caliber of Franco Nero; a multifaceted interpreter whether he is doing comedy or a dramatic role. For his part, Morricone structures the main theme of the movie with a crescendo whose instrumentation is increasingly augmented; and introduced by the amazing modulated whistling of Alessandro Alessandroni, a sound resembling something that might come from Pan's flute.

1968

Diabolik

Danger: Diabolik

45 rpm - PARADE PRC 5052
45 rpm - TIZOC/PARADE ST-47

One of the most sought-after soundtracks in the record production of Ennio Morricone, of which there exists, if we exclude a poor-quality bootleg version, a single version relative to the opening credits: the song is titled, *Deep Down,* sung by Christy, and issued on a Parade Records single and other co-releases Unfortunately, the master tapes with the original recordings directed by Bruno Nicolai have been lost. Recently, a CD was recorded with a new version by the Solisti E Orchestre Del Cinema Italiano. However, slow sales indicate that this version did not meet fans' expectations

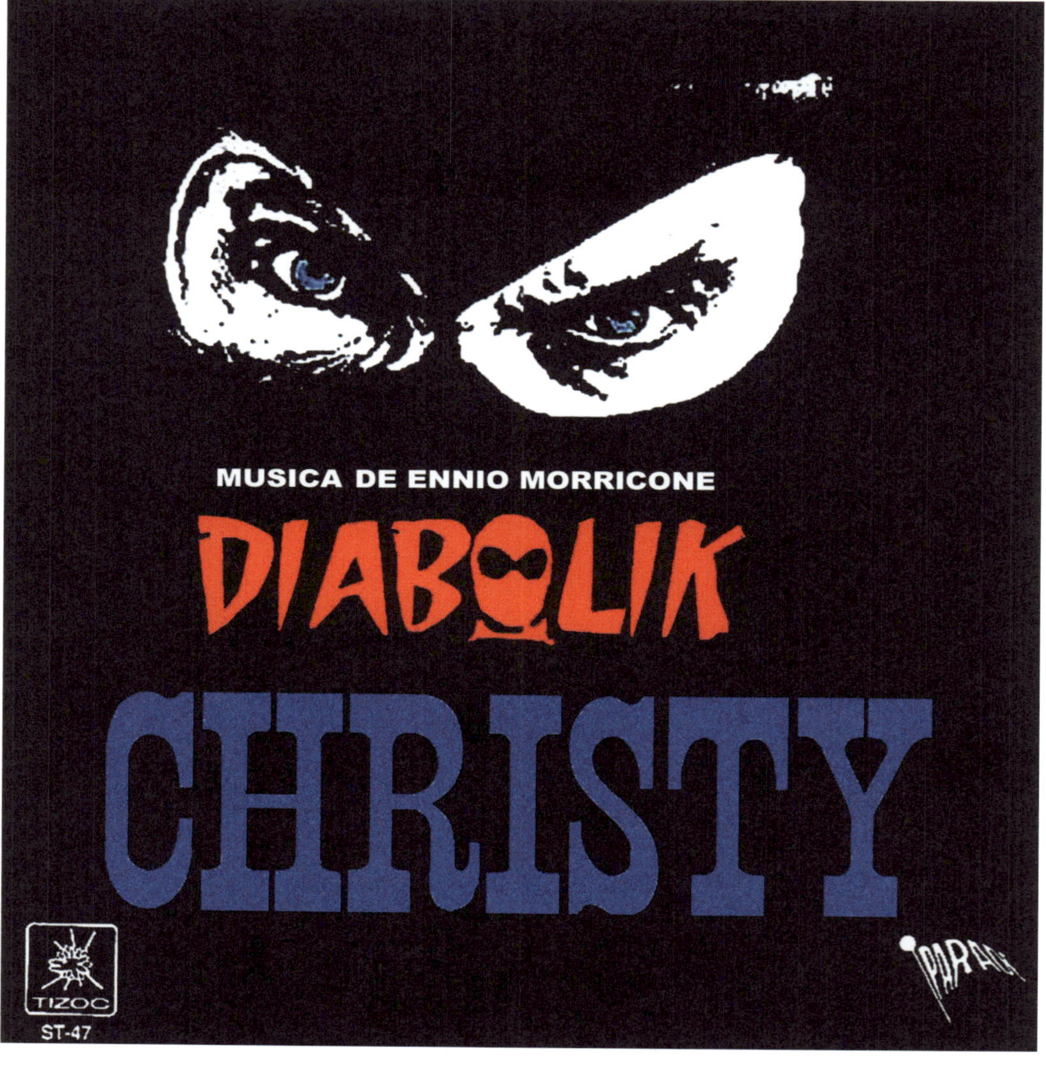

1968
Comandamenti per un gangster
L'enfer avant la mort
LP 33 rpm - CAM MAG 10.014

The soundtrack includes the song, *Solo nostalgia,* sung by Jane Relly and written by Audrey Nohra Stainton, a prolific songwriter living in Italy and the wife of the movie producer Anis Nohra. Nohra Stainton wrote many lyrics for Italian cinema, often collaborating with Armando Trovaioli, Luis Bacalov, and Morricone himself.

1969
H_2S
CD - Bootleg BmgB 00H2S 10 01

1969
Giovanni ed Elviruccia
45 rpm - CAROSELLO CI 20244

1969
Il libro dell'arte: Giotto
Roma come Chicago
Bandits in Rome
CD - RECORDING ARTS SA - x903

1969
Sai cosa faceva Stalin alle donne?
What Did Stalin Do to Women?
Sais-tu ce que Staline faisait aux femmes?
CD - BEAT BCM 9524

1969

Uccidete il vitello grasso e arrostitelo

Kill the Fatted Calf and Roast It

CD - DIGITMOVIES CDDM083

An emblematic score for some breakthrough cinema. Morricone creates a sound that's rhythmical and allegorical and based on modern style, entrusting the lead phrasing to an insistent Hammond organ accompanied by a pervasive sing-song in hypnotic "taste." These are the sound elements in a troubling story that takes place in the sticks. A lot like a musical re-reading inspired by Freud.

1969
Le clan des siciliens
Il clan dei siciliani
The Sicilian Clan
LP 33 rpm - FOX 940.006
45 rpm - CAM AMP 74
LP 33 rpm - FOX GXH 6038

It is truly remarkable that a simple, almost common string of notes following one another repetitively in a descending musical scale, accompanied by a counterpoint of strings and cadenced by the disquieting sound of a Jew's harp (lu marranzanu), has universally come to be associated with all things mafia.

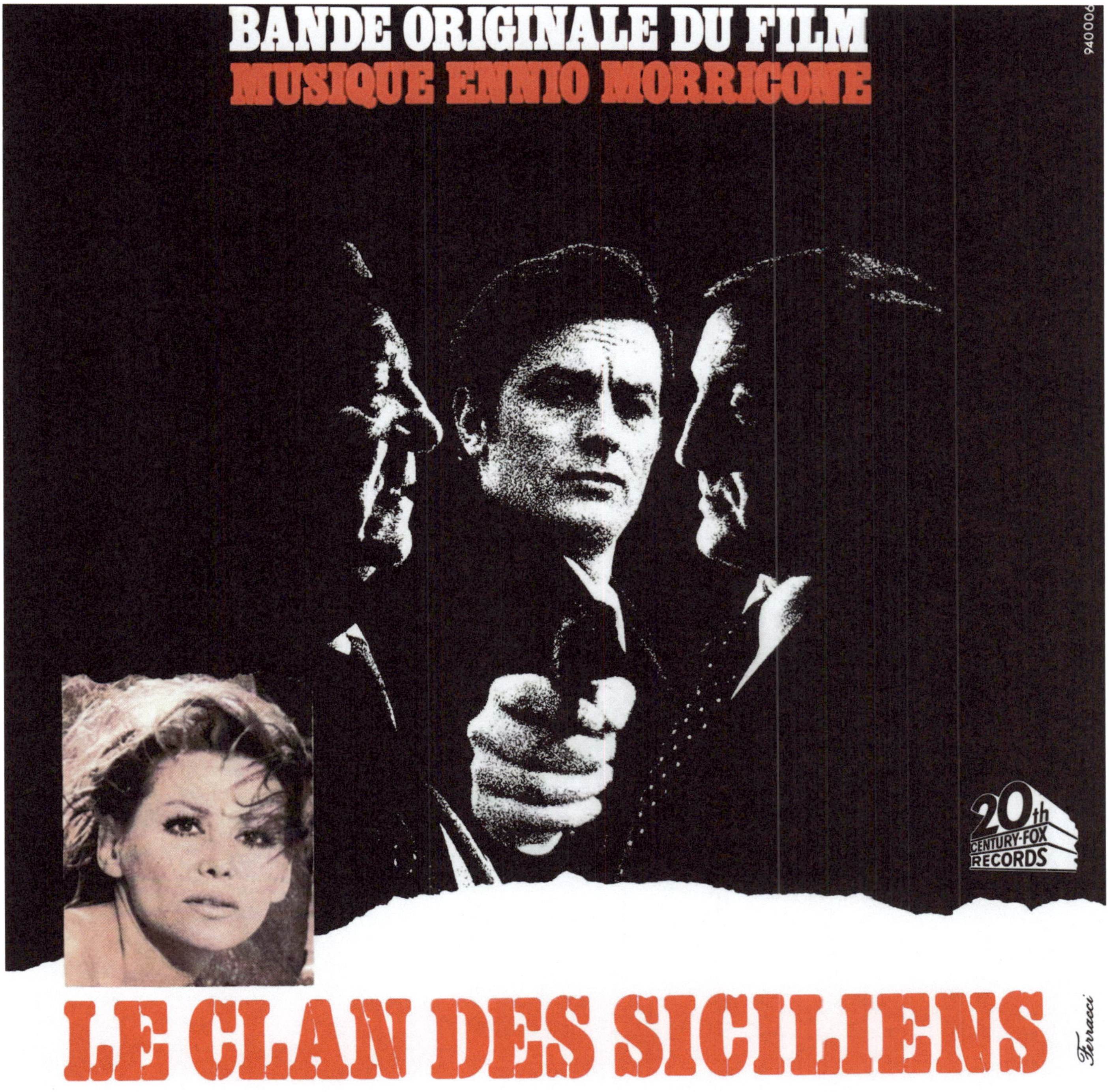
BANDE ORIGINALE DU FILM
MUSIQUE ENNIO MORRICONE
940006
20th CENTURY-FOX RECORDS
LE CLAN DES SICILIENS
Ferracci

CAM AMP 74
MUSICA DI ENNIO MORRICONE
COLONNA SONORA ORIGINALE
IL CLAN DEI SICILIANI

GXH 6038
THE SICILIAN CLAN
Original Motion Picture Soundtrack
20th Century-Fox Presents
A Henri Verneuil-Jacques E Strauss Production
20th CENTURY-FOX RECORDS
stereo

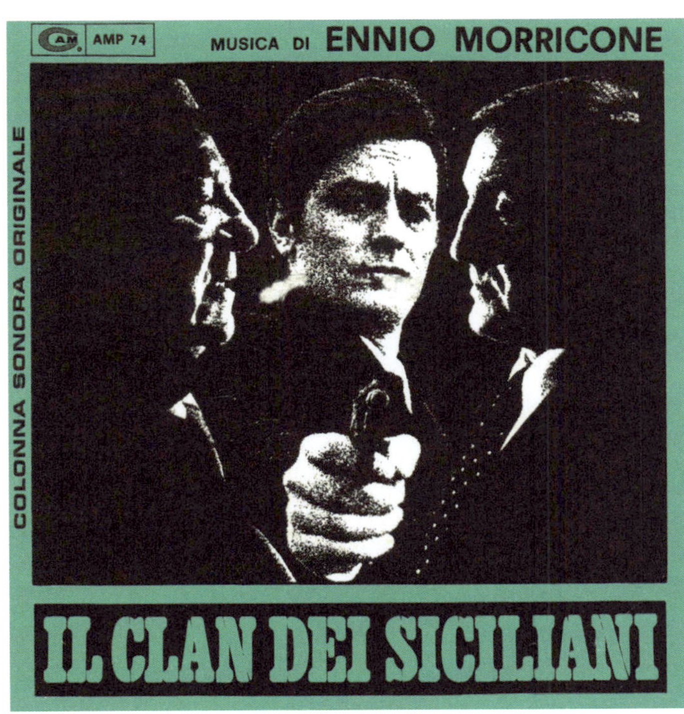

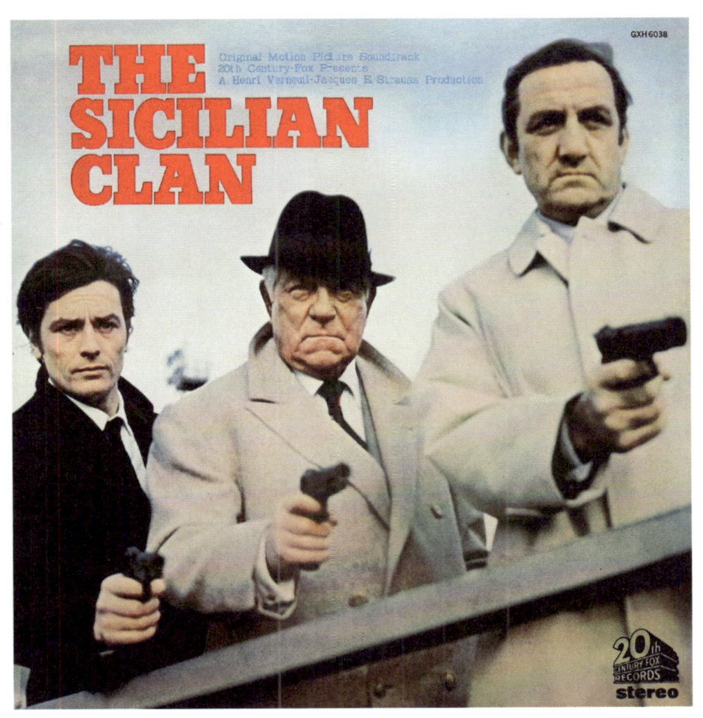

1969
Cuore di mamma
Mother's Heart
LP 33 rpm - MONTE STELLA MSR 1320009

The main theme on the soundtrack for *Mother's Heart* is the touching *Ouverture del mattino*, an andante tune with baroque tones that would be used in at least two more movies: *This Kind of Love*, 1972 and *Il pianeta d'acqua*, 1980.

1969
L'alibi
Alibi
LP 33 rpm - DAGORED RED 242

1969
Ecce homo. I sopravvissuti
Behold Man. The Survivors
LP 33 rpm - DAGORED RED 141-1

1969

Metti, una sera a cena

Love Circle

Disons, un soir à dîner

LP 33 rpm - CINEVOX MDF 33/16

The bossa nova was "reinvented" in a Lounge style by Ennio Morricone for this film, and complemented with imaginative vocals by Edda Dell'Orso. Just as the ingredients for mayonnaise have to be perfectly incorporated and emulsified, this music had just the right timing and just the right amount of input from both artists. This is a masterpiece of musical inventiveness with musical direction by Bruno Nicolai that was a flawless, huge success around the world. It was Morricone's first work to be recorded and released by the historical Cinevox Records.

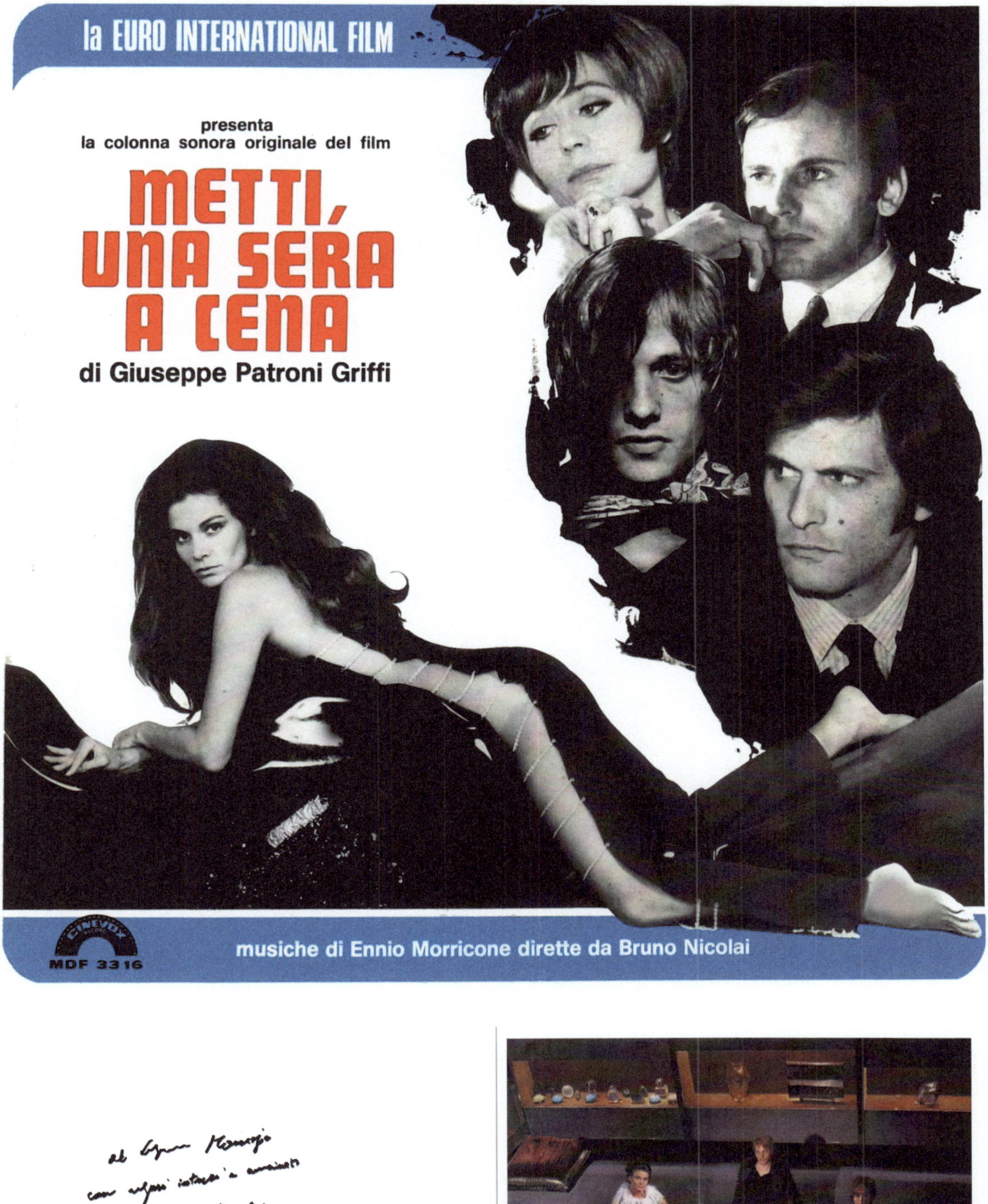

la EURO INTERNATIONAL FILM

presenta
la colonna sonora originale del film

METTI, UNA SERA A CENA

di Giuseppe Patroni Griffi

CINEVOX
MDF 3316

musiche di Ennio Morricone dirette da Bruno Nicolai

al [illegible]
con [illegible]
Ennio Morricone

1969
La monaca di Monza: una storia lombarda
The Lady of Monza
La religieuse de Monza
LP 33 rpm - INTERMEZZO IMGM 001

The music of this tragic 17th-century event is heart-rending and melancholy and was revived from the noble writings of Alessandro Manzoni in his novel, *The Betrothed*. Morricone does not escape the evocativeness and the travail between the sacred and the profane that grip these terrible events, forging music that has a strong emotional impact, and making us want to listen to it even without its cinematic imagery.

1969

Un bellissimo novembre

That Splendid November

Ce merveilleux automne

45 rpm - PARADE PRC 5075

LP 33 rpm - INTERMEZZO IMGM 001

The true authorship of the song, *Nuddu*, sung by Fausto Cigliano in *That Splendid November* is still an unsolved mystery. On the single issued by Parade, the lyricist is listed as Robert Mellin, while on the album *Intermezzo*, the words are attributed to Maria Travia, Maestro Morricone's wife. Other sources, like CD Beat, instead claim that the lyrics were written by Franco Pisano. It is more likely that the song, sung in Sicilian dialect, was indeed written by Maria Travia who is from Sicily.

1969
La stagione dei sensi
Season of the Senses
LP 33 rpm - ARIETE ARLP 2005
45 rpm - CAROSELLO CI 20224

Three songs written by Audrey Nohra Stainton to music by Morricone can be heard on this soundtrack. The songs were sung by Patrick Samson and accompanied by the vocals of Edda Dell'Orso, whose very rare original record, released by Ariete, is still among the most sought after by collectors.

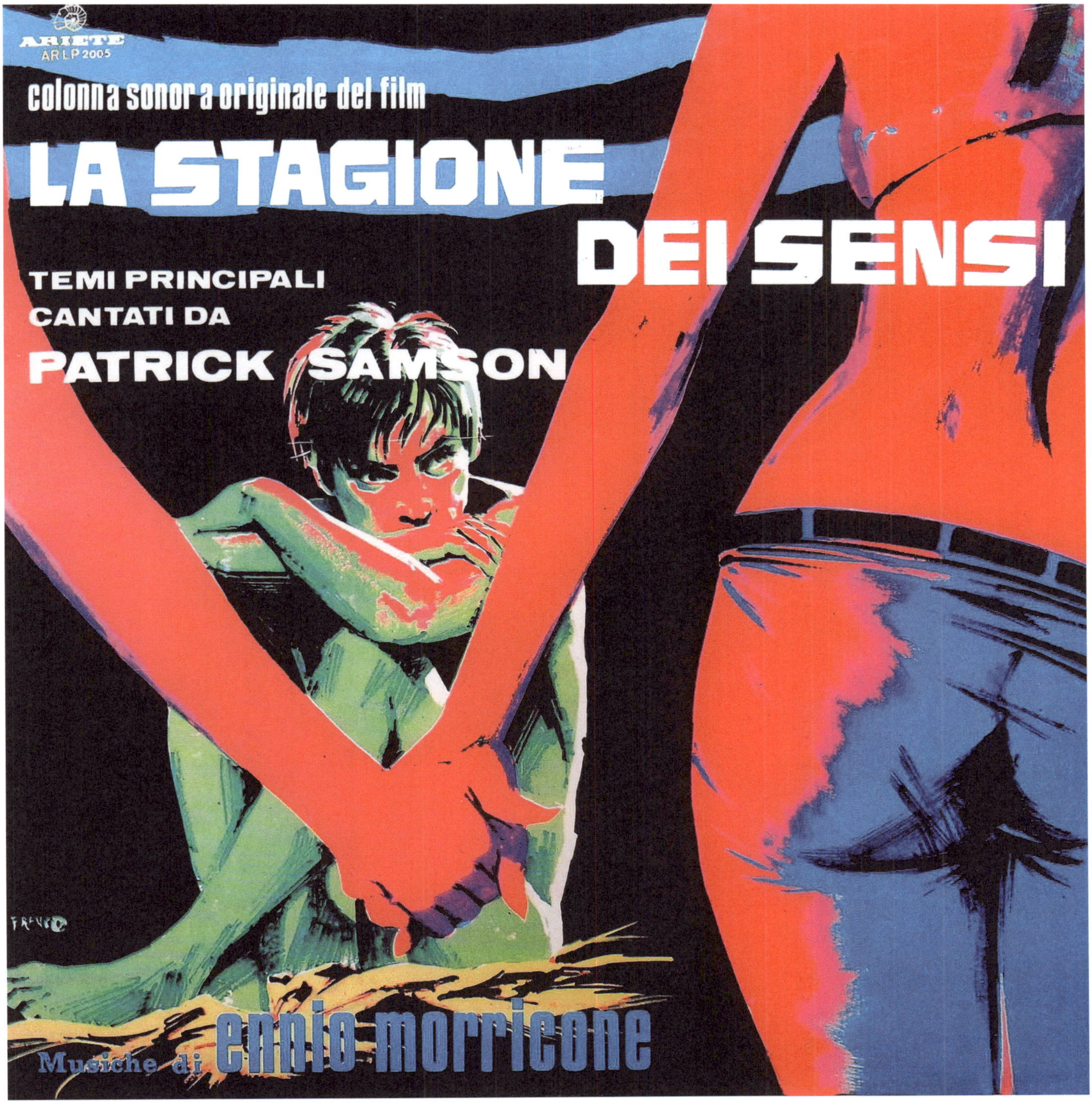
ARIETE
AR LP 2005
colonna sonor a originale del film
LA STAGIONE
DEI SENSI
TEMI PRINCIPALI
CANTATI DA
PATRICK SAMSON
Musiche di ennio morricone

un film di
MASSIMO FRANCIOSA
Prodotto da ITALO ZINGARELLI
CAROSELLO
CI 20224
con UDO KIER LAURA BELLI EDDA DI BENEDETTO
EVA THOLIN SUSANNE VON SASS
COLONNA SONORA ORIGINALE DEL FILM
LA STAGIONE
DEI SENSI
LAILA LAILA
GLORIA
PATRICK SAMSON

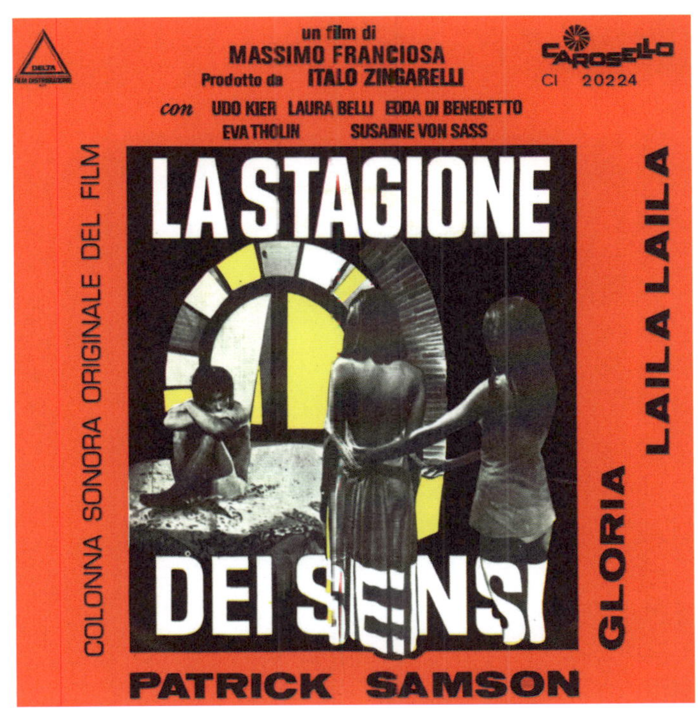

1969
Un esercito di 5 uomini
The 5-Man Army
5 hommes armes
LP 33 rpm - ARIETE ARL 2009

Morricone created specific musical parameters and components for the Spaghetti Western Genre. For this movie, the composer referenced all of them to combine colors, sounds, and vocals for a soundtrack with an almost progressive slant.

1969
Gott Mit Uns
(Dio è con noi)
The Fifth Day of Peace
À l'aube du cinquième jour
45 rpm - RCA PM 3526

1969
Geminus
45 rpm - RCA OC 12

FACCIATA A (1) E. Morricone

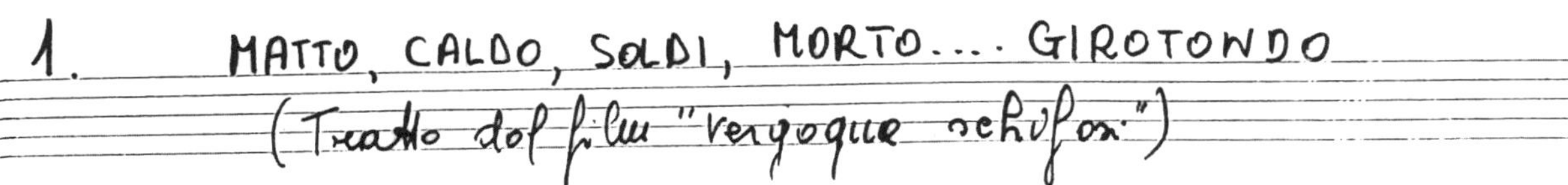

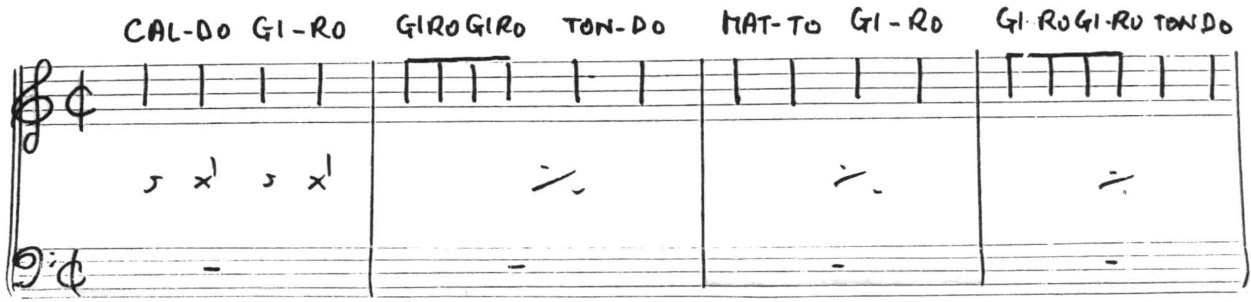

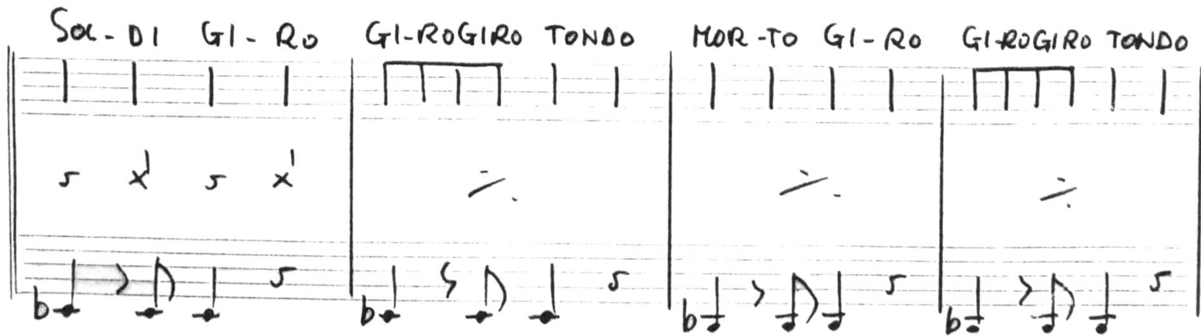

COLONNA SONORA ORIGINALE DEL FILM

VERGOGNA SCHIFOSI

MUSICHE ORIGINALE DI ENNIO MORRICONE

1969
Vergogna schifosi
Dirty Angels
LP 33 rpm - ARIETE ARLP 2003

This splendid score, brimming with bold and penetrating vocals, seems to have surpassed the movie with its quality. Neither the first or last time that Ennio Morricone, happily inspired here, manages to completely embrace the cinematographic work with his music; rescuing a film from oblivion. The rare original record released by Ariete shows an "innocent" typo on the front cover that reads "Musiche *originale*" instead of "Musiche originali." This mistake was only corrected with more recent re-editions.

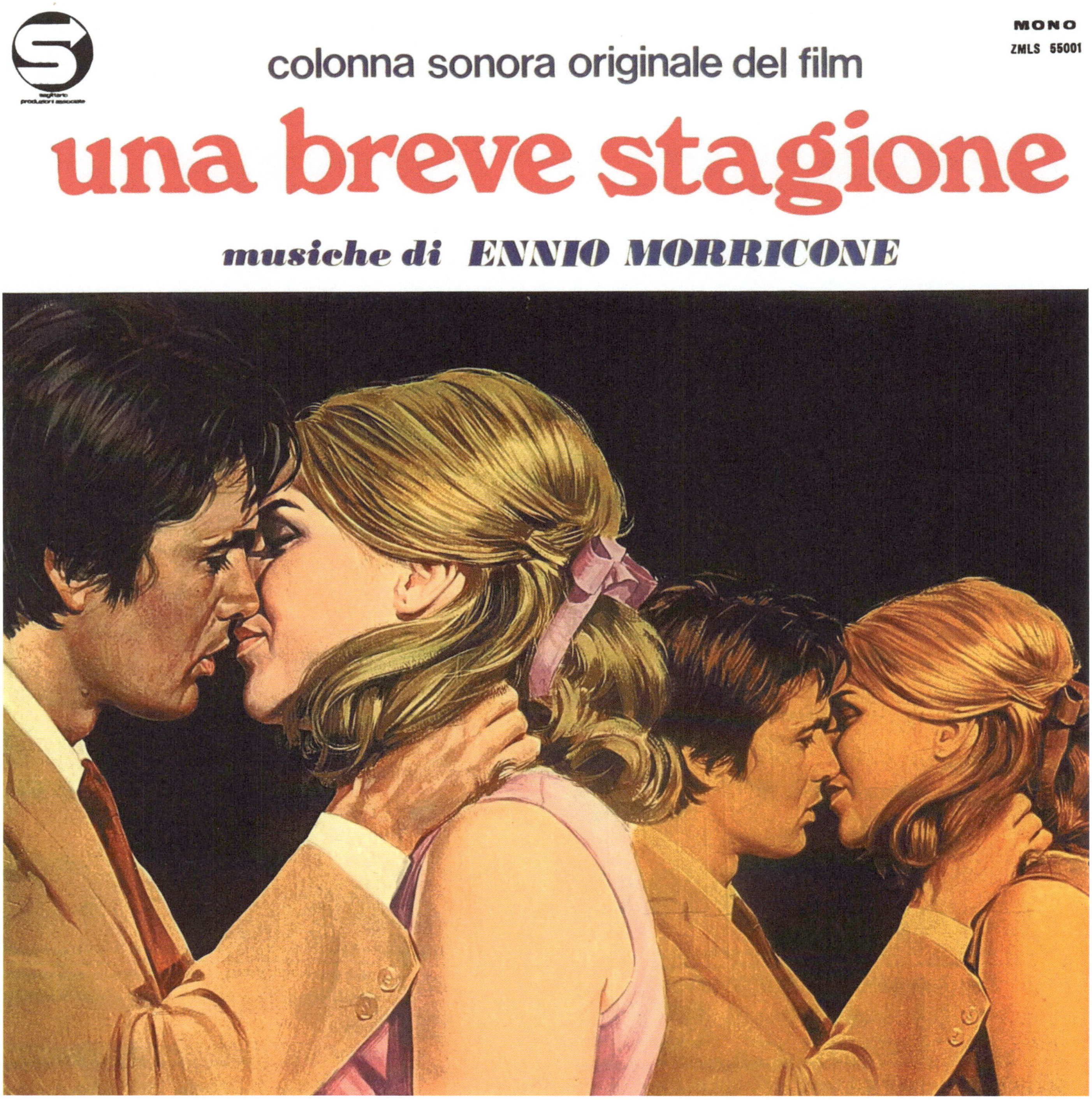

MONO
ZMLS 55001

colonna sonora originale del film

una breve stagione

musiche di ENNIO MORRICONE

1969
Una breve stagione
A Brief Season
LP 33 rpm - SAGITTARIO ZMLS 55001
45 rpm - CETRA SP 1418

In addition to the album released under the Sagittario label, Cetra published a single with the title tune sung by Sergio Endrigo and written by Endrigo, Morricone, and Sergio Bardotti. There were two different covers. One featured a detail from the movie poster and the other, less well known, had an image of the singer. In both cases, the Maestro's name stands out.

1969

L'assoluto naturale

She and He

LP 33 rpm - CINEVOX MDF 33/23

The unnatural affair at the heart of this relatively abstract experimental film belies the original Italian title. Morricone was presented with the opportunity to develop a minimalist, avant-garde soundtrack to accompany the film's sexuality and sometimes torrid scenes. Somewhat surprisingly, instead he opted for tried and true musical idioms that nonetheless augmented this surreal motion picture.

PRESENTA LA COLONNA SONORA ORIGINALE DEL FILM

L'ASSOLUTO NATURALE

musiche di Ennio Morricone dirette da Bruno Nicolai

1969
La donna invisibile
The Invisible Woman
LP 33 rpm - DAGORED RED 109-1

In the 60s, it happened frequently that owing to discographic choices or for other reasons, many movies never saw their soundtracks published. Sometimes instead, their themes at most became compilations for background music; or were used in other movies. This was true about the music composed for *The Invisible Woman,* whose song *Ritratto d'autore,* was recycled in *Giuochi particolari* directed by Franco Indovina in 1970. There is no recording of the latter, but if you listen to the music while watching the movie, you might notice how it was a dress rehearsal for *Duck, You Sucker.*

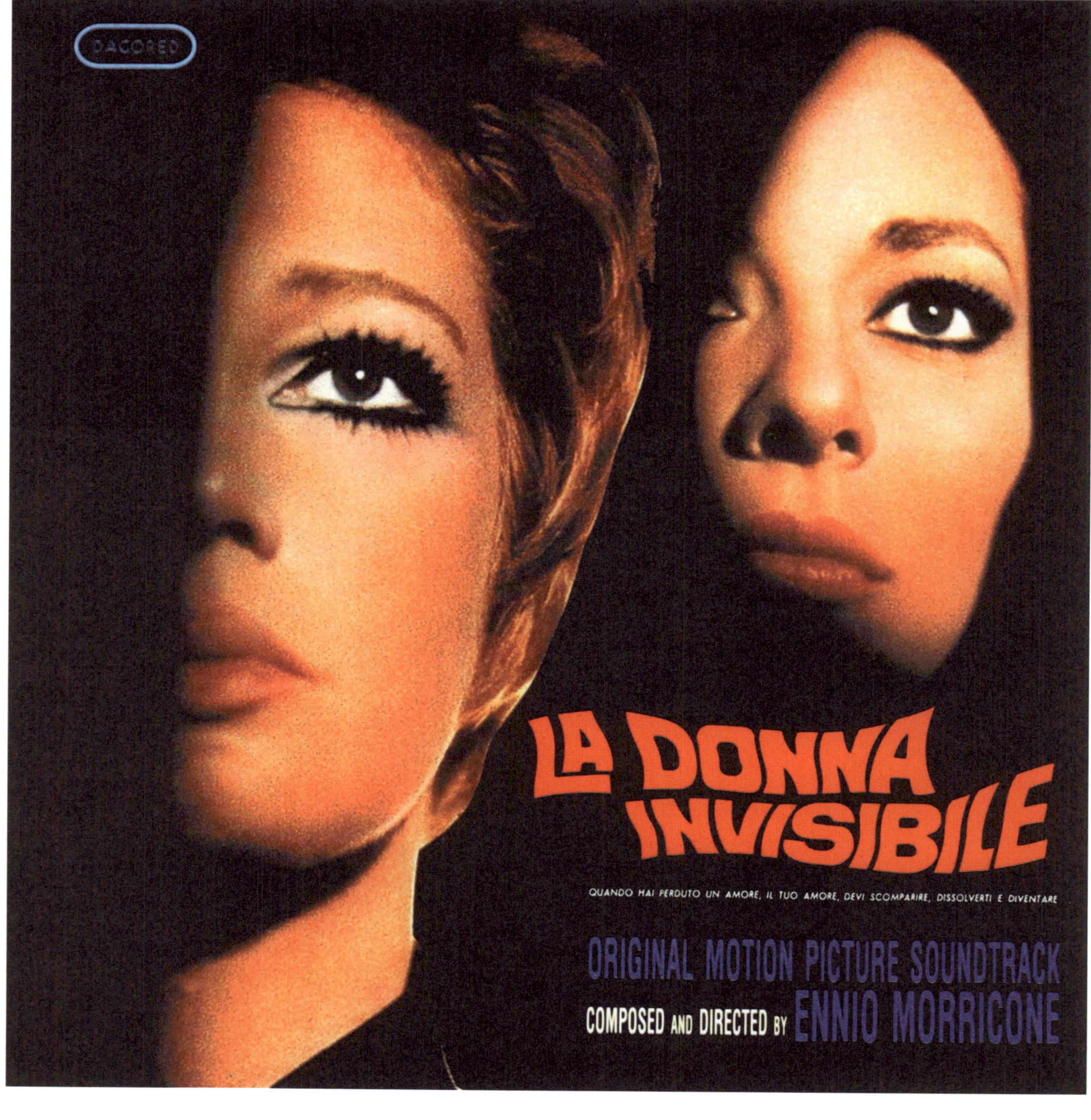

1969
Krasnaya palatka
La tenda rossa
The Red Tent
La tente rouge
LP 33 rpm - SAGITTARIO ZSLS 55006

The Red Tent, an Italian-Russian production of international ambition whose original title was *Krasnaya palatka*, was directed with an all-star cast by the Russian filmmaker Mickail K. Kalatozov. The original music for the film version was composed and directed by Aleksander Zatsepin, while for the international and Italian edition, Ennio Morricone composed the music and Bruno Nicolai conducted.

1969
Queimada
Burn!
45 rpm - UNITED ARTISTS UA 3173
LP 33 rpm - UNITED ARTISTS UA LA 303 G
45 rpm - UNITED ARTISTS UP 35149

Sometimes choices made by record producers seem illogical and incomprehensible to film music enthusiasts. Here, we wonder why United Artists initially limited itself to producing just one single from this amazing soundtrack. *Burn!* is an important film and Ennio Morricone's exotic, ethnic musical contribution is a successful accompaniment for a spectacular and historic film. What's even more disconcerting, is that later it was discovered that a bootleg edition containing most of this splendid film music was circulating in the United States. Dismay became disappointment and anger. Today, the music has been redeemed by numerous re-editions, but the wait for its availability was simply too long.

Original Motion Picture Soundtrack
MARLON BRANDO
in
"BURN!"
A Film by
GILLO PONTECORVO
URN!"
An ALBERTO GRIMALDI Production
with EVARISTO MARQUEZ RENATO SALVATORI
Story and Screenplay by FRANCO SOLINAS and
GIORGIO ARLORIO
Art Director PIERO GHERARDI
Music ENNIO MORRICONE
COLOR by Deluxe
UA

UNITED ARTISTS
bande originale du film
QUEIMADA
musique de Ennio Morricone
doc artistes associés

1969
Senza sapere niente di lei
CD - DIGITMOVIES CDDM050

It was common in the 1960s for many soundtracks to remain unpublished and to record only the main theme. Sometimes, the music would find its way into some hard-to-identify compilation or obscure background in a music album. This was the situation for *Senza sapere niente di lei*.

615

Senza sapere niente di lei - Mº E. Morricone

I5 nab stereo - Rg Fono Roma I8.9.1969

	Iª scatola	
I	generico (romantico); orches tra; moderato in 3 per archi e ritmica; da I,29 a fine canto per celeste e arpa (unisono) anche con corni in contrappunto	2,0I
I8	id. per fiati e ritmica; passaggio decisamente romantico per archi (canto), celeste, arpa, spinetta e ritmica da I I,06 a I,38; n.b. fulla a I,37	2,I0
II	id. introdotto e seguito, anche con lo strumentale completo da fraseggi di spinetta; stesso tema dei brani che precedono con organico via via piu' pieno condotto in prevalenza dai fiati; breve inciso con canto alternato per pianoforte, celeste e chitarra elettrica; vene tristi	2,56
I2	tensivo/introspettivo; lento per spinetta (fraseggi), archi (accordi tensivi) e pianoforte (fraseggi)	2,54
5	generico (romantico); orchestra; moderato in 3 per archi (prevalenti) e ritmica; da I,24 decisamente romantico per pianoforte (canto) e ritmica soli	2,2I
6	id. solo parte per archi (prevalenti) e ritmica; sempre stesso tema	I,20
7	id. per fiati e ritmica	I,02
Ricordo I	flashback; in 3 mod. lento per arpa, celeste, spinetta, flauto e archi (in sottofondo)	3,06
Ricordo 3	flashback/tensivo; lento per archi, celeste e spinetta (solo accenti di questi due all'unisono)	3,0I
2	stacchi/romantici; sul tema a valzer moderato per pianoforte, celeste, spinetta (unisono) e orchestra (archi) con vene tristi	0,22
3	id. (romant/pat t); a valzer lento	0,I8
9	id. per arpa e archi	0,I6
I4 archi	generico (romantico); a valzer sul tema, moderato, per archi (canto in prev.) arpa e pianoforte (inciso)	0,47
2I	tensivo/introspettivo; lento per spinetta (fraseggi), archi (accordi tensivi) e pf. (fraseggi)	I,I2

CAM - DET T 5

VIETATA DUPLICAZIONE E. PUBBLICA ESECUZIONE RADIODIFFUSIONE DI QUESTO DISCO. DEPOSITATO

• FABBRICATO E DIST

1. COME M

2. I

3. UNA DONNA

Dalla Colonna so

"MAD

Composizionl

ENNIO M

ZSLGE 55063

AKA Y 26156

STEREO

CAMPIONE NON COMMERCIABILE

GEN

Orchest

BRUNO

Edizioni

1970–1979

Discography

1970—1979

1970

Compañeros, Sergio Corbucci
Final Shot, Sergio Sollima
Giuochi particolari, Franco Indovina
Hornets' Nest, Phil Karlson
Investigation of a Citizen Above Suspicion, Elio Petri
Lady Caliph, Alberto Bevilacqua
Lui per lei, Claudio Rispoli
Metello, Mauro Bolognini
The Bird with the Crystal Plumage, Dario Argento
The Cannibals, Liliana Cavani
The Forbidden Photos of a Lady Above Suspicion, Luciano Ercoli
The Most Beautiful Wife, Damiano Damiani
The Virginian: Men from Shiloh, Various authors
Two Mules for Sister Sara, Donald Siegel
When Women Had Tails, Pasquale Festa Campanile

1971

4 Flies on Grey Velvet, Dario Argento
Black Belly of the Tarantula, Paolo Cavara
Cold Eyes of Fear, Enzo G. Castellari
Correva l'anno di grazia 1870, Alfredo Giannetti
Duck, You Sucker, Sergio Leone
La scoperta dell'America, Sergio Giordani
Lizard in a Woman's Skin, Lucio Fulci
Lulu the Tool, Elio Petri
Maddalena, Jerzy Kawalerowicz
Nessuno deve sapere, Mario Landi
Romance, Piero Schivazappa
Sacco & Vanzetti, Giuliano Montaldo
Sarah's Last Man, Maria Virginia Onorato
Short Night of Glass Dolls, Aldo Lado
'Tis Pity She's A Whore, Giuseppe Patroni Griffi
The Burglars, Henri Verneuil
The Case Is Closed, Forget It, Damiano Damiani
The Cat o' Nine Tails, Dario Argento
The Decameron, Pier Paolo Pasolini
The Fifth Cord, Luigi Bazzoni
The Wind Blows Free, Folco Quilici
There's a Noose Waiting for You Trinity!, Alfonso Balcazar
Tre donne, Alfredo Giannetti
Tre nel mille, Franco Indovina
Veruschka. Poetry of a Woman, Franco Rubartelli
Winged Devils, Duccio Tessari
Without Apparent Motive, Philippe Labro

1972

Anche se volessi lavorare, che faccio?, Flavio Mogherini
Bluebeard, Edward Dmytryk
Chronicle of a Homicide, Mauro Bolognini
Devil in the Brain, Sergio Sollima
For Love One Dies, Carlo Carunchio
Io e..., Paolo Brunatto, Walter Licastro, Luciano Emmer
L'uomo e la magia, Sergio Giordani
La cosa buffa, Aldo Lado
Life Is Tough, Eh Providence?, Giulio Petroni
My Dear Killer, Tonino Valerii
Sonny & Jed. Far West Story, Sergio Corbucci
The Assassination, Yves Boisset
The Canterbury Tales, Pier Paolo Pasolini
The Master and Margherite, Aleksandar Petrović
The Master Touch, Michele Lupo
The Sicilian Checkmate, Florestano Vancini
This Kind of Love, Alberto Bevilacqua
What Have You Done to Solange?, Massimo Dallamano
When Man Is the Prey, Vittorio De Sisti
Who Saw Her Die?, Aldo Lado
Why, Nino Zanchin

1973

Blood in the Streets, Sergio Sollima
Crescete e moltiplicatevi, Giulio Petroni
E se per caso una mattina, Vittorio Sindoni
Giordano Bruno, Giuliano Montaldo
Here We Go Again, Eh Providence?, Alberto De Martino
La proprietà non è più un furto, Elio Petri
Libera, My Love, Mauro Bolognini
Massacre in Rome, George Pan Cosmatos
My Name Is Nobody, Tonino Valerii
Space: 1999, Lee H. Katzin
The Serpent, Henri Verneuil
The Two Seasons of Life, Samy Pavel
What Am I Doing in the Middle of a Revolution?, Sergio Corbucci
When Love Is Lust, Vittorio De Sisti
Woman Buried Alive, Aldo Lado

1974

A Genius, Two Partners and a Dupe, Damiano Damiani
Allonsanfàn, Paolo e Vittorio Taviani
Almost Human, Umberto Lenzi
Arabian Nights, Pier Paolo Pasolini
Around the World with Peynet's Lovers, Cesare Perfetto
Il segreto di Cristina, Ruggero Deodato
Italiques, Pierre Boursaus
Mistress of the Devil, Juan Luis Buñuel
Moses, Gianfranco De Bosio
Murder on the Bridge, Maximilian Schell
Mussolini: The Last Four Days, Carlo Lizzani
Sex Advice, Vittorio De Sisti
Spasmo, Umberto Lenzi
The Antichrist, Alberto De Martino
The Cousin, Aldo Lado
The Devil Is a Woman, Damiano Damiani
The Human Factor, Edward Dmytryk
The Infernal Trio, Francis Girod
The Murri Affair, Mauro Bolognini
The Prostitution Racket, Carlo Lizzani
The Secret, Robert Enrico
Weak Spot, Peter Fleischmann

1975

Autopsy, Armando Crispino
Down the Ancient Stairs, Mauro Bolognini
Eye of the Cat, Alberto Bevilacqua
Labbra di lurido blu, Giulio Petroni
Last Stop on the Night Train, Aldo Lado
Salò, or the 120 Days of Sodom, Pier Paolo Pasolini
The Divine Nymph, Giuseppe Patroni Griffi
The Flower in His Mouth, Luigi Zampa
The Night Caller, Henri Verneuil
The Sunday Woman, Luigi Comencini

1976

1900, Bernardo Bertolucci
A Sold Life, Aldo Florio
And Agnes Chose to Die, Giuliano Montaldo
For Love, Mino Giarda
Le ricain, Jean-Marie Pallardy
One Way or Another, Elio Petri
San Babila – 8 P.M., Carlo Lizzani
The Desert of the Tartars, Valerio Zurlini
The Inheritance, Mauro Bolognini

1977

Drammi gotici. Nella città vampira (Series), Giorgio Bandini
Exorcist II: The Heretic, John Boorman
Forza Italia!, Roberto Faenza
Hitch-Hike, Pasquale Festa Campanile
Orca: The Killer Whale, Michael Anderson
Rene the Cane, Francis Girod
Stato interessante, Sergio Nasca
The Cat, Luigi Comencini
The Chosen, Alberto De Martino
The Fiend, Luigi Zampa
The Iron Prefect, Pasquale Squitieri

1978

Cock Crows at Eleven, Massimo Pirri
Corleone, Pasquale Squitieri
Days of Heaven, Terence Malik
El Mundial, Sigla dei mondiali di calcio
Il prigioniero, Aldo Lado
L'Italia vista dal cielo: Sardegna, Folco Quilici
La cage aux folles, Edouard Molinaro
Le mani sporche, Elio Petri
Noi lazzaroni, Giorgio Pelloni
One Two Two 122 Rue de Provence, Christian Gion
Pedro Paramo, José Bolanos
Stay as You Are, Alberto Lattuada
Where Are You Going on Holiday? (Segment: *Sarò tutta per te*), Mauro Bolognini

1979

A Dangerous Toy, Giuliano Montaldo
A Trip with Anita, Mario Monicelli
Bloodline, Terence Young
Dedicato al mare Egeo, Masuo Ikeda
Dietro il processo (Segments: *Il caso Pasolini*, *Il caso Montesi*), Franco Biancacci
Good News, Elio Petri
I… For Icarus, Henri Verneuil
Invito allo sport, Folco Quilici
Luna, Bernardo Bertolucci
Μέσα από φυλακή σας γράφω στην Ελλάδα, Poetic collection of Alexandros Panagulis
Operation Ogre, Gillo Pontecorvo
Orient Express, Daniele Danza, Marcel Moussy, Bruno Gentillon
The Humanoid, Aldo Lado
The Meadow, Paolo & Vittorio Taviani
Ten To Survive, Arnoldo Farina e Giancarlo Zagni
Venetian Lies, Stefano Rolla

colonna sonora originale del film

musiche di
ENNIO MORRICONE
dirette da
BRUNO NICOLAI

1970
Metello
LP3 33 rpm - RCA KOLS 1009

The heart-rending main theme that Maestro Morricone wrote for this movie, based on the novel by Vasco Pratolini, is famous. The score recalls the melodrama of one of the most classical of Italian traditions: a family drama and tale of impossible love in a historic setting in the late 19th and early 20th centuries. This is vintage Morricone.

1970
L'uccello dalle piume di cristallo
The Bird with the Crystal Plumage
L'oiseau au plumage de cristal
LP 33 rpm - CINEVOX MDF 33/31

For Dario Argento's debut in the thriller genre, Maestro Morricone used the voice of Gianna Spagnolo to develop the sound of a child singing a nursery rhyme – but in a way that is sinister and terrifying. It is a harbinger of ghastly omens about madness and death. Alfred Hitchcock, a wizard at spine-tingling scenes, apparently had this to say about Dario Argento and his movie: "This young Italian guy is starting to worry me." The English filmmaker's historical composer, Bernard Herrmann, might have added: "With this Morricone guy, I'm already very worried."

1970
La moglie più bella
The Most Beautiful Wife
Seule contre la Mafia
45 rpm - CINEVOX MDF 017
45 rpm - SEVEN SEAS CINEVOX HIT-1929

A "Cosa Nostra Western in an almost progressive rock key ..." This is not meant to be a bizarre definition, but simply one way to describe the feelings triggered when listening to this score. These elements are all there: it sounds like a western; there's a mafioso component and a Jew's harp; but it also resounds grotesquely like a rhythmic rock song.

1970
La califfa
Lady Caliph
LP 33 rpm - CBS 70090

The moving theme of *Lady Caliph* is undoubtedly one of the most beloved among all those composed by Maestro Morricone; and listening to it occasionally is like taking a break from the hustle and bustle of everyday life. Splendid are the versions sung by Milva and Mireille Mathieu to lyrics by the author and filmmaker himself, Alberto Bevilacqua. Since then, this famous song has been recorded by many others.

1970
Le foto proibite di una signora per bene
The Forbidden Photos of a Lady Above Suspicion
Photo interdite d'une bourgeoise
LP 33 rpm - DAGORED RED 106

1970
I cannibali
The Cannibals
Les cannibales
45 rpm - CAM AMP 77

1970

Quando le donne avevano la coda

When Women Had Tails

Quand les femmes avaient une queue

LP 33 rpm - CAM SAG 9032

In spite of electrifying music enlivened by primitive warbling and vocals, and crazy noises and sounds, this film's music was dominated by the feminine grace of the lead character played by Senta Berger. The original record was issued by CAM and American bootleg editions are still much sought after.

E. Morricone

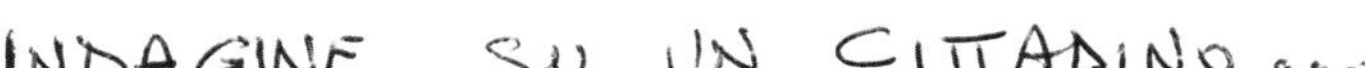

1970

Indagine su un cittadino al di sopra di ogni sospetto

Investigation of a Citizen Above Suspicion

Enquête sur un citoyen au-dessus de tout soupçon

45 rpm - CINEVOX MDF 016
LP 33 rpm - CERBERUS CEM-S 0110
45 rpm - PHILIPS 6009 081

This film helped to revolutionize the canons of composing for the cinema and was directed by Elio Petri. It starred the amazing Gian Maria Volonté who immortalized it with his histrionics. Morricone, who was not new to experimentation, unleashed all his talent and fashioned it using devices from his abstract treasure trove of experience. The result was timeless music for different moods; even problem-solving or trying to soothe one's nerves.

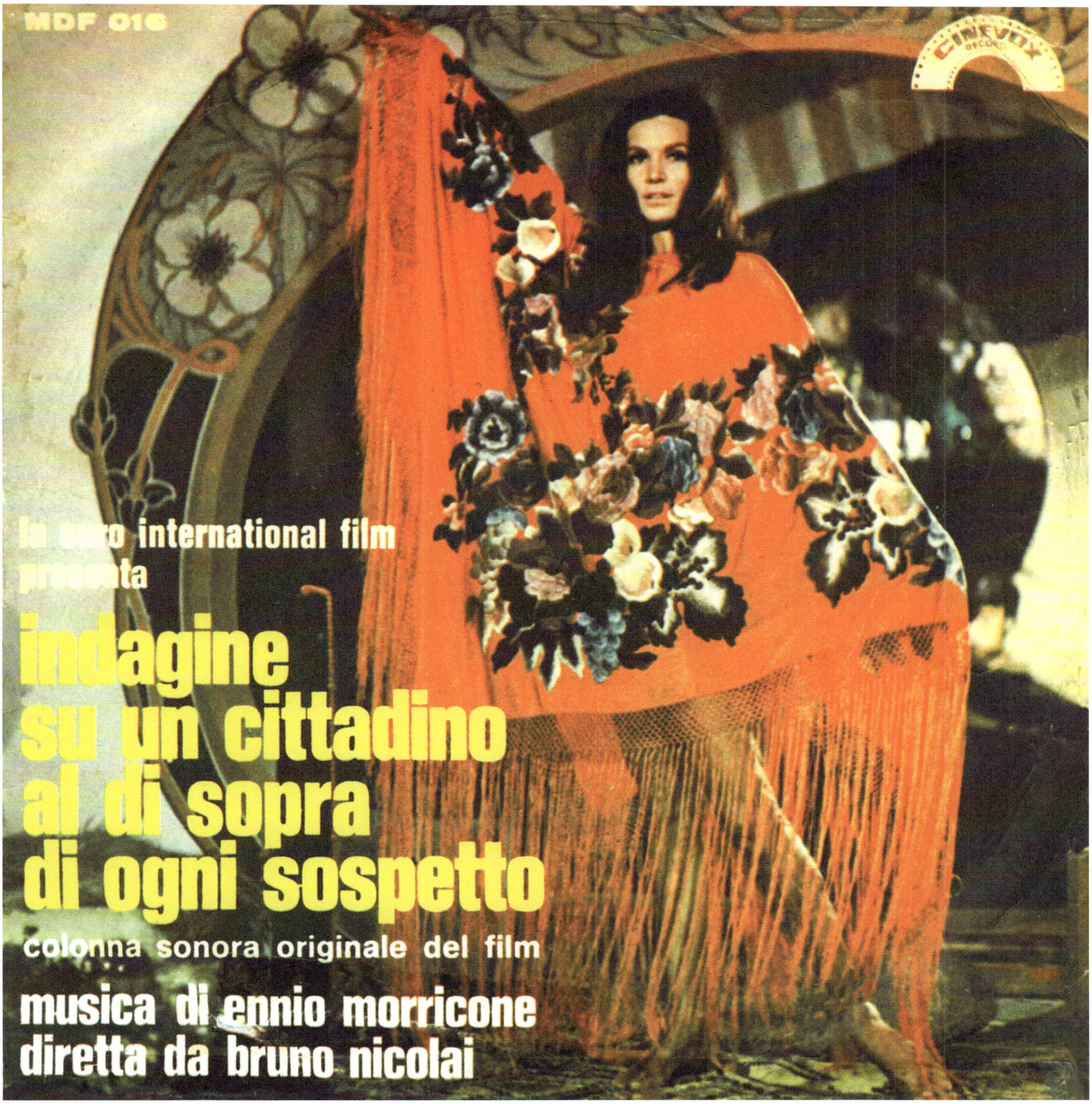

MDF 016

CINEVOX

la euro international film
presenta

indagine
su un cittadino
al di sopra
di ogni sospetto

colonna sonora originale del film

musica di ennio morricone
diretta da bruno nicolai

1970
Vamos a matar, compañeros
Compañeros
45 rpm - iT ZT 7009

In the days when the successful Spaghetti Western genre had begun its inevitable decline, the films that were still being produced seemed to gradually lose their dramatic components. They indulged more in irony and farce. Ennio Morricone, who had lived the genre to the fullest and had actually created its musical style, brilliantly managed to adapt to the new course. The Maestro always managed to elicit genuine latent irony and musical humor from the scores that he wrote during this period.

1970

Two Mules For Sister Sara

Gli avvoltoi hanno fame

Sierra torride

LP 33 rpm - KAPP KRS 5512

In the universe of sounds created by Maestro Morricone for the Spaghetti Western genre, this little-known and under-celebrated soundtrack contains all the required elements for success and recognition. Amidst exotic flutes, untamed violins, mocking zufoli (whistles), and bassoons, there is still room for a mystical choir. The conductor for this highly virtuosic composition has never been identified. Was he Maestro Morricone? Bruno Nicolai? Stanley Wilson? We still wonder.

MAGICO - STRANO - MISTERIOSO - SUBACQUEO
MAGICAL - STRANGE - MYSTERIOUS - UNDERWATER
MAGIQUE - ETRANGE - MYSTERIEUX - SOUS-MARIN
MAGISCH - SELTSAM - GEHEIMNISVOLL - UNTERSEEISCH
MAGICO - EXTRAÑO - MISTERIOSO - SUBMARINO

DISCO DI SONORIZZAZIONE
SCORING RECORD
DISCO DE SONORIZACIÒN

DISQUE DE SONORISATION
BESCHALLUNGS PLATTE
DISCO DE SONORIZAÇÃO

PSICHEDELICO - INTROSPETTIVO - FLASH-BACK
PSYCHEDELIC - INTROSPECTIVE - FLASH-BACK
PSICHEDELIC - INTROSPECTIVE - FLASH-BACK
PSYCHEDELISCH - INTROSPEKTIV - FLASH-BACK
PSICHEDELICO DE INTROSPECCION - FLASH-BACK

DISCO DI SONORIZZAZIONE
SCORING RECORD
DISCO DE SONORIZACIÒN

DISQUE DE SONORISATION
BESCHALLUNGS PLATTE
DISCO DE SONORIZAÇÃO

1970
Lui per lei
LP 33 rpm - CAM CmL 010
LP 33 rpm - CAM CmL 021

1970
The Virginian: Men From Shiloh
Il virginiano
Le Virginien
with various authors
CD - TVT RECORDS 1700-2

1970
Hornets' Nest
I lupi attaccano in branco
L'assaut des jeunes loups
LP 33 rpm - Bootleg - POO LP 105

1970
Città violenta
Final Shot
La cité de la violence
LP 33 rpm - RCA KOLS 1010

With the music he composed for this film, Ennio Morricone insisted on an innovative style that would focus on the power of the orchestra – a style that showed how an orchestra was perfectly capable of creating metropolitan thrillers and spy stories with marked timbres and articulated percussion.

ORIGINAL CAST
STEREO
OLS 4

PRODUZIONE UNIDIS

COLONNA SONORA ORIGINALE DEL FILM
"SACCO E VANZETTI"
MUSICHE DI
ENNIO MORRICONE
JOAN BAEZ
CANTA
LA BALLATA DI SACCO E VANZETTI
HERE'S TO YOU

1971
Sacco e Vanzetti
Sacco & Vanzetti
LP 33 rpm - RCA OLS 4
45 rpm - RCA VICTOR 49748
45 rpm - PHILIPS 6025 047

The story of the two Italian-born anarchists who were persecuted and executed in America was fated to be reassessed historically, and only the politically engaged cinema of Giuliano Montaldo could tell the true story. The film even contributed to a review of the trial by the U.S. government. Ennio Morricone gave his complete support to the filmmaker, and thanks to the collaboration of the famous American folk singer Joan Baez, he was able to write a touching soundtrack that underscored, through music and protest songs, the injustice of the events surrounding the two ill-fated men. The film was an international success and the song, *Here's To You,* became the anthem of a generation.

RCA
VICTOR
49748
BANDE ORIGINALE DU FILM
Sacco et Vanzetti
JOAN BAEZ
ENNIO MORRICONE

la ballata di Sacco e Vanzetti
<LETTERA DI SACCO AL FIGLIO DANTE>
PHILIPS
6025 047
LETTERA A INES
Distribuzione Phonogram s.p.a.
riccardo cucciolla
PHILIPS

1971

Il gatto a nove code

The Cat o' Nine Tails

Le chat à neuf queues

45 rpm - GENERAL MUSIC ZGE 5016
LP 33 rpm - AMS LP 77
45 rpm - BASF 05 19026-3

Maestro Morricone composed the music for this second film in Dario Argento's Animal Trilogy. Rather than seek new musical paths, he returned to sweet melodies in sharp contrast with the subject. So, we find sounds of pure easy listening punctuated by several atonal elements to accentuate the moments of suspense. When the film came out, General Music produced just one single on a 45 rpm, which is now greatly sought after by collectors.

IL GATTO A NOVE CODE
A FILM BY DARIO ARGENTO
MUSIC BY ENNIO MORRICONE

Original-Musik aus dem Constantin-Film
"Die neunschwänzige Katze"
Wiegenlied in blau
(Ninna nanna in blu)
Neunschwänzige Katze
(Il gatto a nove code)
BASF
STEREO 05 19026-3
ENNIO MORRICONE

1971
4 mosche di velluto grigio
4 Flies on Grey Velvet
4 mouches de velours gris
45 rpm - CINEVOX MDF 031

Notwithstanding the originality of the idea, the four flies that bring Dario Argento's trilogy focused on insects to its conclusion, do not seem to convince the viewer. It is instead Maestro Morricone who creates a musical merry-go-round by alternating a series of his typical sound choices that place just the right narrative tension on the story; perhaps in some instances, more so than the images themselves.

DALLA COLONNA SONORA ORIGINALE DEL FILM
VERUSCHKA
POESIA DI UNA DONNA
STEREO
ZGE 50174
VERUSCHKA
POESIA DI UNA DONNA
MUSICHE DI
ENNIO
MORRICONE

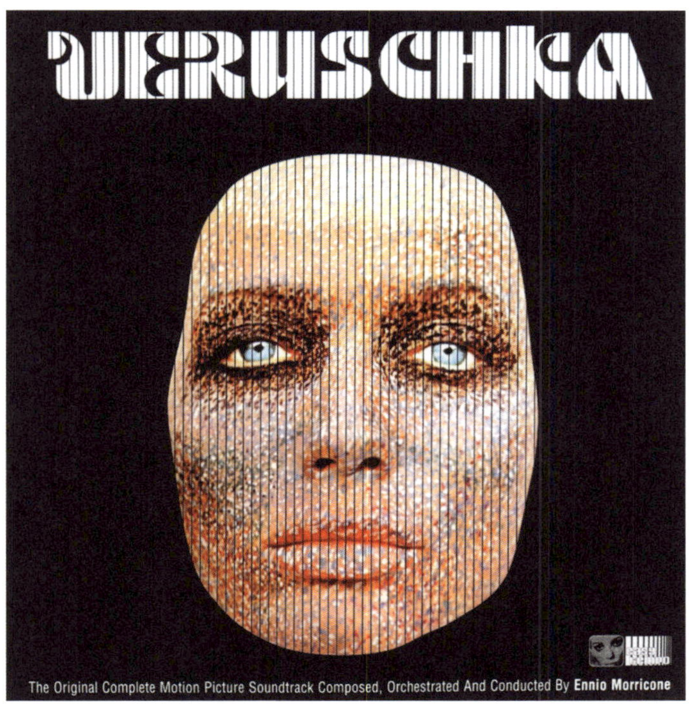

1971
Veruschka.
Poesia di una donna
Veruschka. Poetry of a Woman
45 rpm - GENERAL ZGE 50174
LP 33 rpm - EASY TEMPO ET 934 DLP

The Maestro endeavors to use the same stylistic formula as the one in *Love Circle*, which works, but with somewhat less engaging results. Nonetheless, Edda Dell'Orso's vocals are so enticing that they verge on being a sexual act in themselves.

1971
Giornata nera per l'ariete
The Fifth Cord
Jour maléfique
LP 33 rpm - SPETTRO SP 04

Listeners had to wait twenty-five years to enjoy this soundtrack, whose only previously recorded song is dated from 1971 on an album titled, *Colori*, that was very hard to find at the time. Nonetheless, the funereal musical timbre of the theme song, sung in a sinister cantilena by Edda Dell'Orso, whose voice quivers with lucid madness, does not seem to have aged at all during the wait – actually, quite the opposite.

1971
L'istruttoria è chiusa: dimentichi
The Case Is Closed, Forget It
Nous sommes tous en liberté provisoire
LP 33 rpm - CONTEMPO C02005LP

The director Damiano Damiani didn't want a lot of music for this movie, and Morricone complied with the request in his own way, which was to produce more than what was needed; and the surplus of music remained mostly unused. Electronic music by Walter Branchi, listed in the opening credits, and an initial fanfare composed by Luis Bacalov, complete the sound of this movie denouncing injustice.

1971
Maddalena
LP 33 rpm - GENERAL MUSIC ZSLGE 55063

Not even Ennio Morricone, at his finest with this splendid score, managed to use his music to fully describe the voluptuousness, the sensuality of Lisa Gastoni as *Maddalena*. Truly a challenge, in spite of the fact that the actress, who while no longer a 20-year-old, still revealed herself to be a river overflowing with eroticism.

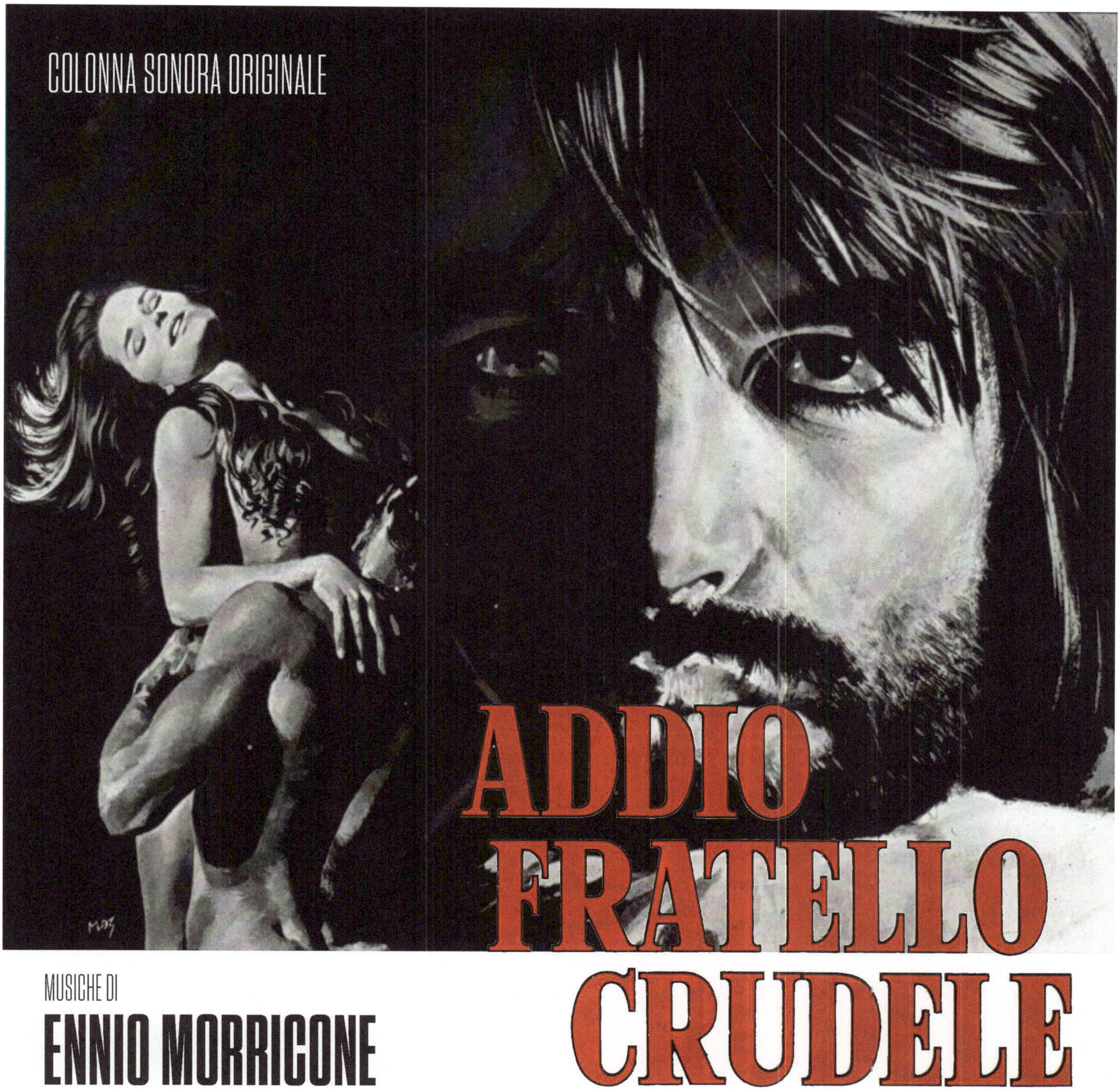

COLONNA SONORA ORIGINALE
MUSICHE DI
ENNIO MORRICONE
ADDIO FRATELLO CRUDELE

MORRICONE
BANDES SONORES ORIGINALES ORIGINAL SOUNDTRACKS ADDIO FRATELLO CRUDELE \ INCONTRO

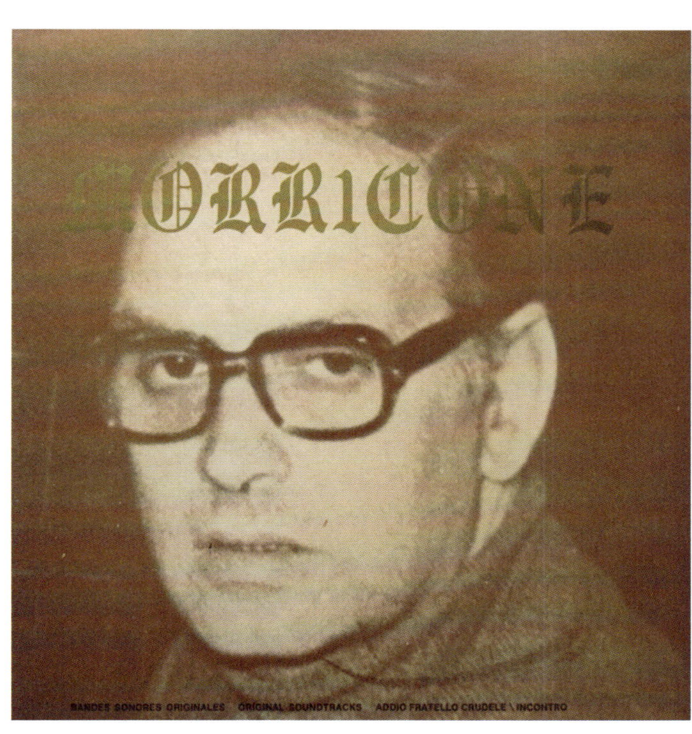

1971
Addio fratello crudele
'Tis Pity She's A Whore
Dommage qu'elle soit une putain
CD - Bootleg
LP 33 rpm - CAM 500 002

With a rather unusual move, CAM issued the soundtrack of *'Tis Pity She's A Whore* in France on a double album and in tandem with the music of the movie, *Incontro*. The cover, reproduced here, was thought by most enthusiasts to be insignificant, if not downright ugly. The combination of the photo and heavy-handed typography is questionable at best.

1971
La tarantola dal ventre nero
Black Belly of the Tarantula
La tarentule au ventre noir
LP 33 rpm - CERBERUS CEM - S 0116

1971
La corta notte delle bambole di vetro
Short Night of Glass Dolls
CD - DAGORED RED 160-2

1971

Una lucertola con la pelle di donna

Lizard in a Woman's Skin

Le venin de la peur

LP 33 rpm - DAGORED RED 110

LP 33 rpm - ACETATO INEDITO

At the height of the period when animals and thrillers were the latest thing in Italian cinema, Morricone defied the conventional and the banal with his composing for film, no doubt coming up against obtuse requests by directors and producers on more than one occasion. In this case, the problem was indecision by RCA's record producers. At the time, they prepared an acetate test pressing with all the music from the movie, however, it was never produced as a commercial record (photo of test record).

1971
Gli occhi freddi della paura
Cold Eyes of Fear
LP 33 rpm - DAGORED RED 119

1971
Forza G
Winged Devils
La patrouille du ciel
45 rpm - CINEVOX MDF 034

morricone
la musica nel cinema di pasolini

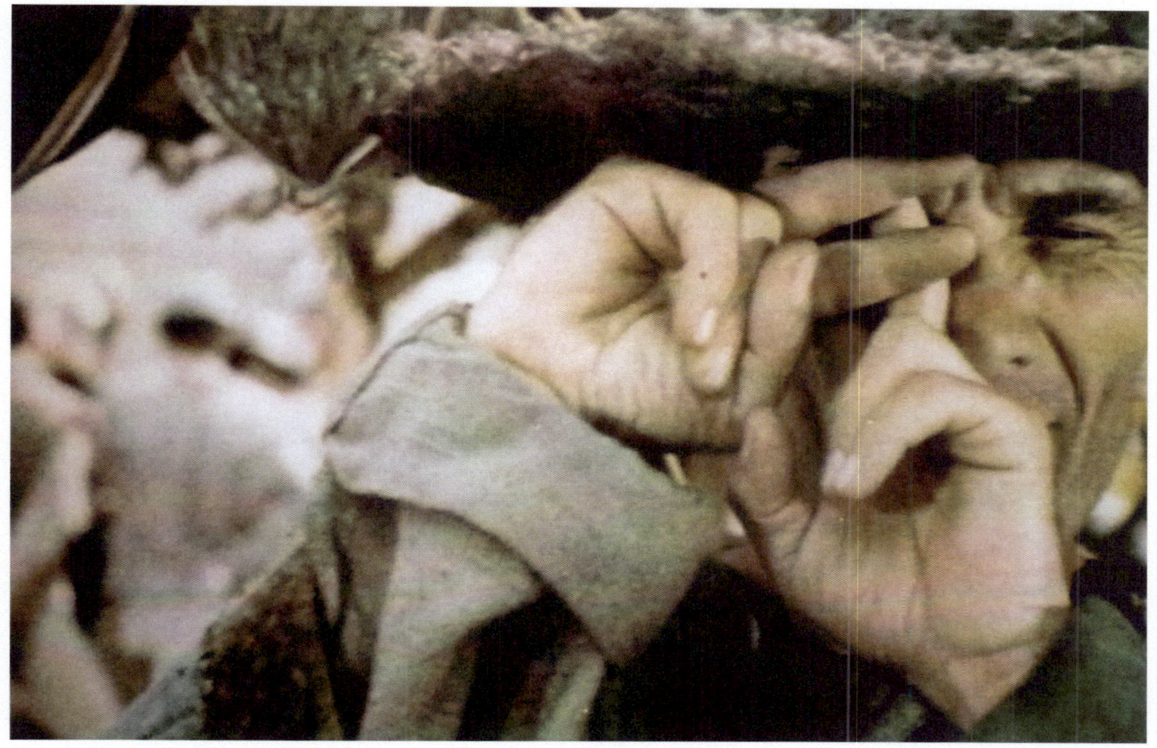

1971
Il Decameron
The Decameron
Le Décaméron

1972
I racconti di Canterbury
The Canterbury Tales
Les contes de Canterbury

1974
Il fiore delle mille e una notte
Arabian Nights
Les mille et une nuits

1975
Salò o le 120 giornate di Sodoma
Salò, or the 120 Days of Sodom
Salo ou les 120 journées de Sodome

1983
La musica nel cinema di Pasolini
LP 33 rpm - GENERAL MUSIC GM 73001

It must not have been easy for Ennio Morricone to work with Pasolini who clearly preferred classical music for his movies. But perhaps the opposite was true, seeing that the composer was never condescending to his directors; and he delivered excellent work.

1971
La classe operaia va in Paradiso
Lulu the Tool
La classe ouvrière va au paradis
LP 33 rpm - RCA SP 8038
LP 33 rpm - RCA PL 37644

Finally, here is a topic about which the composer can develop that small universe of sounds and noises that have always distinguished his great talent. The score for this movie, one part – *Final Shot* and the other – *Investigation of a Citizen Above Suspicion* … is perfect for an unusual context, offering a chance for the composer to "make all the noise he wants."

ORIGINAL CAST
STEREO
SP 8038

1971
La scoperta dell'America
CD - SAIMEL BANDAS SONORAS 3995310

1971
Tre nel mille
LP 33 rpm - COMETA CMT 1006/16

1971
Il ritorno di Clint il solitario
There's a Noose Waiting for You Trinity!
CD - RECORDING ARTS 5X057

1971
Nessuno deve sapere
CD - RECORDING ARTS 2X903

1971
Oceano
The Wind Blows Free
LP 33 rpm - RCA OLS 10

For Folco Quilici's exotic documentary, Maestro Morricone used the same musical structure as the one that is heard in the snow-capped *The Great Silence*. The films share a dominant element: water, which the sweet vocal vibrato by Gianna Spagnolo synthesizes with the same grace as Manfredo Acerbo's paintbrush for the combination of forms in the movie's splendid poster.

1971
Le casse
Gli scassinatori
The Burglars
LP 33 rpm - BELL 2308 018 L

If it really were possible to positively qualify a soundtrack based on a film's success and the number of recordings produced, critical judgment might be insufficient, and even unflattering. On the other hand, even genius and creativity need to take a break every now and then.

1971
Incontro
Romance
LP 33 rpm - CAM SAG 9036
45 rpm - CAM AMP 92

1971
Giù la testa
Duck, You Sucker
Il était une fois… la révolution
LP 33 rpm - CINEVOX MDF 33/50
45 rpm - CINEVOX MDF 030
45 rpm - CINEVOX MDF 029

This was another success for both the movie and the record thanks to the duo Leone/Morricone, who once again hit their target. With this soundtrack, Maestro Morricone capitalizes on his experience up until then and composes a sound fresco of strong emotional impact; and also one that closely adheres to the theme with the prolific creativity that increasingly distinguishes his work. Vocals by Edda Dell'Orso, at the top of her game here, contribute to its success. It triumphed at the box office and had stratospheric record sales.

MDF 029
dalla colonna sonora originale del film
GIU' LA TESTA
un film di
SERGIO LEONE
GIU' LA TESTA · DOPO L'ESPLOSIONE
MUSICHE COMPOSTE E DIRETTE DA ENNIO MORRICONE
N.1

colonna sonora originale del film
GIU' LA TESTA

CINEVOX
MDF 030
N.2
musiche composte e dirette da
ENNIO MORRICONE
MARCIA DEGLI ACCATTONI · MESA VERDE

CAM AMP 91

La RAI
Radio Televisione Italiana
presenta

ANNA MAGNANI

TRE DONNE

colonna sonora originale di ENNIO MORRICONE

original soundtrack recording in stereo on 2 discs set

ANNA MAGNANI IN
TRE DONNE
CORREVA L'ANNO DI GRAZIA 1870

FOUR MOVIES FOR TELEVISION DIRECTED BY **ALFREDO GIANNETTI**

MUSIC BY **ENNIO MORRICONE**

1971
Tre donne
45 rpm - CAM AMP 91

1971
Correva l'anno di grazia 1870
CD - DIGITMOVIES CDDM 038

ZGE 50242
STEREO
distribuito dalla RCA S.p.A.

RCA

STEREO
PM 3705

l'ultimo
UOMO
di Sara

CARMEN
VILLANI

1971
Sans mobile apparent
Senza movente
Without Apparent Motive
45 rpm - GENERAL MUSIC ZGE 50242

1971
L'ultimo uomo di Sara
Sarah's Last Man
45 rpm - RCA PM 3705

1972
Cosa avete fatto a Solange?
What Have You Done to Solange?
Jeux particuliers
LP 33 rpm - INTERMEZZO/RCA SP 8062

Though the film was made in 1972, the soundtrack was recorded for the first time in 1986, thanks to the Intermezzo label with permission from RCA. As a rule, this type of revival in music doesn't produce proper, well-deserved interest, but because the composer was Ennio Morricone, luckily for us, this was different and succeeded.

▸

1972
Mio caro assassino
My Dear Killer
LP 33 rpm - DEATH WALTZ DW 114

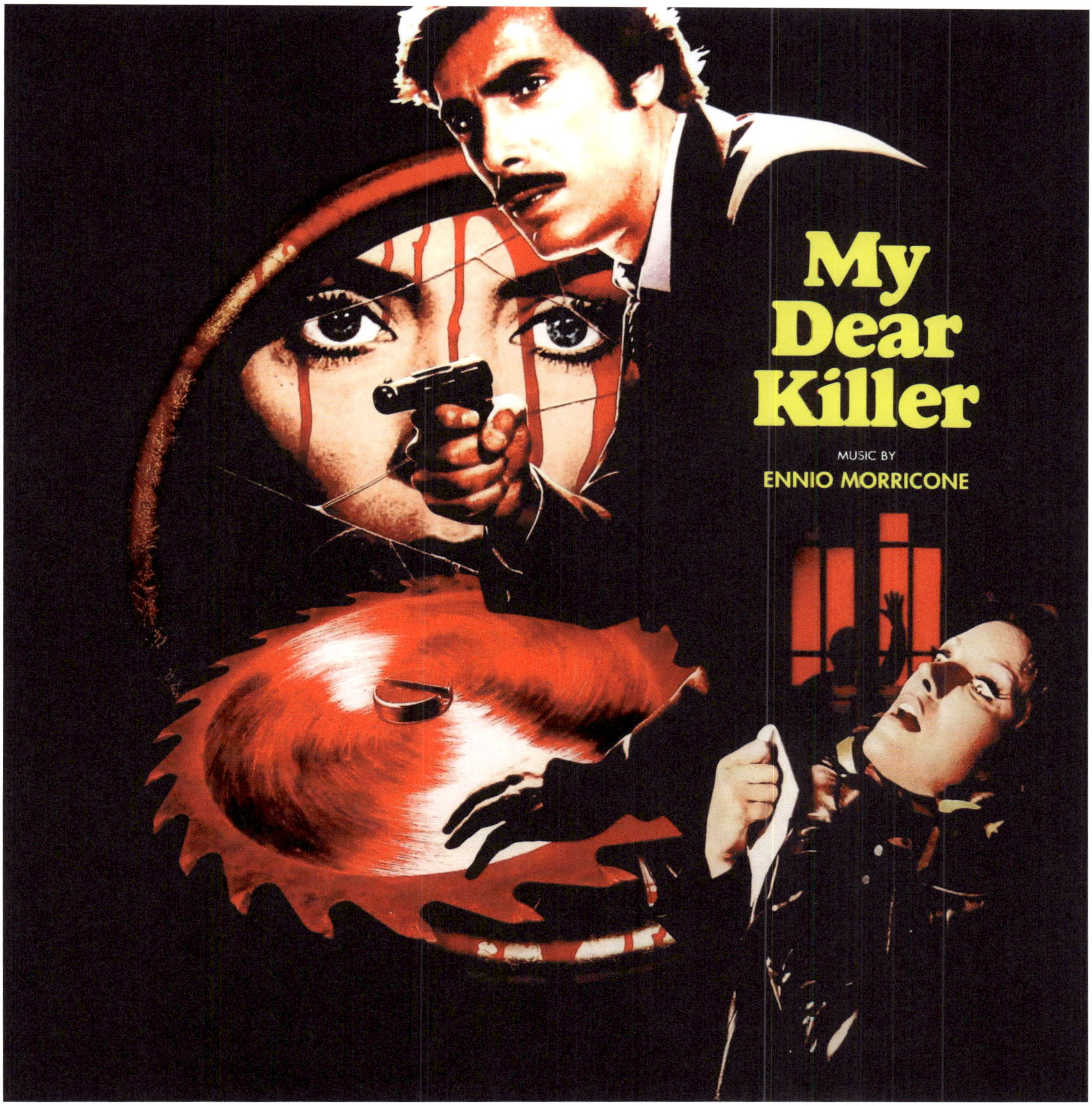
My
Dear
Killer
MUSIC BY
ENNIO MORRICONE

Mio caro Assassino

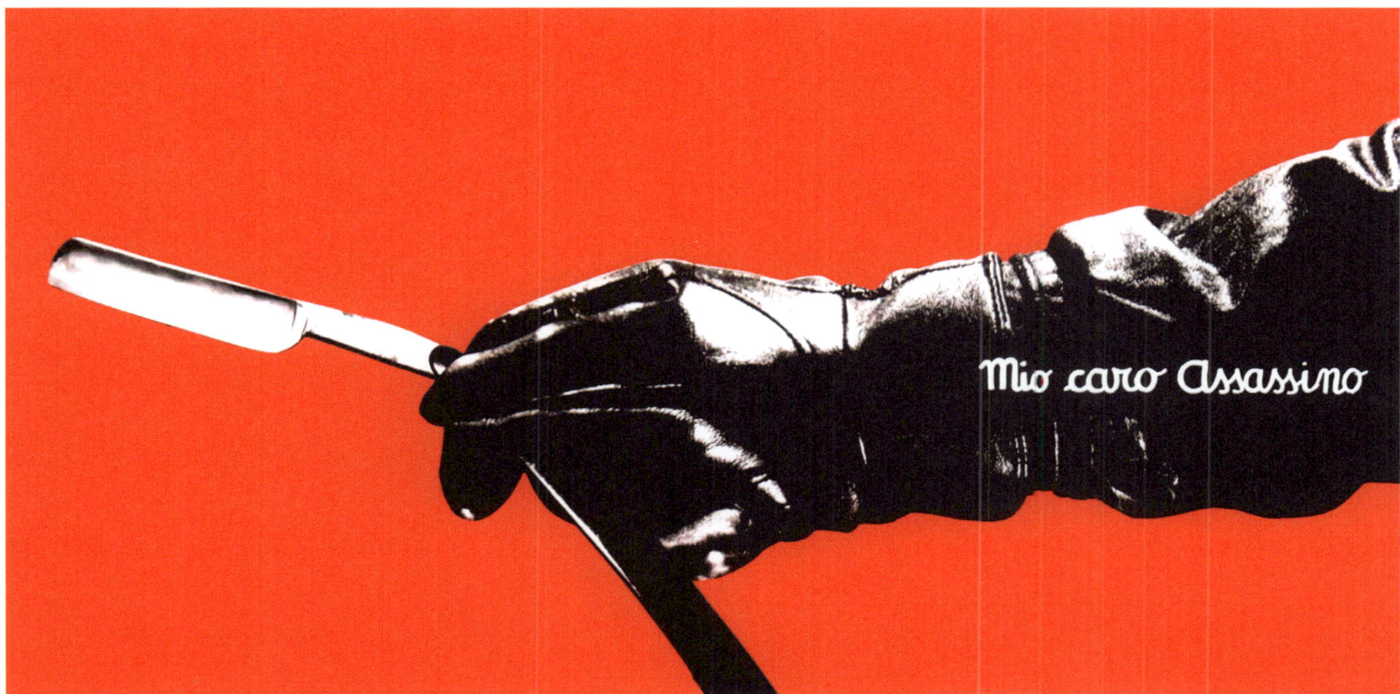

colonna sonora originale del film

LA BANDA J.&S.

cronaca criminale del far west

1972
La banda J.&S.
Cronaca criminale del Far West
Sonny & Jed. Criminal Story Of An Outlaw Couple
45 rpm - CAM AMP 101
LP 33 rpm - CERBERUS RECORDS CEM-S 0111

When Morricone decides to break the viewer/listener's heart with a song that oozes with nostalgia and feeling, he is so successful that the result is suited to every situation where there's sadness and sorrow; even when it has nothing to do with the soundtrack. *Sweet Susan* is a case in point, from the movie, *Sonny & Jed. Criminal Story Of An Outlaw Couple*

1972
L'attentat
L'attentato
The Assassination
LP 33 rpm - FESTIVAL FLD 592
LP 33 rpm - GENERAL MUSIC zslge 55121

Before 1972, Ennio Morricone had already successfully used avant-garde and experimental formulae for some of his soundtracks. In this case, you might even be persuaded to talk about pure musical impressionism as it relates to perfection: the element of suspense that drives the plot was based on a true story.

1972
Bluebeard
Barbablù
Barbe-bleue
LP 33 rpm - GENERAL MUSIC zslge 55122

To underscore the dire and tragic tale of Bluebeard, set here in a period that is equally grim, Morricone chooses to use a Hungarian cimbalom, an ancient chordophone of Eastern European origin whose subtle, creepy sound becomes a harbinger of sinister omens and unconfessable secrets. Musical direction was by Franco Tamponi with Leonida Torrebruno on the disturbing chords of the cimbalon.

1972
La violenza: quinto potere
The Sicilian Checkmate
Les mafiosis
LP 33 rpm - COMETA CMT 1012/26

1972
Majstor i Margarita
Il maestro e Margherita
The Master and Margherite
Le maître et Marguerite
45 rpm - RCA OC 27

The main theme of the film *Incontro* was used here and also several years later for the TV series, *Orient Express;* for which Morricone composed only the theme song.

1972
Chi l'ha vista morire?
Who Saw Her Die?
Qui l'a vue mourir?
LP 33 rpm - COMETA GG.ST. 10.017

1972
L'uomo e la magia
LP 33 rpm - COMETA CMT 1

The theme song for the *Faith* series (Fowlkes/ Morricone) was sung by Rocky Roberts and recorded on a very rare single issued by General Music (GMS 0014).

1972
La cosa buffa
LP 33 rpm - CINEVOX MDF 33/60

Here we find airy and cadenced orchestral sounds with a Venetian theme that includes the sharp, malevolent sounding vocals of Edda Dell'Orso; and a conspicuous series of dance songs that all together make an enjoyable score. Unfortunately, it was represented by an album cover unanimously believed to be one of the ugliest and most insignificant of all of Morricone's discography. Using the intriguing poster with its puzzle motif might have turned around its poor reception.

1972
Il diavolo nel cervello
Devil in the Brain
Le diable dans la tête
LP 33 rpm - GENERAL MUSIC ZSLGE 55076

The rarefied atmospheres evoked by Morricone's music for this film were recycled, often anonymously, as commentary for documentaries or newspaper reporting; with the common denominator being a link to the mysterious and the paranormal. In this way, existing musical material was channeled into many records as background music for diverse themes.

1972
Anche se volessi lavorare, che faccio?
LP 33 rpm - CINEVOX MDF 33/56

1972
Imputazione di omicidio per uno studente
Chronicle of a Homicide
Chronique d'un homicide
LP 33 rpm - CGD FG 5099

The film contains three sung tunes: *Un po' per giorno* (Bigazzi/Morricone), sung by the leading actor Massimo Ranieri; *Scappa scappa* (Falzoni/Morricone), sung by Maria Monti; and the song *Gente grida* sung by Federico Pietrabruna and Marina Fiorentini was added as an afterthought.

original motion picture soundtrack

LA VITA, A VOLTE, E' MOLTO DURA, VERO PROVVIDENZA?

music by
ENNIO MORRICONE

STEREO

ORIGINAL MOTION PICTURE SOUNDTRACK
MUSIC by ENNIO MORRICONE

I FIGLI CHIEDONO PERCHE'

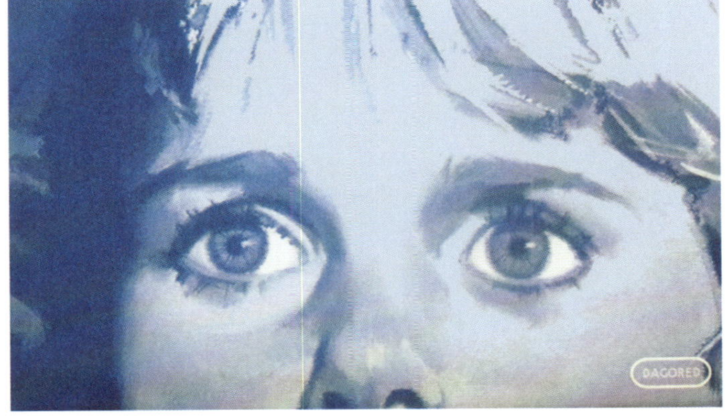

1972
La vita, a volte, è molto dura, vero Provvidenza?
Life Is Tough, Eh Providence?
On m'appelle Providence
LP 33 rpm - GDM LP 6706

1972
I figli chiedono perché
Why
LP 33 rpm - DAGORED RED 146-1

1972
Un uomo da rispettare
The Master Touch
Un homme à respecter
LP 33 rpm - CBS 70117

In the movie music industry, the design of the album cover has always been particularly important, leaving lots of room for the creativity of both artists and designers. The results at times are questioned depending on whether or not a listener appreciates a cover based on personal taste or for other reasons. No doubt, a cover like the one presented on this page sets an example, and most people agree that because of its immediacy and the design itself, the work of Pietro Ermanno Iaia, it is successful.

1972
Questa specie d'amore
This Kind of Love
Un amour insolite
LP 33 rpm - GENERAL MUSIC ZSLGE 55077

For this movie, the song, *Ouverture del mattino,* was chosen. It was originally composed for the 1968 movie, *Mother's Heart*. The practice of re-using work does not denote, as might be assumed, that there is a lack of ideas for composing a soundtrack, but rather means that the type of song is particularly suited to the film situation. This can often be said for background music too.

1972
D'amore si muore
For Love One Dies
LP 33 rpm - GDM LP 6711

1972
Quando la preda è l'uomo
When Man Is the Prey
LP 33 rpm - CERBERUS CEM-SP 0118

ennio morricone/colonna sonora originale

1973
Revolver
Blood in the Streets
La poursuite implacable
LP 33 rpm - GENERAL MUSIC zslge 55496

The theme song for this soundtrack is the beautiful *Un ami (Un amico)* sung by the French singer, Daniel Beretta, who plays the role of Al Niko in the movie. The song was written by Alberto Bevilacqua and Catherine Desage to music by Morricone. It is somewhat curious that a single was never released of this marvelous piece that instantly grabs a listener's ear and would no doubt have sold well. Was this a faux pas by General Music? We'll never know, but we do know that the Japanese company Seven Seas was quick to produce it (FSM-48).

1973
Ci risiamo, vero Provvidenza?
Here We Go Again, Eh Providence?
with Bruno Nicolai
LP 33 rpm - GDM LP 6710

Morricone and Nicolai composed and completed a soundtrack together only a few times; and this film was the next-to-last chance for them to do so. The two theme songs extracted from the second part of *Provvidenza* were recorded on a single released by RCA (OC 44), completing the *Original Cast* series. However, it seems that no one has ever actually seen this record, and there are many who strongly doubt that it even exists. What is certain is that Intermezzo, licensed by RCA, had prepared for the publication of the album (SP 8063) with an entire score. The album was to conclude the historical series SP 8000, but the project never materialized for reasons that are still unknown.

1973
Quando l'amore è sessualità
When Love Is Lust
LP 33 rpm - CERBERUS CEM-S 0113

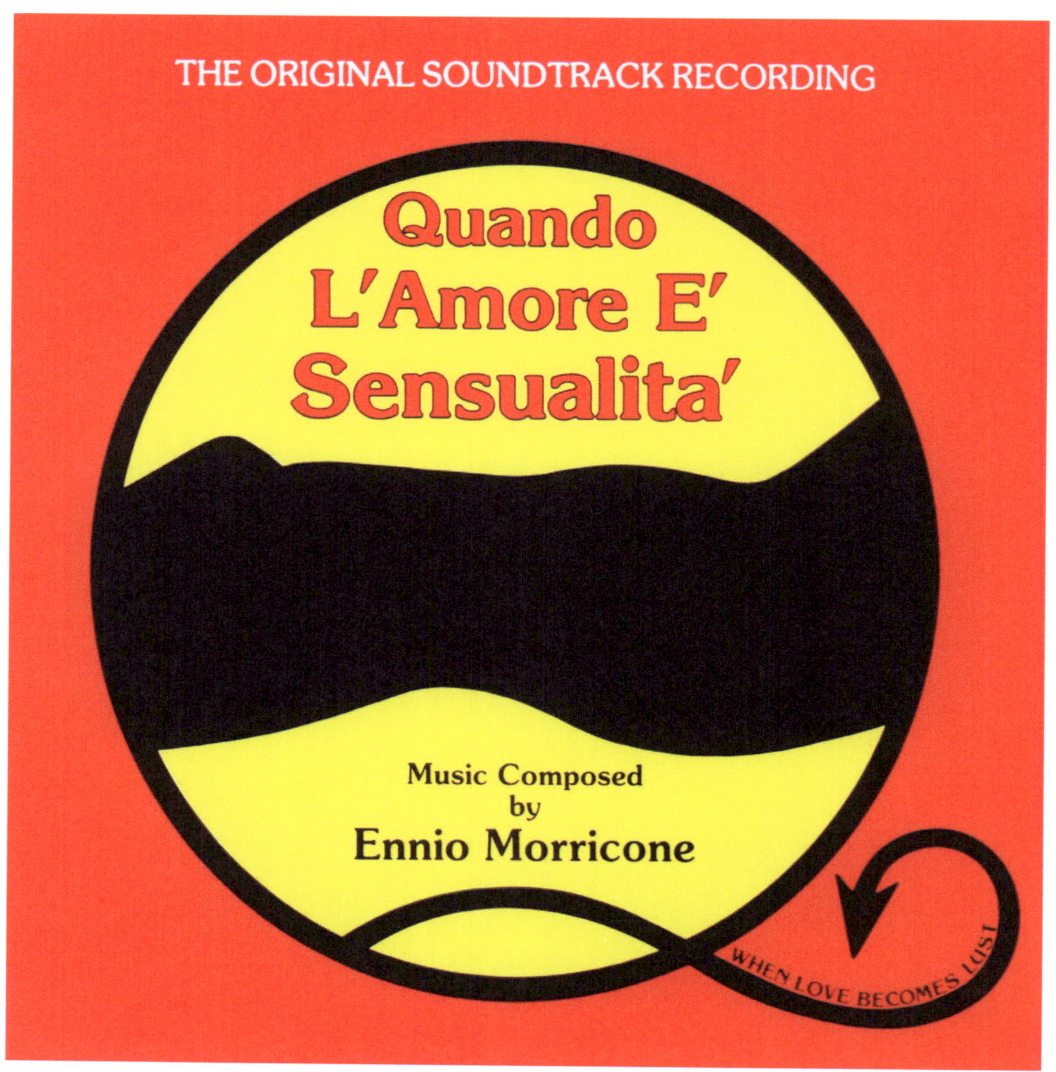

1973
Che c'entriamo noi con la rivoluzione?
What Am I Doing in the Middle of a Revolution?
Mais qu'est-ce que je viens foutre au milieu de cette révolution?
LP 33 rpm - DAGORED RED 145-1

1973
Space: 1999
Spazio: 1999
Cosmos 1999
LP 33 rpm - DEATH WALTZ DW102

1973
Rappresaglia
Massacre in Rome
Représailles
CD - GDM CLUB 6075

1973
Le serpent
Il serpente
The Serpent
LP 33 rpm - RCA VCTOR 440758

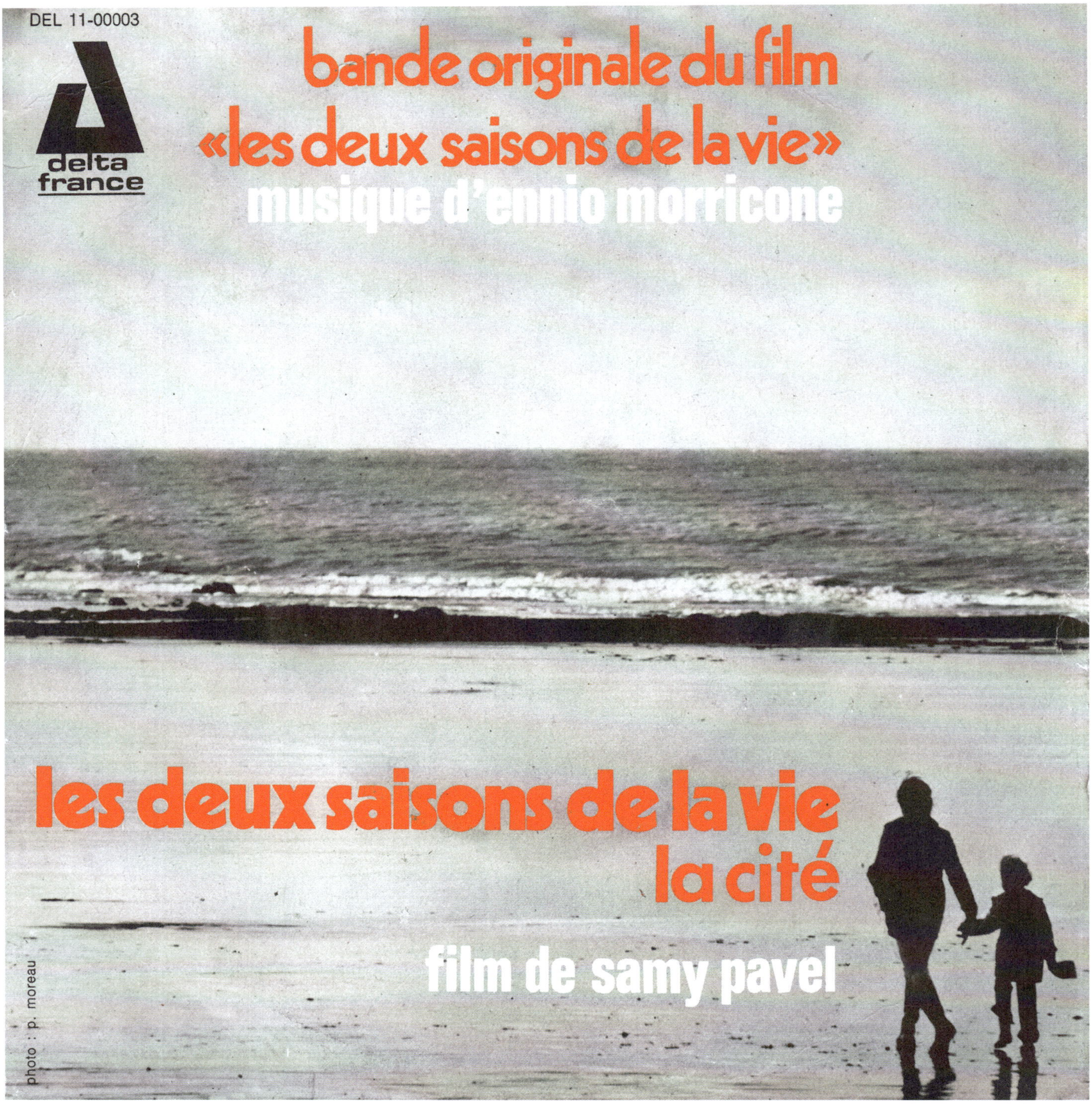

DEL 11-00003
delta france
bande originale du film
«les deux saisons de la vie»
musique d'ennio morricone
les deux saisons de la vie
la cité
film de samy pavel
photo : p. moreau

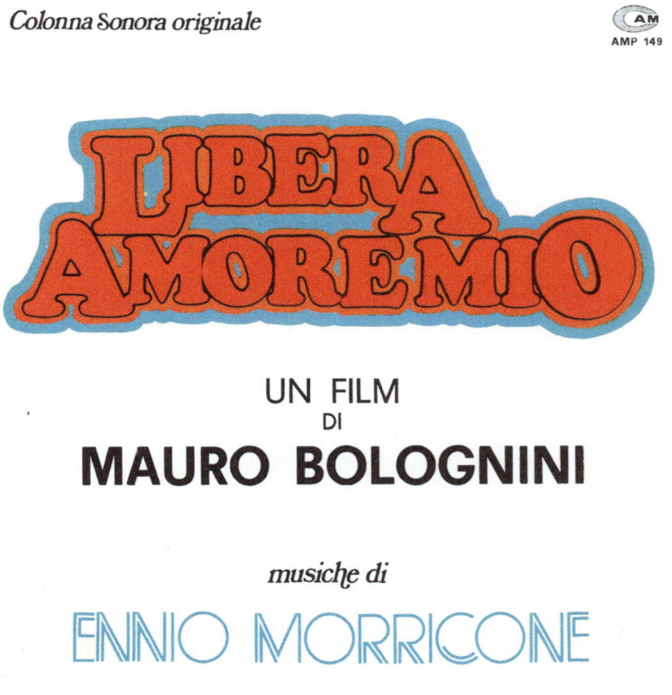

Colonna Sonora originale
CAM
AMP 149
LIBERA AMORE MIO
UN FILM
DI
MAURO BOLOGNINI
musiche di
ENNIO MORRICONE

1973
Les deux saison de la vie
Le due stagioni della vita
The Two Seasons of Life
45 rpm - DELTA FRANCE DEL 11-00003

1973
Libera amore mio
Libera, My Love
Libera mon amour
45 rpm - CAM AMP 149

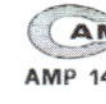

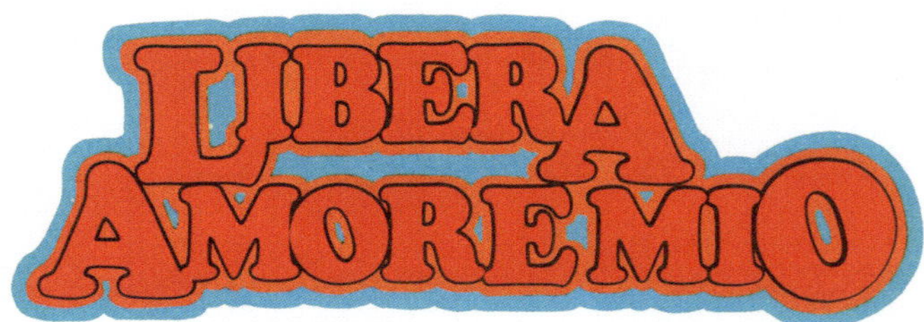

1973
Crescete e moltiplicatevi
Mais... Laissez nous succomber à la tentation
CD - GDM CLUB 7012

1973
Sepolta viva
Woman Buried Alive
La tour du désespoir
LP 33 rpm - BEAT LPF 021

For this period romance, Morricone adapts his unmistakable style and personalizes the main theme, entrusting it at times to the oboe; at others to the violin. While the movie suffers some weaknesses, once again the Maestro's music saves it from oblivion.

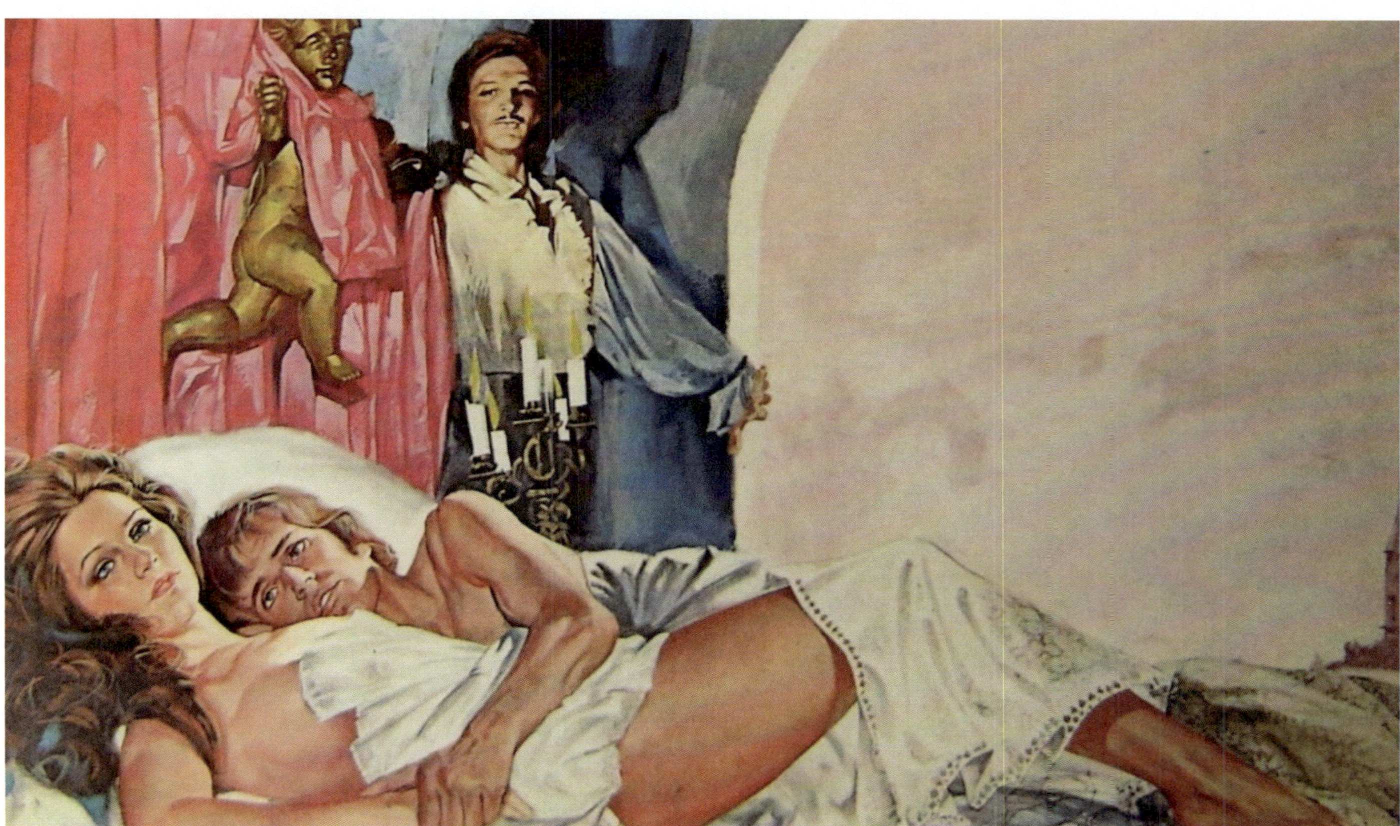

IL MIO NOME E' NESSUNO
colonna sonora originale
ENNIO MORRICONE

SERGIO LEONE presenta

stereomono dzslge 55497

TERENCE HILL HENRY FONDA
in
IL MIO NOME E' NESSUNO
diretto da
TONINO VALERII
prodotto da FULVIO MORSELLA musiche di ENNIO MORRICONE

1973
Il mio nome è nessuno
My Name Is Nobody
Mon nom est personne
LP 33 rpm - GENERAL MUSIC dzslge 55497

This film was a partially successful attempt to re-energize the Italian Western genre at a time when it was in a state of free fall. The music of Maestro Morricone, hovering between the classical tradition of the genre and new sounds, dashes the commonplace and elicits a timeless classiness that is a hallmark of the expert composer. *Mucchio selvaggio* is amazing; and the *Cavalcata delle Valchirie*, interrupted by the sound of a car horn, is genius.

1973
La proprietà non è più un furto
Property Is No Longer A Theft
La proprièté, c'est plus le vol
LP 33 rpm - RCA OLS 19

ORIGINAL CAST
STEREO
OLS 19

colonna sonora originale del film
LA PROPRIETA' NON E' PIU' UN FURTO
Musiche composte e strumentate da
ENNIO MORRICONE
Orchestra diretta da
BRUNO NICOLAI

1973
Giordano Bruno
LP 33 rpm - RCA OLS 21

ORIGINAL CAST
STEREO
OLS 21

colonna sonora originale del film
GIORDANO BRUNO
MUSICHE COMPOSTE E STRUMENTATE DA
ENNIO MORRICONE

ORIGINAL CAST
STEREO
SP 8051

colonna sonora originale del film

musiche di
ENNIO MORRICONE

1974
Allonsanfàn
LP 33 rpm - RCA SP 8051 (unpublished)

We have only a mock-up album cover of the only known example of a test pressing of this soundtrack that was supposed to be released in RCA's 8000 series (SP 8051), but never saw the light of day. Later, this score was matched with the music of Egisto Macchi's in the film, *Padre padrone,* in a Linea Tre album, also by RCA.

◂

1974
Der Richter Und Sein Henker
Il giudice e il suo boia
aka Assassinio sul ponte
Murder on the Bridge
CD - BEAT RECORDS CDCR 90

1974
Mussolini ultimo atto
Mussolini: The Last Four Days
45 rpm - CINEVOX MDF 053

Military rhythms accompany the decadent musical structure, deliberately studded with solo instruments that play distortedly and efficiently comment on the end of the evil and vainglorious era of its leader, Benito Mussolini.

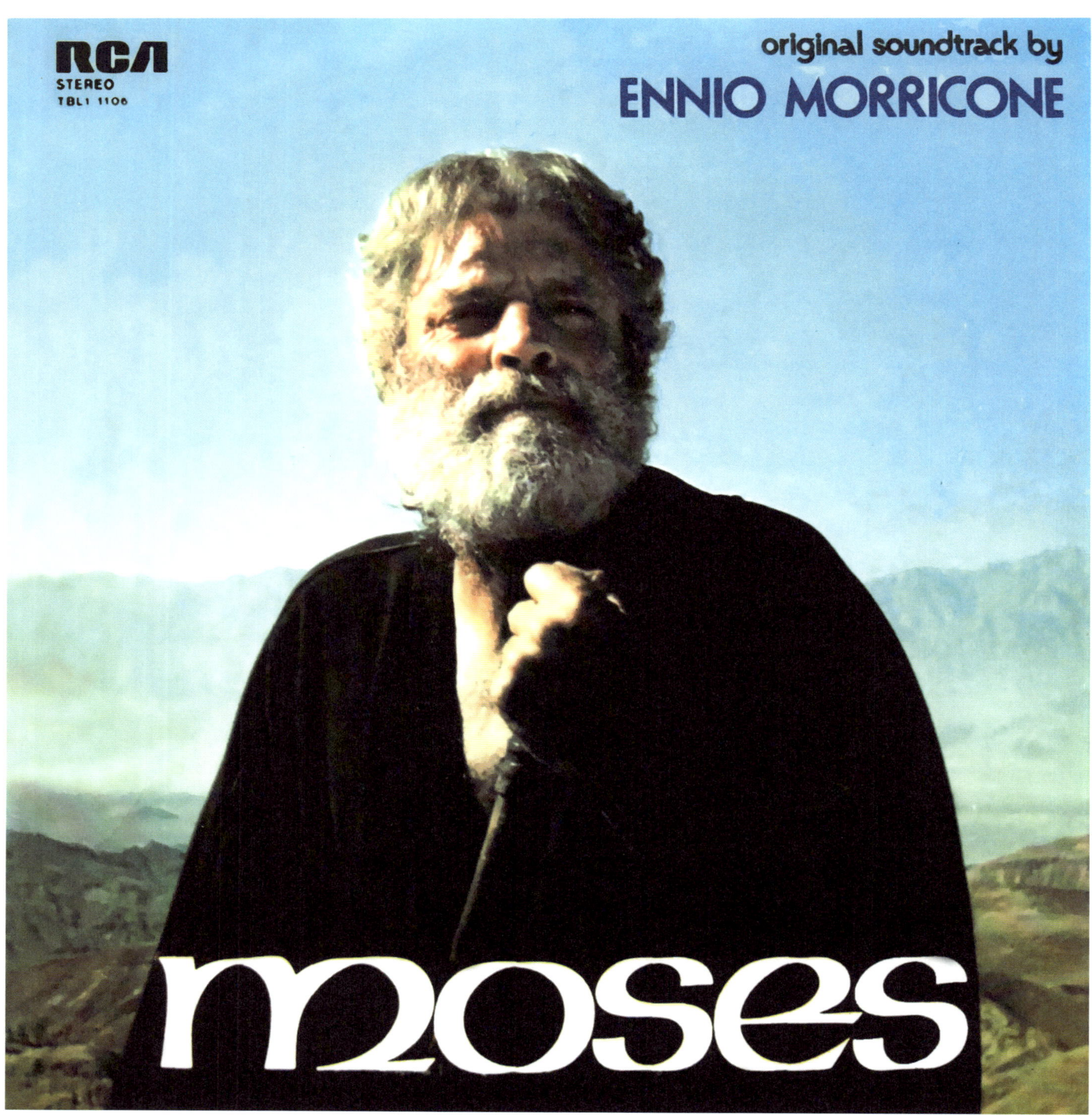

1974
Mosé.
La legge del deserto
Moses
Moïse
LP 33 rpm - RCA TBL1 1106

A mega-hit, this highly successful production by RAI has an international cast and a soundtrack that is far-reaching and worthy of a Bible epic. In addition to the theme song and the piece entitled, *Israel,* are the spine-tingling lamentations from amazing vocals by Gianna Spagnolo. Another little-known yet splendid apocryphal interpretation of the Moses theme song is by Maria Carta, entitled *Diglielo al tuo Dio*.

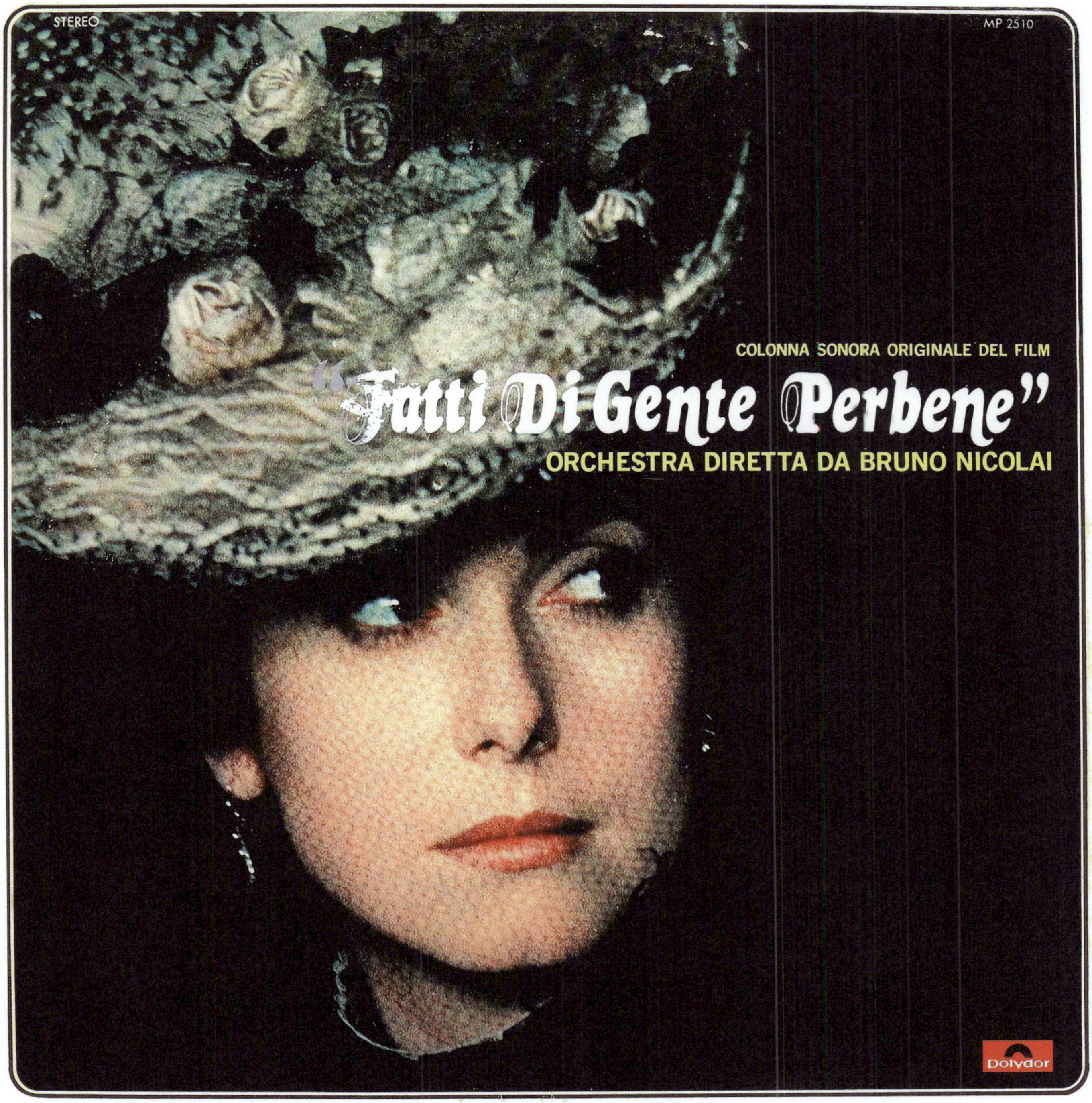
STEREO
MP 2510
COLONNA SONORA ORIGINALE DEL FILM
"Fatti Di Gente Perbene"
ORCHESTRA DIRETTA DA BRUNO NICOLAI
Polydor

CINEVOX
MDF 062
colonna sonora originale del film
FATTI DI GENTE PERBENE
di mauro bolognini
musiche di
ennio morricone
dirette da
bruno nicolai

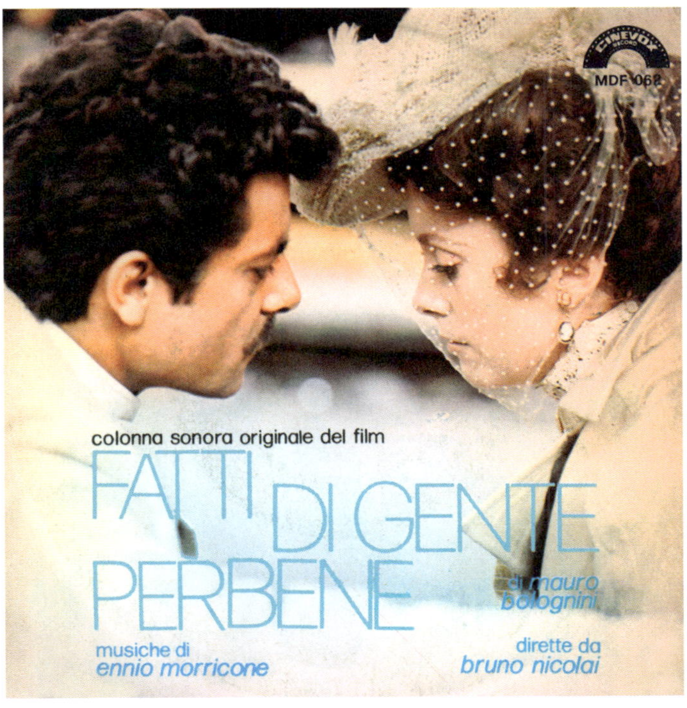

1974
Fatti di gente perbene
The Murri Affair
La grande bourgeoise
LP 33 rpm - POLYDOR MP 2510
45 rpm - CINEVOX MDF 062

Heartbreaking and mournful, the music for Mauro Bolognini's movie is dominated by the violin which converses with the discreet notes of the piano; and with the delicate sound of a music box. This combination takes listeners back to their most distant memories; perfect for a gray, rainy autumn day.

1974
L'anticristo
The Antichrist
L'antéchrist
with Bruno Nicolai
45 rpm - BEAT BTF 089

Significantly offsetting the wild viola of *Il buio* with the more vibrant solemnity of the pipe organ in *La luce*, Morricone and Bruno Nicolai in their last work together demonstrate their high degree of professionalism and rigor in service of film composition for this collaboration.

RCA
STEREO
TBBO 1018
Tratto dal film
SPASMO
Bambole
Spasmo
musiche di
ENNIO MORRICONE

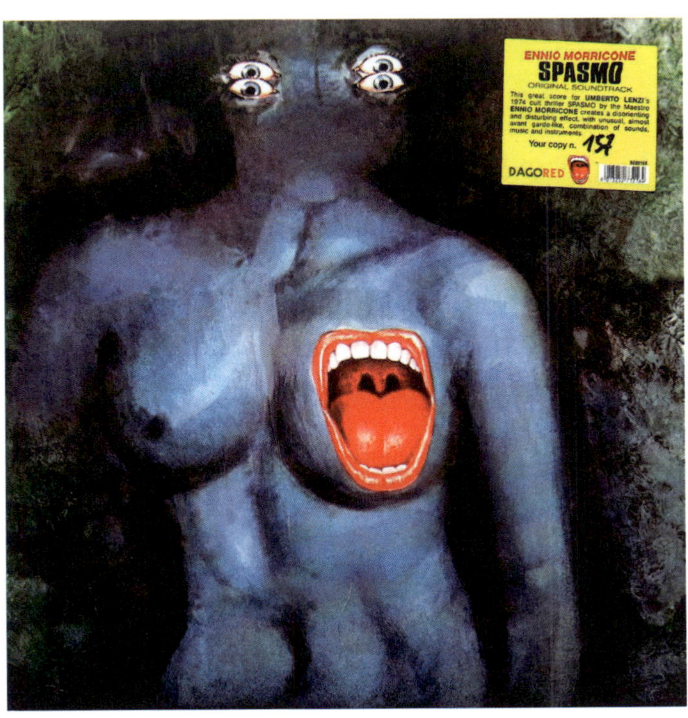

1974
Spasmo
45 rpm - RCA TBBO 1018
LP 33 rpm - DAGORED 216X

The music of *Spasmo* seems strange in that it recalls *The Great Silence*, romanticized in a way that is also reminiscent of *The Anonymous Venetian*. Morricone offered little that was new here for the last definitive soundtrack conducted by his friend, Bruno Nicolai.

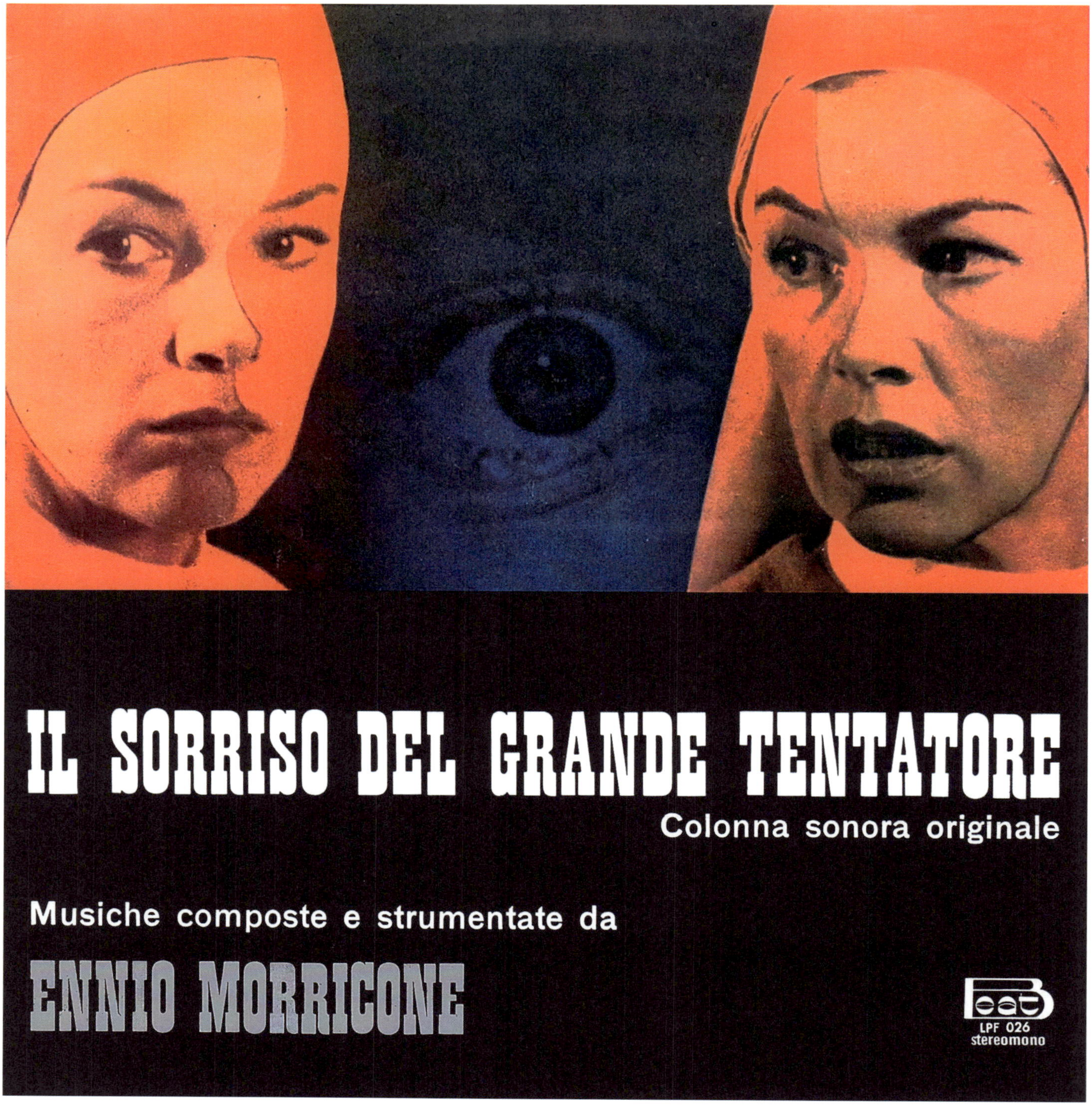

IL SORRISO DEL GRANDE TENTATORE
Colonna sonora originale
Musiche composte e strumentate da
ENNIO MORRICONE
Beat
LPF 026
stereomono

1974
Il sorriso del grande tentatore
The Devil Is a Woman
LP 33 rpm - BEAT LPF 026

1974
The Human Factor
Il giustiziere
La guerre des otages
CD - RCA OST 123

1974
Léonor
Mistress of the Devil
CD - GDM 2016

1974
Sesso in confessionale
Sex Advice
CD - BEAT RECORDS CD CR 20

1974
Storie di vita e malavita
The Prostitution Racket
CD - SCREEN TRAX CDST 318

1974
Le tour du monde des amoureux de Peynet
Il giro del mondo
degli innamorati di Peynet
Around the World
with Peynet's Lovers
with Alessandro Alessandroni
LP 33 rpm - EMI/MONTE STELLA MSR 1320003

1974
Le trio infernal
Il trio infernale
The Infernal Trio
45 rpm - YUKI MUSIC N 871001

1974
La faille
La smagliatura
Weak Spot
LP 33 rpm - YUKI MUSIC 873003

1974
Il fiore delle mille e una notte
Arabian Nights
Les mille et une nuits
CD - GDM CD CLUB 7020

To score the film for a demanding director like Pier Paolo Pasolini, Ennio Morricone was forced to adhere closely to classicism. He could not be spontaneous and had no room for other musical expressions; nor for any ethnic or exotic forays of the film which it may have deserved.

1975
Salò o le 120 giornate di Sodoma
Salò, or the 120 Days of Sodom
Salo ou les 120 journées de Sodome
CD - MEDIANE MED 11021

original motion picture score in full stereo
IL FIORE DELLE MILLE
E UNA NOTTE
ARABIAN NIGHTS
music composed, orchestrated and conducted by
ENNIO MORRICONE

1974
Le secret
Il segreto
The Secret
45 rpm - UNITED ARTISTS UA 35785

▸

1974
Un genio, due compari, un pollo
A Genius, Two Partners and a Dupe
Un génie, deux associés, une cloche
LP 33 rpm - CBS 69231

In 1981, Sergio Leone directed a commercial for a well-known automobile. The images of a car in chains that roars and burns rubber in the dust to free itself inside an ancient Roman amphitheater were accompanied by a brilliant combination of Western music and the famous notes from Ludwig van Beethoven's *Für Elise.* This singular song, that very few recognized, is indeed called *Cavalcata … per Elisa*, from the soundtrack for this film. The splendid gatefold cover was designed by Renato Casaro.

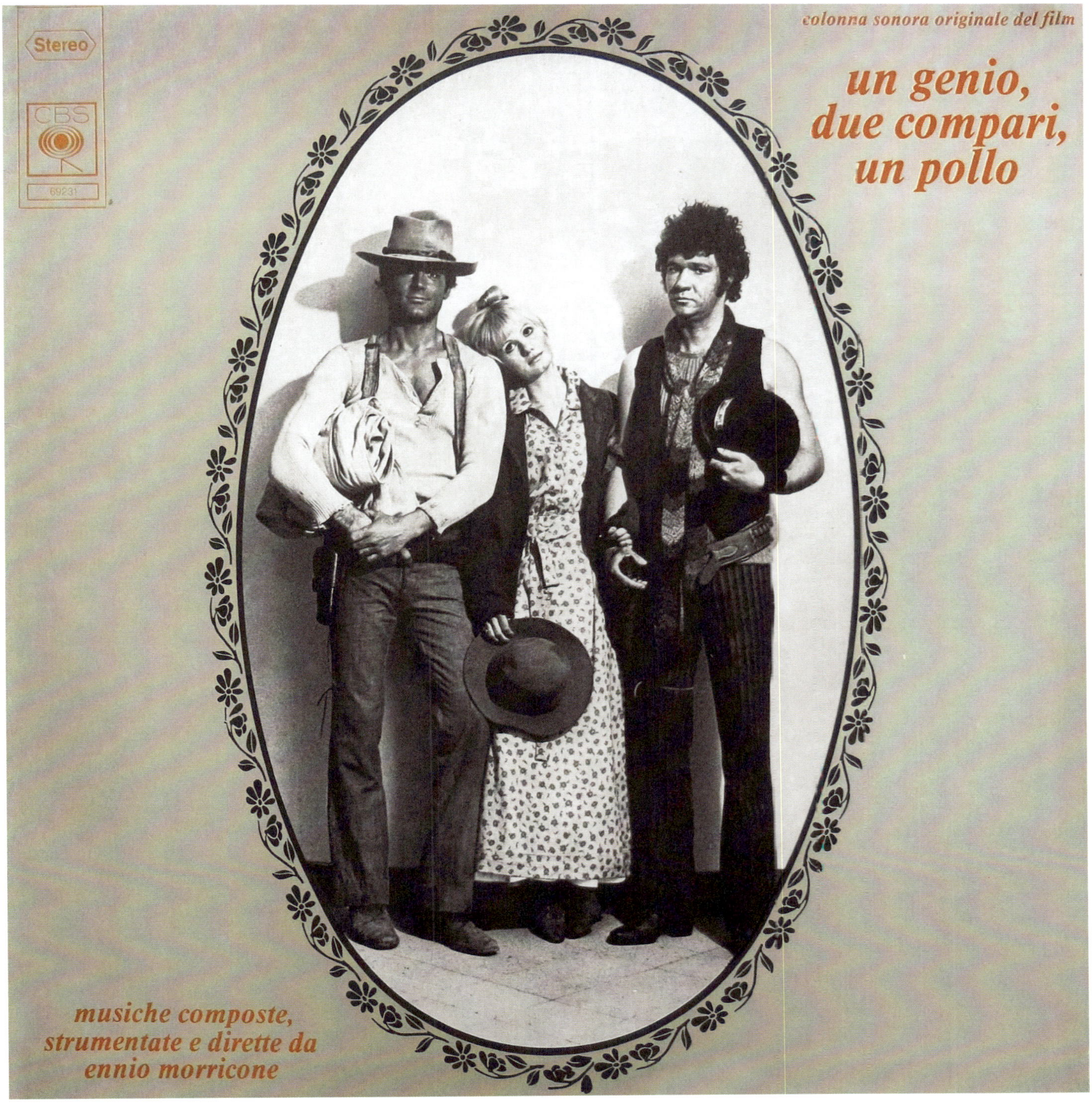
Stereo
CBS
69231
colonna sonora originale del film
un genio, due compari, un pollo
musiche composte, strumentate e dirette da ennio morricone

colonna sonora originale del film
UN GENIO, DUE COMPARI, UN POLLO
musiche composte, strumentate e dirette da ennio morricone

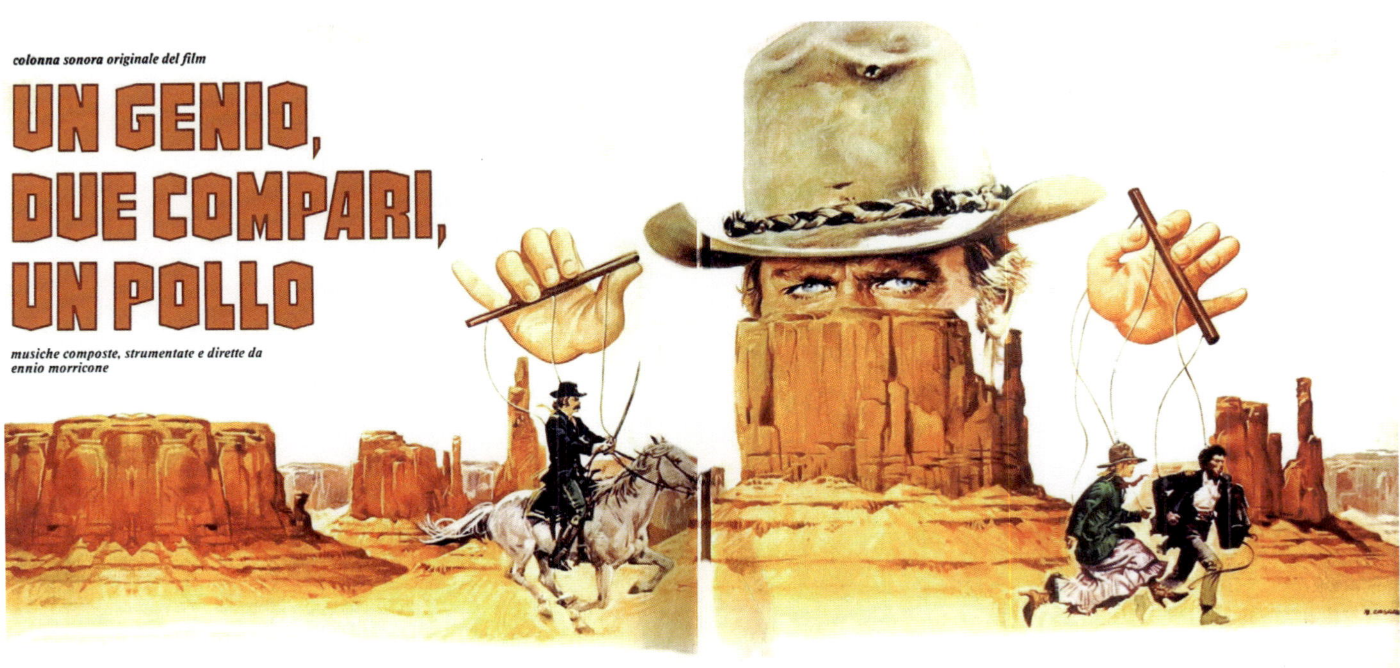

1974
La cugina
The Cousin
La cousine
LP 33 rpm - OVERDRIVE ODR036LP

1974
Milano odia:
la polizia non può sparare
Almost Human
La rançon de la peur
LP 33 rpm - GDM LP 6501

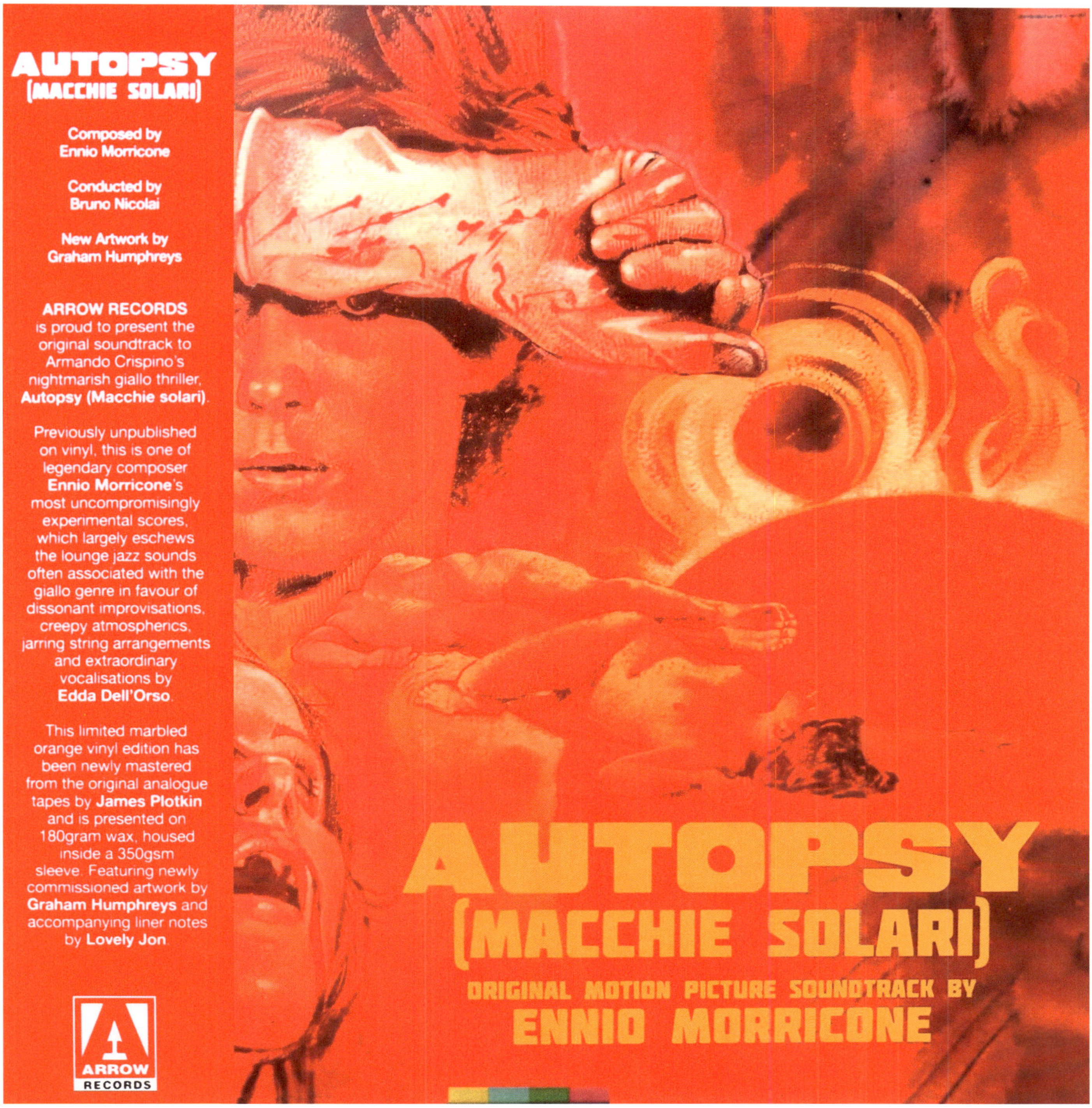

1975
Macchie solari
Autopsy
Frissons d'horreur
LP 33 rpm - ARROW RECORDS AR 007
45 rpm - SEVEN SEAS/CAM FMS 9

The revival of vinyl on the record market and the obscure path taken by the Compact Disc, of which fewer and fewer are being published today, made it possible to find never-before-published musical works that had long fallen into oblivion. A case in point is the unknown score by Maestro Morricone for this meteorology-based thriller, *Autopsy*.

1975
La donna della domenica
The Sunday Woman
La femme du dimanche
45 rpm - CINEVOX MDF 087

1975
Attenti al buffone
Eye of the Cat
LP 33 rpm - COMETA CMT 3

1975
L'ultimo treno della notte
Last Stop on the Night Train
Le dernier train de la nuit
45 rpm - CINEVOX MDF 072

1975
Peur sur la ville
Il poliziotto della
brigata criminale
The Night Caller
LP 33 rpm - WEA 56135

STEREO
TBBO1164

PER LE ANTICHE SCALE / CARNEVALE
Musiche composte e dirette da

ENNIO MORRICONE

dalla colonna sonora originale del film

prodotto dalla Italian International Films per la regia di Mauro Bolognini

1975
Per le antiche scale
Down the Ancient Stairs
Vertiges
45 rpm - RCA TBBO 1164

"Subdued" is the correct adjective to describe the musicality of *Down the Ancient Stairs*, where the viola and the flute become intimate accomplices of the string section. The strings are subtle and dim, and make no attempt to burst forward. The only extra sound is a popular carnival melody.

1975
Divina creatura
The Divine Nymph
Divine créature
music by Cesare Andrea Bixio
LP 33 rpm - CINEVOX MDF 33/95

1975
Gente di rispetto
The Flower in His Mouth
Les maîtres
LP 33 rpm - GDM LP 6714

1976
L'Agnese va a morire
And Agnes Chose to Die
45 rpm - GENERAL MUSIC GM 354

It might have been more logical and easier for Morricone to compose the music surrounding the dramatic events of Agnese's tale in the context of the Resistance by using hard orchestral sounds that recall the nation's liberation. Instead, the Maestro chose to celebrate the protagonist here – her courage, her sacrifice. It is a delicate musical tribute to this bold figure with just a whisper of emotion.

1976
L'eredità Ferramonti
The Inheritance
L'héritage
LP 33 rpm - CAM SAG 9067

1976
Per amore
For Love
with Luis Enríquez Bacalov
LP 33 rpm - RCA TBL1 1234

STEREO
TBL1 1221

COLONNA SONORA ORIGINALE DEL FILM

Musiche di

ennio morricone

1976
Novecento
1900
LP 33 rpm - RCA TBL 1 1221

If we did not know for certain that Ennio Morricone is of Roman origins, listening to the score of *1900,* we might assume that he was born in Emilia-Romagna like Giuseppe Verdi, whose death is announced as Bernardo Bertolucci's film begins. As the opening credits unfold, we hear Giuseppe Pellizza da Volpedo's celebrated *Il quarto stato*, but viewers are likely already imagining rows of poplars, canals, and the scent of mown wheat fields.

33
41
49

1976
Il deserto dei tartari
The Desert of the Tartars
Le désert des Tartares
LP 33 rpm - GENERAL MUSIC GML 10005

The desert in Dino Buzzati's celebrated novel, an indispensable title in the canon of 20th-century Italian literature, is a closed room without walls in which what happens over the course of a lifetime, is only expectation. Morricone seems to fully understand this significance, and composes a theme song in which there are no endless horizons, but instead there is music that is slow and incessant; and that becomes more and more claustrophobic like the protagonist soldier's life.

colonna sonora originale

CAM
SAG 9073

1976
Todo modo
One Way or Another
CD - RECORDING ARTS SA-2X903

1976
Una vita venduta
A Sold Life
LP 33 rpm - CAM SAG 9073

2393152

1976
San Babila ore 20: un delitto inutile
San Babila – 8 P.M.
Tuer pour tuer
CD - SCREEN TRAX CDST 318

1977
René la Canne
Tre simpatiche carogne
Rene the Cane
LP 33 rpm - POLYDOR 2393 152

1977
Stato interessante
CD - GDM CLUB 7049

1977
Holocaust 2000
The Chosen
Holocauste 2000
LP 33 rpm - BEAT LPF 040

1977
Il mostro
The Fiend
Qui sera tué demain?
45 rpm - BEAT BTF 102

1977
Forza Italia!
LP 33 rpm - COMETA CMT 1002-9

1977
Autostop rosso sangue
Hitch-Hike
La proie de l'autostop
LP 33 rpm - COMETA 1001

The entire movie seems to be pervaded by the misplaced. Director Pasquale Festa Campanile, King of Comedy, tries his hand at a hard-core road thriller, where Abruzzo as a film location is not quite the California that it is supposed to represent. Ennio Morricone, showing his pop side here, indulges excessively with the banjo, and Edda Dell'Orso's dramatic voice fails to render a genuine country blues sound.

COLONNA SONORA ORIGINALE DEL FILM

AUTOSTOP ROSSO SANGUE

ENNIO
MORRICONE

1977
Orca: Killer Whale
L'orca assassina
Orca
45 rpm - PHILIPS-6172077

1977
Il gatto
The Cat
Qui a tué le chat?
LP 33 rpm - CINEVOX MDF 33.117

1977
Exorcist II: The Heretic
L'esorcista II – L'eretico
L'hérétique (L'exorciste II)
LP 33 rpm - WARNER BROS BS 3068

Morricone was almost certainly aware of the musical controversies surrounding the first film in this franchise, *The Exorcist*. For this reason, and to avoid encountering problems in a foreign project where he didn't have free rein, he wisely scored a more traditional soundtrack.

1977
Il prefetto di ferro
The Iron Prefect
L'affaire Mori
LP 33 rpm - BEAT LPF 041

The brand-new narrative of this score develops in the best popular tradition of telling infamous stories of crime and bloodshed in song. The long *La ballata del prefetto Mori,* written by Ignazio Buttitta, a Sicilian poet and singer-songwriter, to music by Morricone, is developed like a three-part story with guitar sounds and Rosa Balistreri's gravelly voice. This is truly a soundtrack to accompany an imagined "History of Sicily Through Music."

1977
Drammi gotici.
Nella città vampira
LP 33 rpm - RUSTBLADE RBLLP 020

1978
L'Italia vista dal cielo:
Sardegna
LP 33 rpm - COMETA CMT 45

1978
Noi lazzaroni
LP 33 rpm - CAM SAG 9086

1978
One Two Two
122 Rue de Provence
One Two Two
Madame Claude n. 3
LP 33 rpm - GENERAL MUSIC GM 803 024

1978

Corleone

CD - SCREENTRAX - CDST 338
CD - POINT RECORDS PRCD 112

Something funereal shrouds the music for this film, even when the orchestra plays its sweeter romantic themes. The bad omen that it expresses leads to a chain of bloody events with a domino effect. It's pure Morricone in a state of grace.

1978
L'immoralità
Cock Crows at Eleven
LP 33 rpm - CAM SAG 9091

A gentle peacefulness envelops the listener in this score, which falls short of telling a dark and unsavory story. This film was of dubious quality and did poorly at the box office and with critics. The soundtrack is more enjoyable when listened to on a record rather than while watching the film.

THE ORIGINAL SOUNDTRACK FROM THE MOTION PICTURE

1978

Days of Heaven

I giorni del cielo

Les moissons du ciel

LP 33 rpm - PACIFIC ARTS PAC8-128

CD - FILM SCORE MONTHLY FSM V.14 No. 12

This was the first Oscar nomination for Morricone in the "Best Film Score" category. The music here has both classical renditions and country music for a film with a rural setting.

1978
Dove vai in vacanza?
Where Are You Going on Holiday?
Où es-tu allé en vacances?
LP 33 rpm - RCA BL 31453

1978
Così come sei
Stay as You Are
La fille
LP 33 rpm - CINEVOX MDF 33.122

1978
La cage aux folles
Il vizietto
LP 33 rpm - CAM SAG 9090

Morricone's spot-on musical solution for the first chapter of *Il vizietto* exploits the Music Hall while, at the same time, adds sounds and noises typical of his most tongue-and-cheek productions.

1978
Il prigioniero
45 rpm - CAM AMP 207

1978
El Mundial
45 rpm - RCA BB 6191

This was not the first time that Morricone wrote music for sports, like the previous *Invito allo sport*. In 1978, his fame and his prestige were already so great that he was asked to write the official El Mundial World Cup theme that was recorded and produced around the world.

1978
Le mani sporche
LP 33 rpm - CAM SAG 9089

1978
Invito allo sport
LP 33 rpm - GENERAL MUSIC GML 10012

LA RAI
RADIOTELEVISIONE
ITALIANA
PRESENTA

ADATTAMENTO TELEVISIVO E TRADUZIONE DI
ELIO PETRI
MUSICHE ORIGINALI COMPOSTE E DIRETTE DA
ENNIO MORRICONE
EDIZIONI MUSICALI CAM S.p.A.

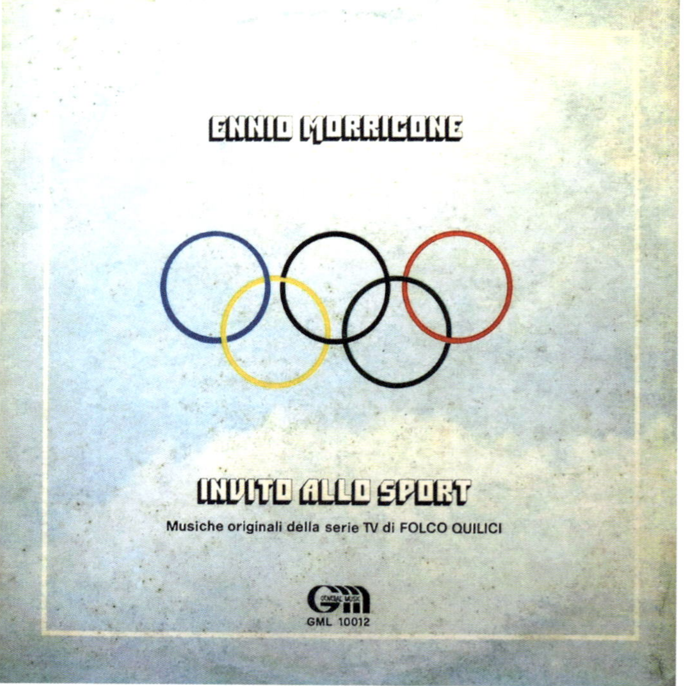

1979
Il giocattolo
A Dangerous Toy
Un jouet dangereux
LP 33 rpm - CINEVOX MDF 33.128

Hastily branded as a sort of *Death Wish* Italian-style, Guiliano Montaldo's movie is instead ahead of its time as it addresses one of the most important issues today: the safety of each citizen with both the political and social implications. Maestro Morricone is the perfect accomplice squaring the circle with the dramatic musical timbres in the manner of *Final Shot* and the dreamy sound of a delicate music box. Mysterious and highly descriptive, the music encompasses the triple essence of this thorny and unsolved problem: man (the protagonist), the metropolis (the setting), and the object (the weapon).

1979
Il prato
The Meadow
LP 33 rpm - CAM SAG 9100

For his second and last collaboration with the Taviani brothers, Morricone creates background music of a bucolic nature, leaving much room to interact with flute solos by the talented Marianne Eckstein.

1979
Dietro il processo
LP 33 rpm - GENERAL MUSIC GM 30703

ennio morricone/oscar valdambrini
antologia di musiche da film scritte da ennio morricone per oscar valdambrini

COLONNA SONORA ORIGINALE DEL FILM
DI PAOLO E VITTORIO TAVIANI

PRODOTTO DA GIULIANI G. DE NEGRI
PER LA RAI-RADIOTELEVISIONE ITALIANA E LA FILMTRE s.r.l.

MUSICHE COMPOSTE E DIRETTE
DA ENNIO MORRICONE

1979
Ogro
Operation Ogre
LP 33 rpm - PHOENIX PHCAM 04

This film is a harsh, scathing commentary on a story from the political news of a Spain in the years of Basque terrorism. There are many, albeit inappropriate, analogies with *The Battle of Algiers* by the same director, Gillo Pontecorvo. *Operation Ogre* remains a chapter on its own, as does the musical score, which can only be appreciated within the context of the movie. Here and there, Morricone also breaks the tension with a few short musical "scherzos."

ORIGINAL SOUND TRACK FROM THE MOTION PICTURE

MUSIC BY ENNIO MORRICONE

VOLUME 4: OGRO / BY GILLO PONTECORVO

1979
Viaggio con Anita
A Trip with Anita
CD - SCREEN TRAX CDST 336

1979
Bugie bianche (Professione figlio)
Venetian Lies
CD - GDM 4328

1979
Orient Express
45 rpm - RCA BB 6396

1979
Μέσα από φυλακή σας γράφω στην Ελλάδα
Non devi dimenticare. Vi scrivo da un carcere in Grecia
LP 33 rpm - RCA PL 31328

1979
Bloodline
Linea di sangue
Liés par le sang
LP 33 rpm - VARESE STV 81131

1979
L'umanoide
The Humanoid
L'humanoïde
LP 33 rpm - RCA BL 31432

This film by Aldo Lado was an Italian attempt to exploit the world success of *Star Wars*. Ennio Morricone does not give in to the easy and perhaps expected emulation of American composer John Williams, instead scoring the space science fiction movie in his own way, with surprising results as proven by the absolute jewel, *Estasi stellare*.

1979
Dedicato al mar Egeo
LP 33 rpm - COLUMBIA LX 7062

1979
I… comme Icare
I… come Icaro
I… For Icarus
LP 33 rpm - GENERAL MUSIC 803 006

Colonna sonora originale del film

Buone Notizie

Musiche di ENNIO MORRICONE

Original Sound Track

Ten to Survive

dedicated to unicef

UNITED NATIONS CHILDREN'S FUND

LUIS BACALOV • FRANCO EVANGELISTI

EGISTO MACCHI

ENNIO MORRICONE • NINO ROTA

MOTION PICTURE ACADEMY AWARD 1980

1979
Buone notizie
Good News
LP 33 rpm - COMETA CMT 1013/27

1979
Ten To Survive
Dieci per vivere
with Luis Enríquez Bacalov,
Nino Rota, Egisto Macchi,
Franco Evangelisti
LP 33 rpm - WEA - T 58442

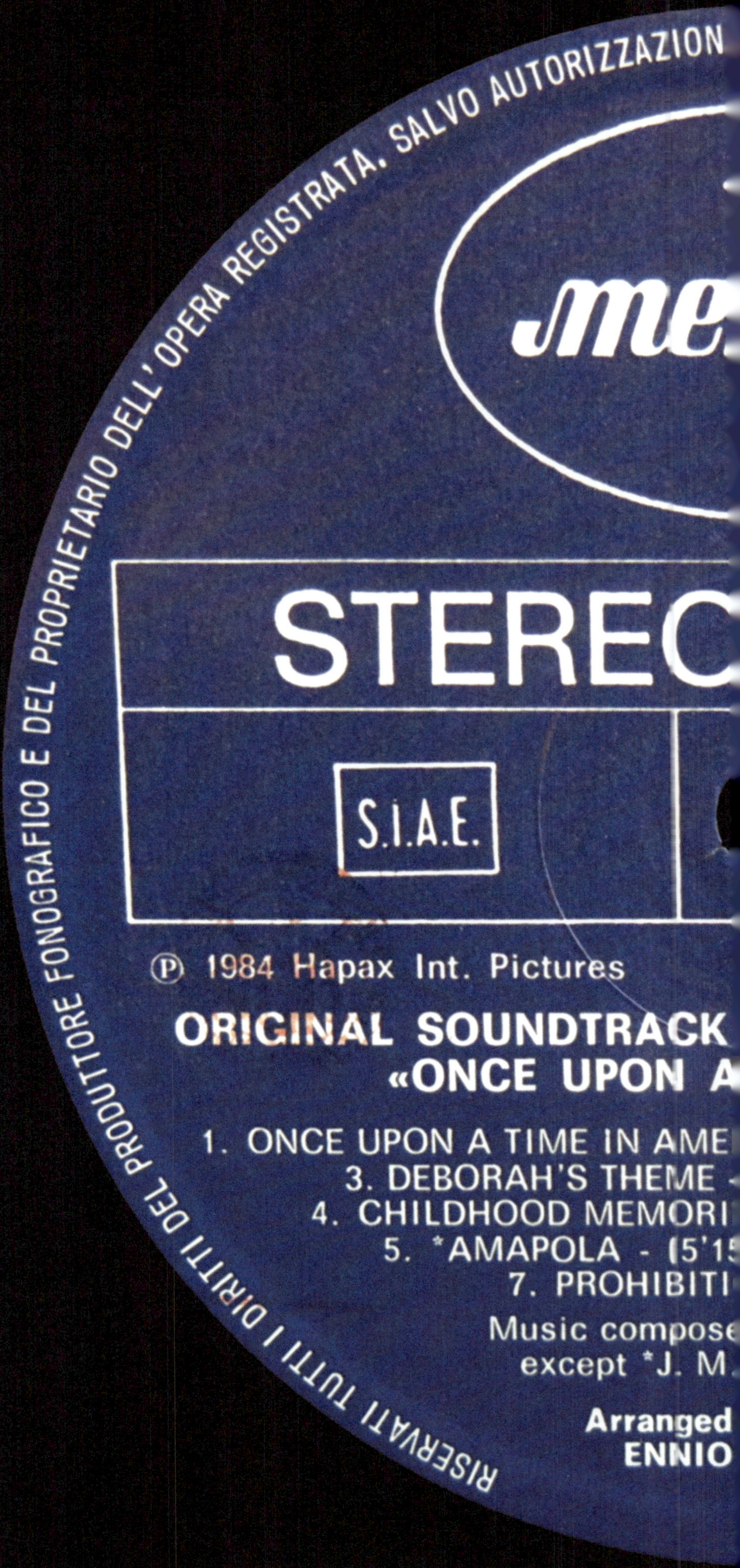

me

STEREO

S.I.A.E.

ORIGINAL SOUNDTRACK
«ONCE UPON A

1. ONCE UPON A TIME IN AME
3. DEBORAH'S THEME -
4. CHILDHOOD MEMORI
5. *AMAPOLA - (5'15
7. PROHIBITI

Music compose
except *J. M.

Arranged
ENNIO

1980 —1989

Discography 1980—1989

1980
Birds of a Feather 2, Edouard Molinaro
Fun Is Beautiful, Carlo Verdone
Il pianeta d'acqua, Carlo Alberto Pinelli
La via del silenzio, Franco Brocani
Si salvi chi vuole, Roberto Faenza
Stark System, Armenia Balducci
The Blue-Eyed Bandit, Alfredo Giannetti
The Fantastic World of M.C. Escher, Michele Emmer
The Good Thief, Pasquale Festa Campanile
The Island, Michael Ritchie
The Lady Banker, Francis Girod
Uomini e no, Valentino Orsini
Windows, Gordon Willis

1981
Bianco, rosso e Verdone, Carlo Verdone
Buddy Goes West, Michele Lupo
La disubbidienza, Aldo Lado
Lady of the Camelias, Mauro Bolognini
The Life and Times of David Lloyd George (Series), John Hefin
The Professional, Georges Lautner
Tragedy of a Ridiculous Man, Bernardo Bertolucci
So Fine, Andrew Bergman

1982
A Time to Die, Matt Cimber
Butterfly, Matt Cimber
Espion, lève-toi, Yves Boisset
Flatlandia, Michele Emmer
Le ruffian, José Giovanni
Maja Plisetskaja, Istvan Szintai
Marco Polo, Giuliano Montaldo
The Link, Alberto de Martino
The Thing, John Carpenter
Treasure of the Four Crowns, Ferdinando Baldi
White Dog, Samuel Fuller

1983
Hundra, Matt Cimber
Order of Death, Roberto Faenza
Nana, the True Key of Pleasure, Dan Wolman
Sahara, Andrew V. McLaglen
The Key, Tinto Brass
The Outsider, Jacques Deray
The Scarlet and the Black, Jerry London

1984
Die Försterbuben, Peter Patzak
Don't kill God, Jacqueline Manzano
Once Upon A Time In America, Sergio Leone
Thieves After Dark, Samuel Fuller
Wer War Edgar Allan?, Michael Haneke

1985
Chimica e agricoltura, Luciano Emmer
Dead Fright, Giuseppe Patroni Griffi
La Cage aux Folles 3: the Wedding, Georges Lautner
Red Sonja, Richard Fleischer
Via Mala, Tom Toelle

1986
Au Louvre: le plus grand musée du monde, Jean-Marc Leuven e Daniel Lander
C.A.T. Squad. Stalking Danger, William Friedkin
Quartiere, Silvano Agosti
The Mission, Roland Joffé
The Octopus 2, Florestano Vancini
The Repenter, Pasquale Squitieri
The Venetian Woman, Mauro Bolognini

1987
Farewell Moscow, Mauro Bolognini
Gli angeli del potere, Giorgio Albertazzi
La piovra 3, Luigi Perelli
Mind Control, Giuliano Montaldo
Rampage, William Friedkin
The Gold Rimmed Glasses, Giuliano Montaldo
The Untouchables, Brian De Palma

1988

A Time of Destiny, Gregory Nava
Camillo Castiglioni oder die Moral der Haifsche, Peter Patzak
C.A.T. Squad: Python Wolf, William Friedkin
Cinema Paradiso, Giuseppe Tornatore
Frantic, Roman Polanski
Gli indifferenti, Mauro Bolognini
Secret of the Sahara, Alberto Negrin

1989

12 registi per 12 città (Segments: *Udine e Firenze*), Gillo Pontecorvo, Franco Zeffirelli
Casualties of War, Brian De Palma
Fat Man and Little Boy, Roland Joffé
La piovra 4, Luigi Perelli
The Betrothed, Salvatore Nocita
The Endless Game, Bryan Forbes
Time to Kill, Giuliano Montaldo

1980
La banquière
La banchiera
The Lady Banker
LP 33 rpm - GENERAL MUSIC GM 803 015

For this movie, Morricone recycled three songs previously composed for *Murder on the Bridge*, 1975, including *Fox astratto* and *Affresco con bambino,* and he completed everything with arias in chamber music for violin and piano.

1980
Stark System
CD - BEAT RECORDS BCM 9528

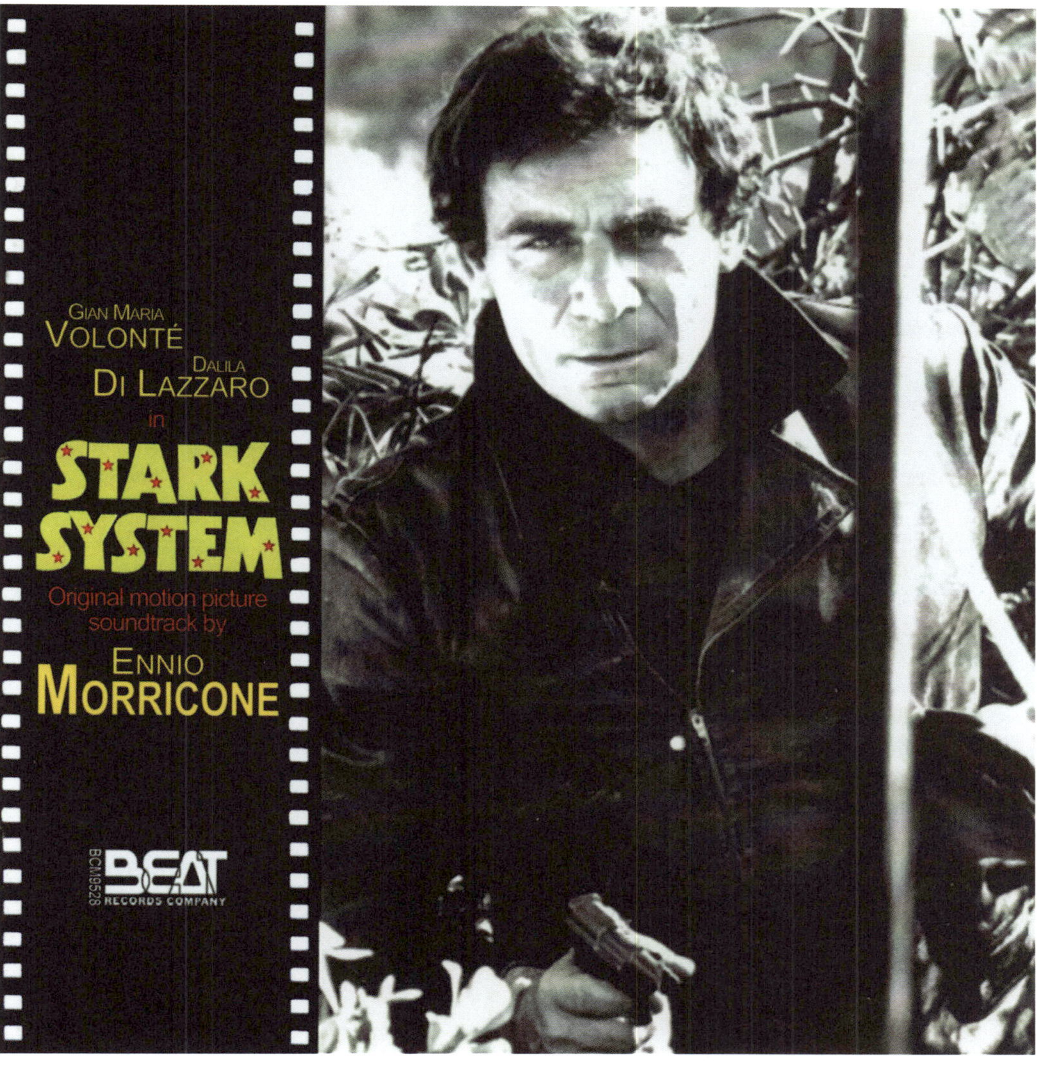

1980
Un sacco bello
Fun Is Beautiful
45 rpm - CINEVOX MDF 127

For his first movie with Carlo Verdone, Maestro Morricone tries his hand at rock; and in the opening credits he brilliantly "apes" the funky *Train Time* by Cream (1968). He continues by producing a tongue-in-cheek commentary ennobled by Oscar Valdambrini on the saxhorn and by the whistling of Alessandro Alessandroni, without ever losing sight of the humor. The music has a modern and captivating sound – elements that are indispensable for such a fun film.

1980
Il ladrone
The Good Thief
Le larron
LP 33 rpm - RCA BL 31502

1980
Il pianeta d'acqua
CD - COMETA CMT 10017

1980
The Island
L'isola
L'île sanglante
LP 33 rpm - VARESE STV 81147

1980
Uomini e no
CAM SOUNDTRACK ENCYCLOPEDIA

The cover art created by CAM for this release exists only in the digital realm. It was created to accompany the music for streaming and online sales, as an actual LP was never released.

1980
Il bandito dagli occhi azzurri
The Blue-Eyed Bandit
Le bandit aux yeux bleus
LP 33 rpm - CERBERUS CEM S 0113

This is another case where the soundtrack of an Italian film is published abroad several years before; in this case in the United States by Cerberus Records. The title of the song *For Enrico, Riccardo and Roberto* highlights the musicians who collaborated with Morricone on the score: Enrico Pieranunzi, Riccardo Del Fra, and Roberto Gatto.

1980
La cage aux folles II
Il vizietto II
Birds of a Feather 2
LP 33 rpm - WEA WB 56234

The theme song was composed for the first film in the series, and then used again as a leitmotif and recycle of the piece, *Bianco e nero* from the soundtrack of *Malamondo*.

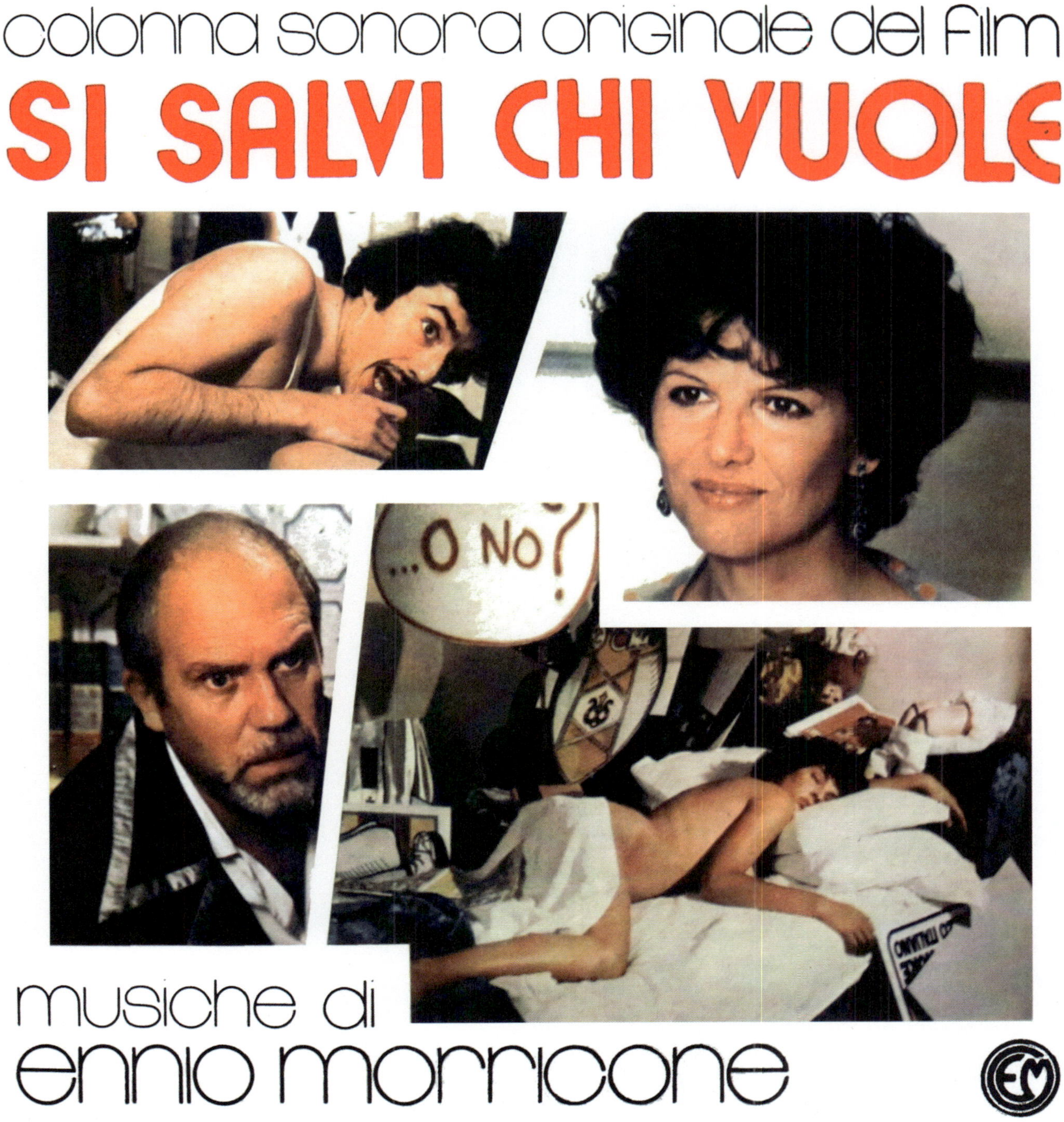
colonna sonora originale del film
SI SALVI CHI VUOLE
...O NO?
musiche di
ennio morricone

ORIGINAL MGM MOTION PICTURE SOUNDTRACK
WINDOWS
MUSIC COMPOSED, ORCHESTRATED AND CONDUCTED BY ENNIO MORRICONE

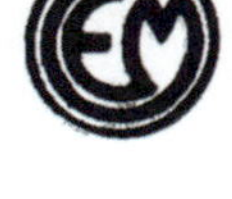

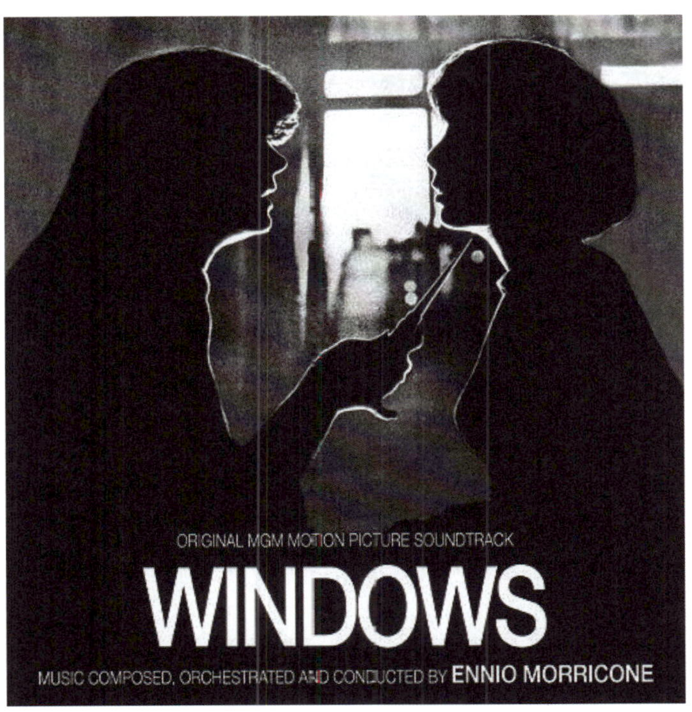

1980
Si salvi chi vuole
LP 33 rpm - COMETA CMT 1014/28

1980
Windows
CD - QUARTET RECORDS QRSCE 031

Stereo
MDF 33/144

La storia vera della Signora dalle Camelie

colonna sonora originale del film

musiche di

ENNIO MORRICONE

1981
La storia vera della signora dalle camelie
Lady of the Camelias
La dame aux camélias
LP 33 rpm - CINEVOX MDF 33/144

Inspired by the famous novel by Alexandre Dumas, Mauro Bolognini's film includes cameo roles for the actresses, Carla Fracci and Luciana Turina, who also sings *Petite crèature*, written by the director himself to music by Morricone.

1981
Bianco rosso e Verdone
45 rpm - CINEVOX MDF 135

With popular themes and a few moments of fake tongue-in-cheek charm for the entertaining Italian-style road movie by Carlo Verdone, this film was divided into three parts like the colors of the Italian national flag. Morricone plays along with it and brilliantly indulges the marvelous actor and director. We don't know whether the Maestro ever saw the completed movie, but if he did, he must have laughed heartily. Morricone's music was nominated for a David di Donatello Award for "Best Musical Score."

LA TRAGEDIA DI UN UOMO RIDICOLO

1981
La tragedia di un uomo ridicolo
Tragedy of a Ridiculous Man
La tragédie d'un homme ridicule
LP 33 rpm - BUBBLE BLU 19605

Released by Bubble Record and labeled Gruppo Editoriale Bixio, there are many who say that since the soundtrack of the movie was by Ennio Morricone, it deserved a more "illustrious" recording company. This opinion is debatable but meanwhile, it did not prevent the release from being unjustly snubbed.

1981
Le professionel
Joss il professionista
The Professional
LP 33 rpm - GENERAL MUSIC GM 808 026

Although it's an action film, the songs composed for it are calibrated for string instruments and are rather "calm". Additionally, it has a well-known theme song, *Chi mai*, reused from the film, *Maddalena*. The song also comes in a disco version and was recorded as a rare 12-inch single entitled, *Ennio Morricone Disco78,* for use by disc jockeys; and many different recordings of the soundtrack were also released.

1981
Occhio alla penna
Buddy Goes West
On m'appelle Malabar
LP 33 rpm - CINEVOX MDF 33.145

Maybe we've all heard the story before, but the music and the film are still lots of fun, with an entertaining score and several especially touching moments. Many instruments have solos and include the Indian flute, played by Morricone himself.

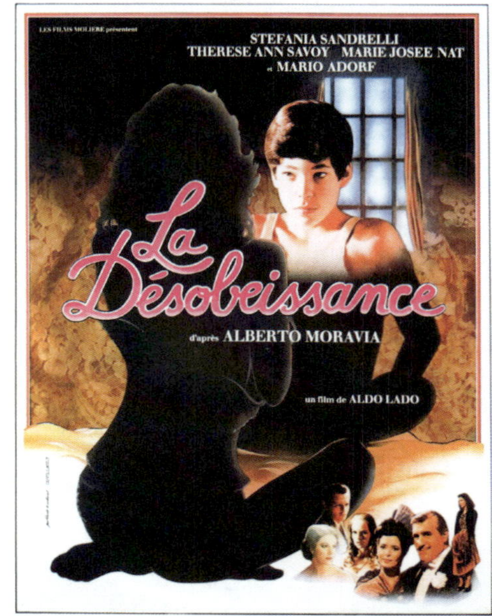

1981
So Fine
Jeans dagli occhi rosa
Les fesses à l'air
CD - MUSIC BOX RECORD (2) - MBR -101

1982
White Dog
Dressé pour tuer
CD FILM SCOORE MONTHLY FSM Vol. 13 n. 3

1981
La disubbidienza
La désobéissance
LP 33 rpm GENERAL MUSIC 803 021

1982
Butterfly
Butterfly. Il sapore del peccato
LP 33 rpm - APPLAUSE APLP 1017

1982
A Time To Die
Tempo di morire
V comme vengeance
with Robert O. Ragland
LP 33 rpm - CERBERUS CEM-S 0119

1982
Extrasensorial
The Link
LP 33 rpm - DUSE ELP 074

1982
Il tesoro delle 4 corone
Treasure of the Four Crowns
Le trésor des quatres couronnes
LP 33 rpm - GENERAL MUSIC 803 053

1982
Le ruffian
Una cascata tutta d'oro
LP 33 rpm - GENERAL MUSIC 803 042

1982

Espion lève-toi

Alzati spia

LP 33 rpm - GENERAL MUSIC 803 028

In this movie an earlier composition is once again re-purposed. *Ombre sospese* was borrowed from the 1974 film score for *The Secret*. It was published for the first time by General Music in 1978 on an obscure album that was not available for sale. This piece is difficult to identify because it was first renamed *Nebulosa* for the "complete score" and then in 1982, called *Ambres suspendues* in *Espion leve-toi*, the French version of the 1981 film, *Alzati spia*.

1982
The Thing
La cosa
LP 33 rpm - MCA 4164

Welcome to Arctic isolation, the terror of the unknown, and the frightening alien revelation in a climate of deeply distressing solitude and impotence against unimaginable events. All this is masterfully underscored in the amazing fusion between John Carpenter's film and Ennio Morricone's music. A masterpiece from every angle.

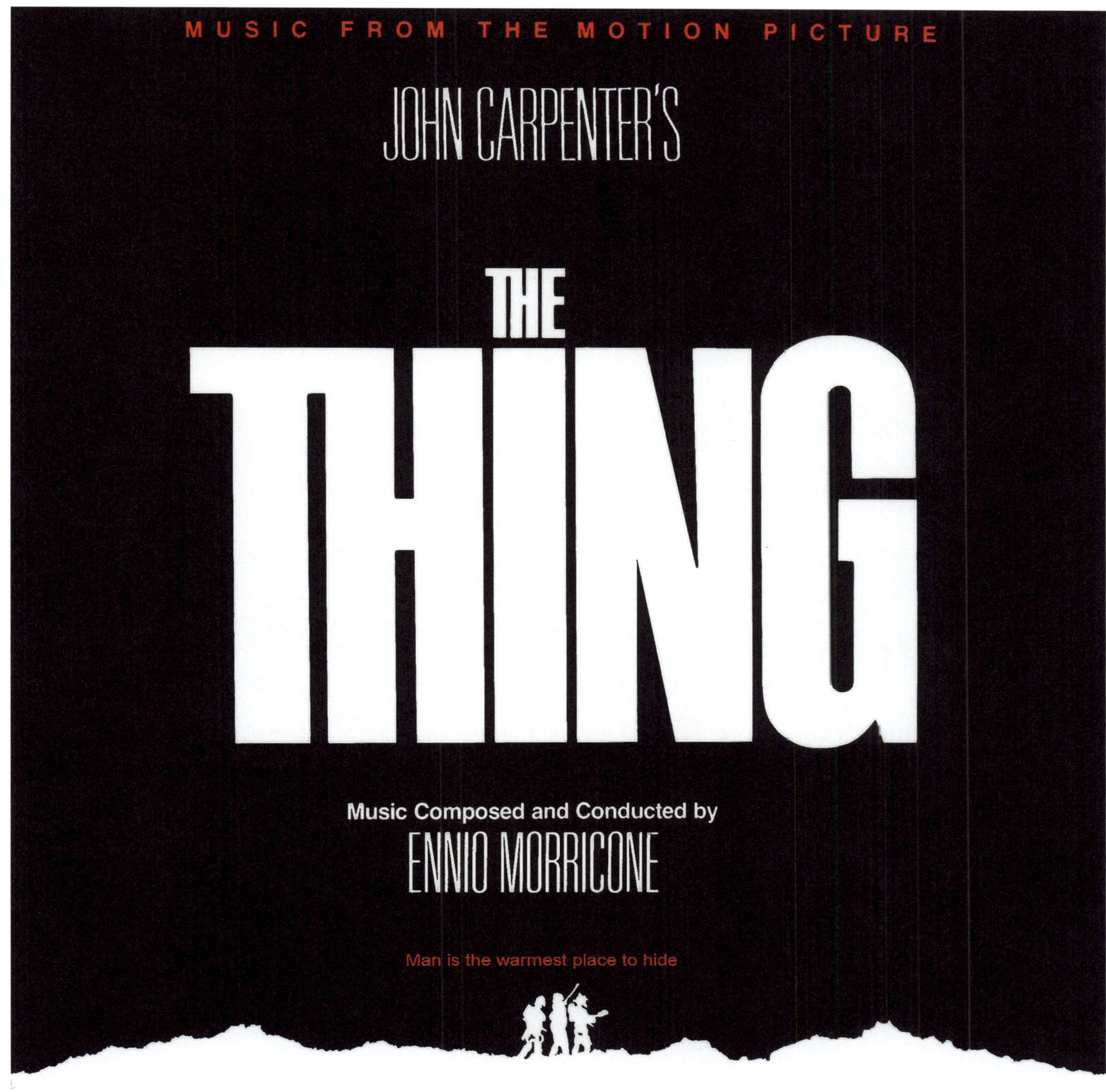

1982

Marco Polo

LP 33 rpm FONIT CETRA LPX 108

This was another major Italian television production entrusted to the Maestro whose focus is the theme of the journey. This is understood as both an inner and physical journey that the young protagonist faces as he heads toward the unknown; but simultaneously it is about his personal growth and education. The soundtrack is suited to accompany a traveler toward any destination, set to the hypnotic and lulling *Verso l'Oriente* (*Viaggio*).

MARCO POLO

COLONNA SONORA ORIGINALE

ENNIO MORRICONE

1983
The Scarlet and the Black
Scarlatto e nero
La pourpre et le noir
LP 33 rpm - CERBERUS CEM-S 0120

1983
Nana
Nana. La vera chiave del piacere
Nana, the True Key of Pleasure
Nana: Le désir
LP 33 rpm - CINEVOX MDF 33.161

1983
Copkiller.
L'assassino dei poliziotti
Order of Death
À couteau tiré
LP 33 rpm - GENERAL MUSIC 803 074

1983
Hundra
Hundra. La regina di fuoco
LP 33 rpm - MECOLA MRC 903

1983
La chiave
The Key
La clef
LP 33 rpm - TRIPLE TIME ZPLTT 34208

Varied and intriguing, the music of this movie becomes the accomplice of the director on a par with his unbiased vision of eroticism. Morricone catches us off-guard with a series of different themes that range from the Baroque to dance music.

MUSIQUE DE ENNIO MORRICONE

Bande Originale du Film

BELMONDO

CÉRITO ET LES FILMS ARIANE PRÉSENTENT

LE MARGINAL

UN FILM DE

JACQUES DERAY

◄

1983
Le marginal
Professione: poliziotto
The Outsider
LP 33 rpm - GENERAL MUSIC 803 056

This smooth, modern score is instantly recognizable from the first notes as Morricone. The Maestro asserts his typical cadenced style, one of his numerous hallmarks.

1983
Sahara
LP 33 rpm - RED BUS RECORDS - RED 33905

1984

Once Upon A Time In America

C'era una volta in America

Il était une fois en Amérique

LP 33 rpm - MERCURY 818 697

45 rpm - MERCURY 7PP-147

45 rpm - MERCURY 818 699-7 Q

45 rpm - MERCURY PROMO 281-7

There is an invisible thread represented by the passing of time that closely links the two souls of *C'era una volta in America*; one is the epic story of the lead character and his friends stretching over a 40-year period; and the other is, in parallel, the gestation and making of the movie itself. After its release, its hopes for success were disappointing. But over the course of the years, Time restores the true value of a work and this one is not just deemed a great film today, but an absolute masterpiece in cinema history. And covering all of it, like a precious veil, is Maestro Ennio Morricone's timeless music.

7PP-147
¥700
N·9·1
東宝東和提供「ワンス・アポン・ア・タイム・イン・アメリカ」オリジナル・サウンドトラック盤
アマポーラ～愛のテーマ
AMAPOLA
最高のスタッフと豪華キャストを総結集した超大作映画「ワンス・アポン・ア・タイム・イン・アメリカ」
'84年度カンヌ映画祭の話題を独占！
映画音楽の巨匠、エンニオ・モリコーネがアメリカ神話の影を今、鮮烈に甦えらせる!!
ONCE UPON A TIME IN AMERICA
Side 2
アマポーラ～パートII
AMAPOLA-PART 2
〈音楽〉エンニオ・モリコーネ
Music arranged by Ennio Morricone
mercury

GHEORGHE ZAMFIR
Cockeye's Song
ES WAR EINMAL IN AMERIKA
818 699-7 Q

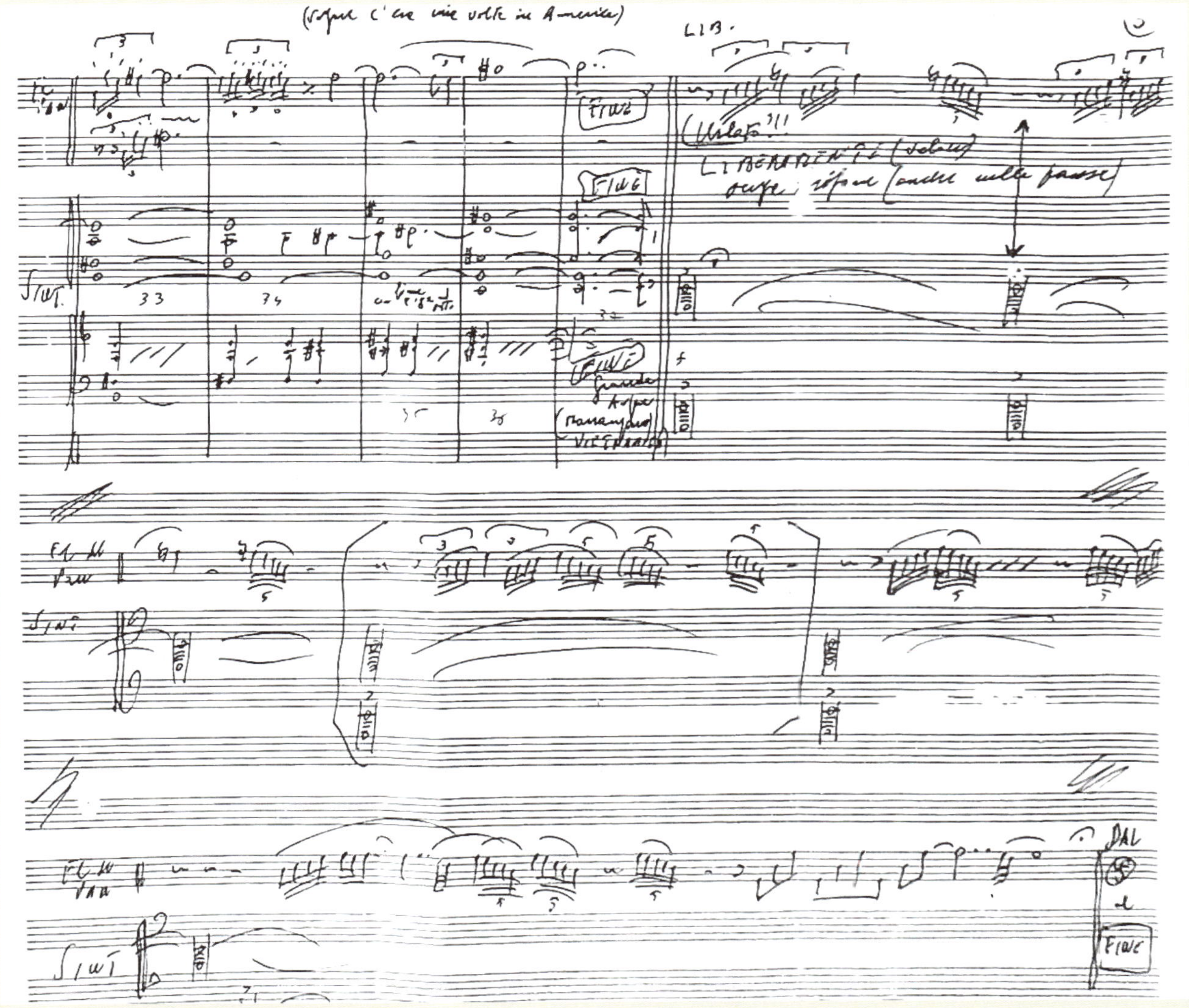

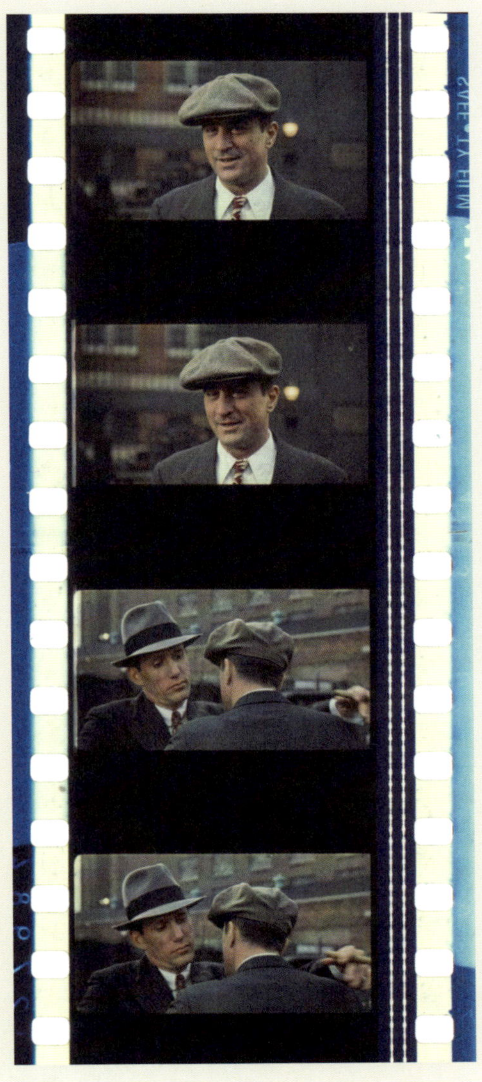

PRO 281-7
ONCE UPON A TIME IN AMERICA
MAIN THEME 3:33
(POVERTY)
Composed, Arranged &
Conducted by
ENNIO MORRICONE
From the forthcoming soundtrack album, "Once Upon A Time in America"
© 1984 PolyGram Records, Inc.
Manufactured and Marketed by PolyGram Records, Inc., 810 Seventh Avenue, New York, New York 10019.
All Rights Reserved. Unauthorized Duplication is a Violation of Applicable Laws. Printed in U.S.A.
PolyGram Records

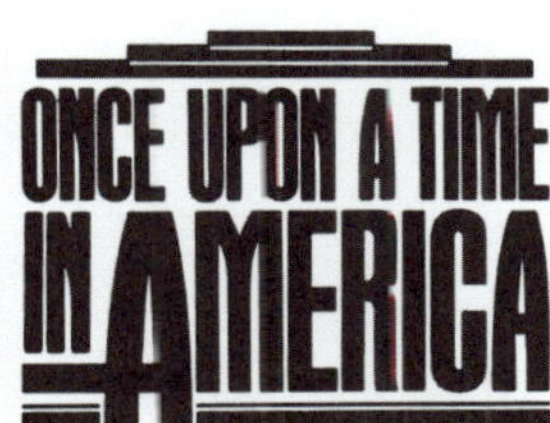

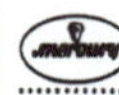

1984
Les voleurs de la nuit
Thieves After Dark
LP 33 rpm - GENERAL MUSIC 803 054

1985
Via Mala
LP 33 rpm - GENERAL MUSIC 803 075

1985
Red Sonja
Yado
Kalidor. La légende du talisman
LP 33 rpm - VARESE STV 81248

1985
La cage aux folles III. Elles se marient
Matrimonio con vizietto (Il vizietto III)
La Cage aux Folles 3: The Wedding
LP 33 rpm - GENERAL MUSIC 30718

1985
La gabbia
Dead Fright
L'enchaîné
LP 33 rpm - INTERMEZZO IM 006/
GENERAL MUSIC GM 30717

This film has lively, modern musical commentary, perhaps uncharacteristic for Morricone, but with good jazzy sounds thanks to musicians of the caliber of Oscar Valdambrini and Enrico Pieranunzi, who participated in the recordings along with Roberto Fabbriciani and Mario Caporalani; all of whom were directed by Morricone.

1986
Il pentito
The Repenter
CD - POINT RECORDS PRCD 112

1986
La venexiana
The Venetian Woman
La vénitienne
LP 33 rpm - GENERAL MUSIC 30721

1986
Quartiere
CD - GDM 2941

1986
Au Louvre.
Le plus grande musée du monde
LP 33 rpm - KING K28 P 632

This is a musical commentary for a TV documentary about the Louvre Museum. The Maestro is in complete harmony with the accompanying narrative, writing music that is classical, rigorous, and pertinent; except when he adds something that is entirely unrelated to the subject, the leitmotif from the movie *Lady Caliph*. The 1970 Franco-Italian drama film directed by Alberto Bevilacqua was used for the theme song. Numerous records were released for this work, but the original Japanese version is a must-have for collectors.

COPIA CONFORME ALL'ORIGINALE
AUTOGRAFA di ENNIO MORRICONE

1986

The Mission

Mission

Mission

LP 33 rpm - VIRGIN V 2402
45 rpm - VIRGIN 7-99484

This movie is unanimously believed to have one of the most beautiful soundtracks ever made. Ennio Morricone, more inspired than ever, directs the prestigious London Symphony Orchestra and both the heavenly *On Earth as It Is in Heaven* and the delicate *Gabriel's Oboe*, instantly become universal symbols of peace and hope that were borrowed by media around the world. The centrality of this work within the composer's oeuvre in general contains a treasure trove; its musical essence embellished here by representing the difficult rapport of ecumenical spirituality in a savage world. The ethnic contribution was by an uncredited South American folk group and the music received a nomination for Best Original Music Score at the Oscars.

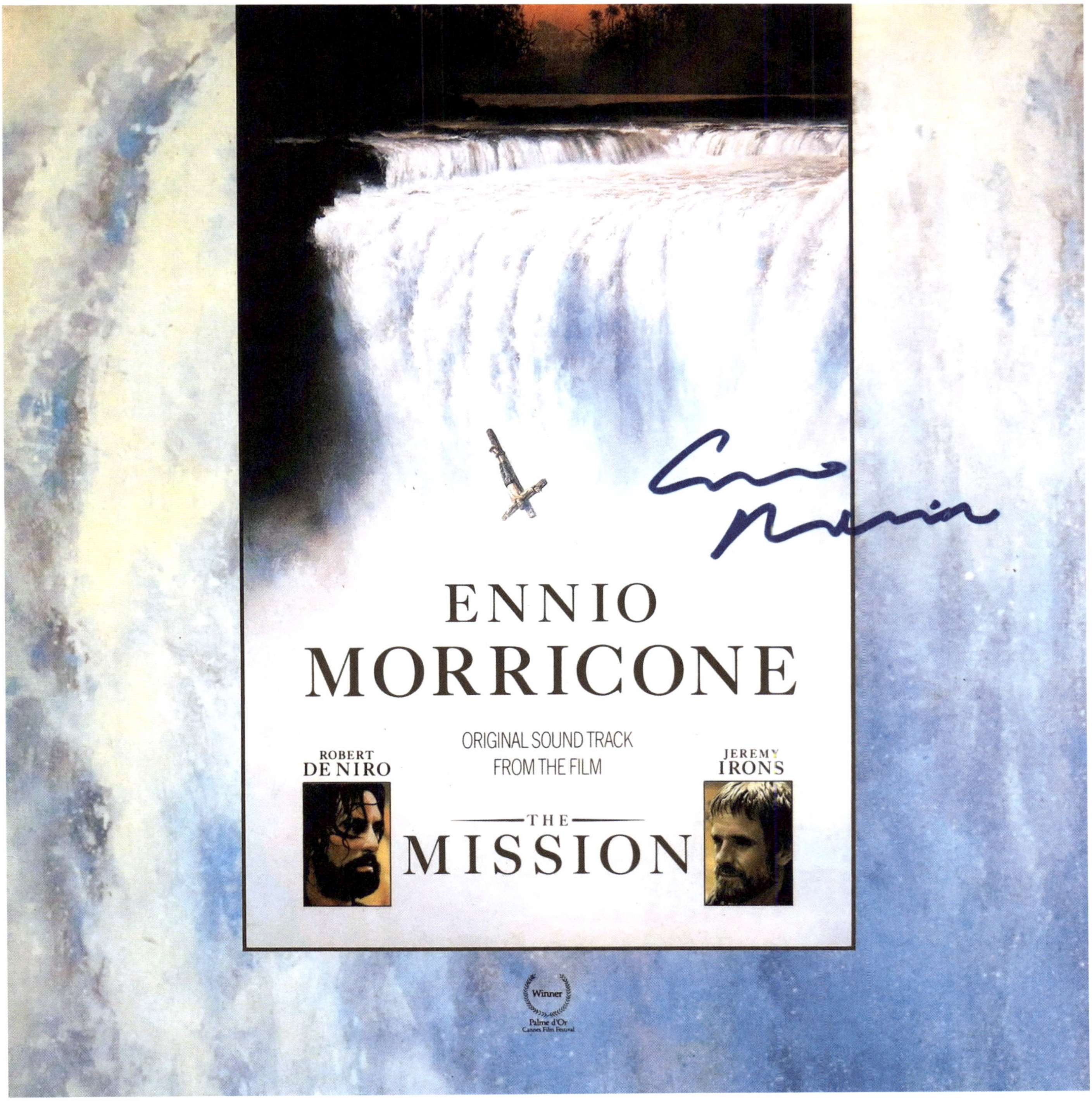
ENNIO
MORRICONE
ORIGINAL SOUND TRACK
FROM THE FILM
ROBERT
DE NIRO
JEREMY
IRONS
THE
MISSION
Winner
Palme d'Or
Cannes Film Festival

ENNIO MORRICONE
THEME FROM
THE
MISSION
TAKEN FROM THE ORIGINAL SOUNDTRACK ALBUM "THE MISSION"

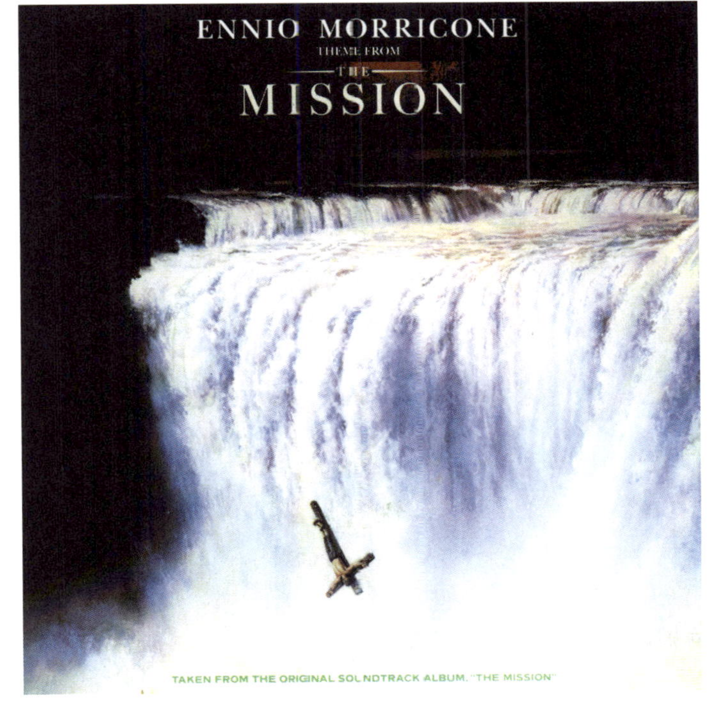

1986
La piovra 2
The Octopus 2
La Mafia 2
CD - FONIT CETRA CDL 263

The Octopus 2, a groundbreaking Italian TV series about the grip of the Mafia in Sicily, could not have found a better composer to score most of its hit seasons. For this series, popular both within Italy and beyond, the Maestro effectively refreshes musical themes for which he was already famous, successfully evoking Sicilian clans, Corleonese mafiosi, and iron-willed magistrates.

2006
La piovra
Music from the soundtracks of the TV series
CD - RAI TRADE FRT 420

1986
La piovra 2
1987
La piovra 3
1989
La piovra 4
1990
La piovra 5
1992
La piovra 6

1995
La piovra 7
2001
La piovra 10

1987
Il giorno prima
Mind Control
Contrôle
CD - SCREEN TRAX CDST 319

1987
Gli occhiali d'oro
The Gold Rimmed Glasses
Les lunettes d'or
CD - SCREEN TRAX CDST 302

This musical score won the 1988 David di Donatello Award thanks to the arias composed for *Metello in 1970;* and at the same time, was a field test for the soon to be released *Cinema Paradiso*.

1987
Rampage
Assassino senza colpa?
Le sang du châtiment
LP 33 rpm -VIRGIN 208609

1987
Gli angeli del potere
CD - FONIT CETRA CDM 2097

1987
Mosca addio
Farewell Moscow
Adieu Moscou
LP 33 rpm - GENERAL MUSIC/CGD 20630

In this film, the Maestro had an opportunity to experiment with new sounds cross-pollinated by references to traditional Russian music, but the dramatic visual tale told by Mauro Bolognini takes him back instead to a sadder and more subdued musical/visual emotion. The song *Lavori forzati* from this film was recycled in 1988 for the soundtrack of the TV miniseries, *Il segreto del Sahara* directed by Alberto Negrin.

TROMBA in Do

M 20

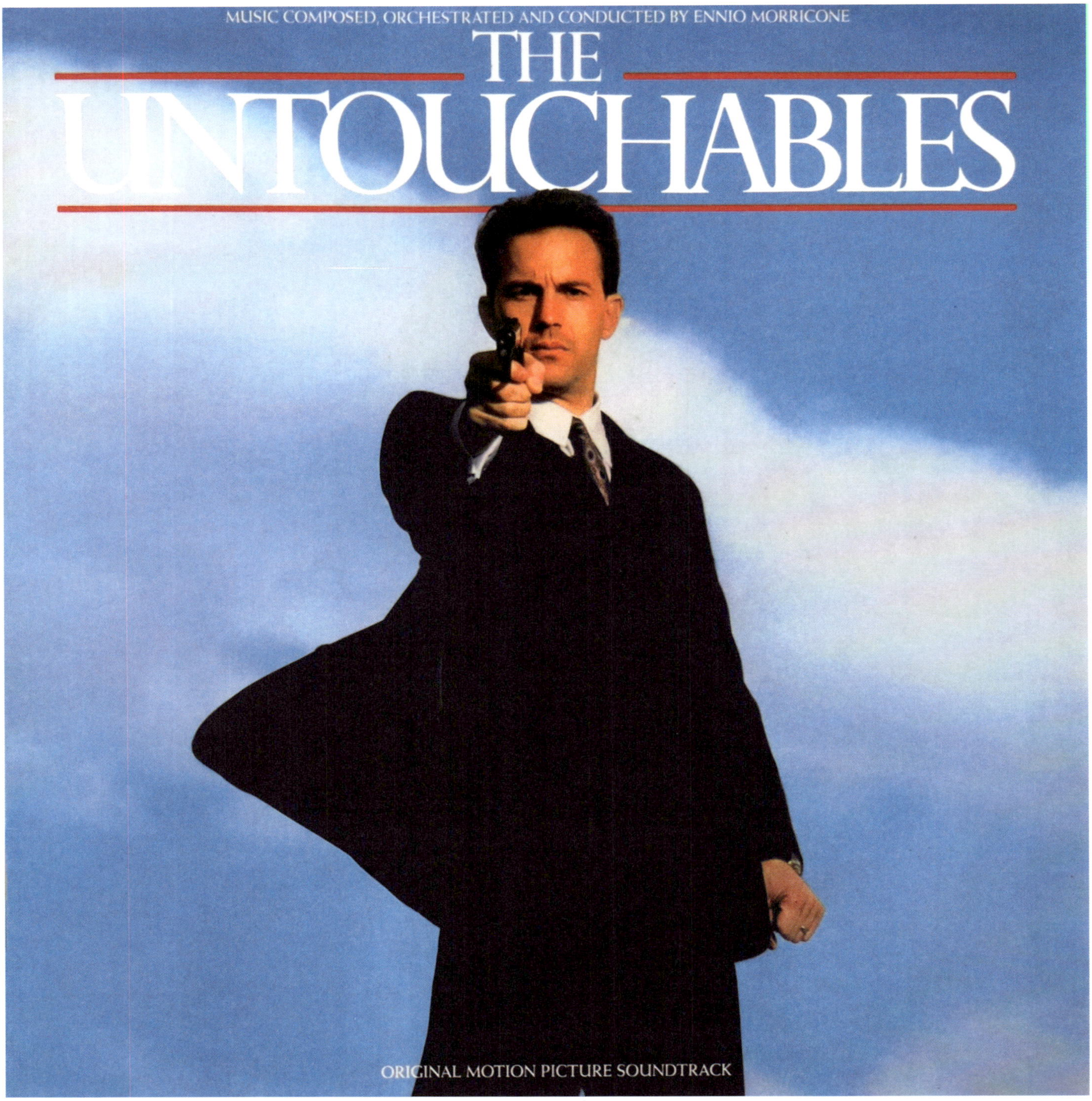

1987
The Untouchables
The Untouchables
– Gli intoccabili
Les incorruptibles
LP 33 rpm - A&M RECORD SP 3909

This film received an Oscar nomination for its splendid soundtrack score, but its failure to win the award brought disappointment and dismay to the Maestro's admirers. The score is rich with the ingredients that all film music should have; and all the sentiment required to compose and direct it. It is masterful work that goes hand-in-hand with the tale. Its rhythm is perfectly in line with the times and setting of 1930s Chicago; and has themes that are heart-rending yet never hackneyed. A big little masterpiece!

1988

Frantic

LP 33 rpm - ELEKTRA 670.4147

CD - FILM SCORE MONTHLY - FSM V14 No.17

The haunting melody of a tragic stroll through Paris offsets the progressive rock sound of a bass guitar played by Nanni Civitenga and becomes an original basis for a story filled with mystery. Morricone is not new to revivals in a pop rock key with his compositions so when he decides to pursue it, it's unbelievable!

1988

Il segreto del Sahara

Secret of the Sahara

Le secret du Sahara

LP 33 rpm - RCA BL 71559

A romantic desert is scored by the composer for this highly successful TV series. Romanticism is expressed with sweetness in the theme song, *Sahara dream,* sung by the velvety voice of Amii Stewart. For the occasion, Morricone added two already famous themes: *The Mountain* and *The Golden Door*, originally composed in 1964 for the musical screen test for John Huston's *The Bible*; and respectively for *La creazione* and *La torre di Babele*, both present here in the original version conducted by Franco Ferrara. Perhaps the album cover deserved a more creative treatment.

1988
A Time of Destiny
Il grande odio
Le temps du destin
LP 33 rpm - VIRGIN 790938

1988
Gli indifferenti
LP 33 rpm - RCA BL 71684

TOTÒ E ALFREDO
MUSICA DI ENNIO MORRICONE
E ANDREA MORRICONE

1988
Nuovo Cinema Paradiso
Cinema Paradiso
Cinéma Paradiso
with Andrea Morricone
LP 33 rpm - MERCURY 836 810-1

This is an amazing, at times moving and nostalgic, but authentic view of Italian life that discusses cinema through cinema. Audiences laugh heartily when they see this marvelous movie by Giuseppe Tornatore. It won an Oscar for Best Foreign Film in 1990 (two years after it was made), followed by a prestigious Golden Globe Award. This film that lingers in the collective memory as a symbol of the past and the ever-glorious movie theater. Andrea Morricone, who hadn't earned his diploma from the Conservatory yet, collaborated with his father on this score, giving listeners a taste of his potential, and composing a beautiful love theme later also awarded a BAFTA (British Academy of Film and Television Arts) Award.

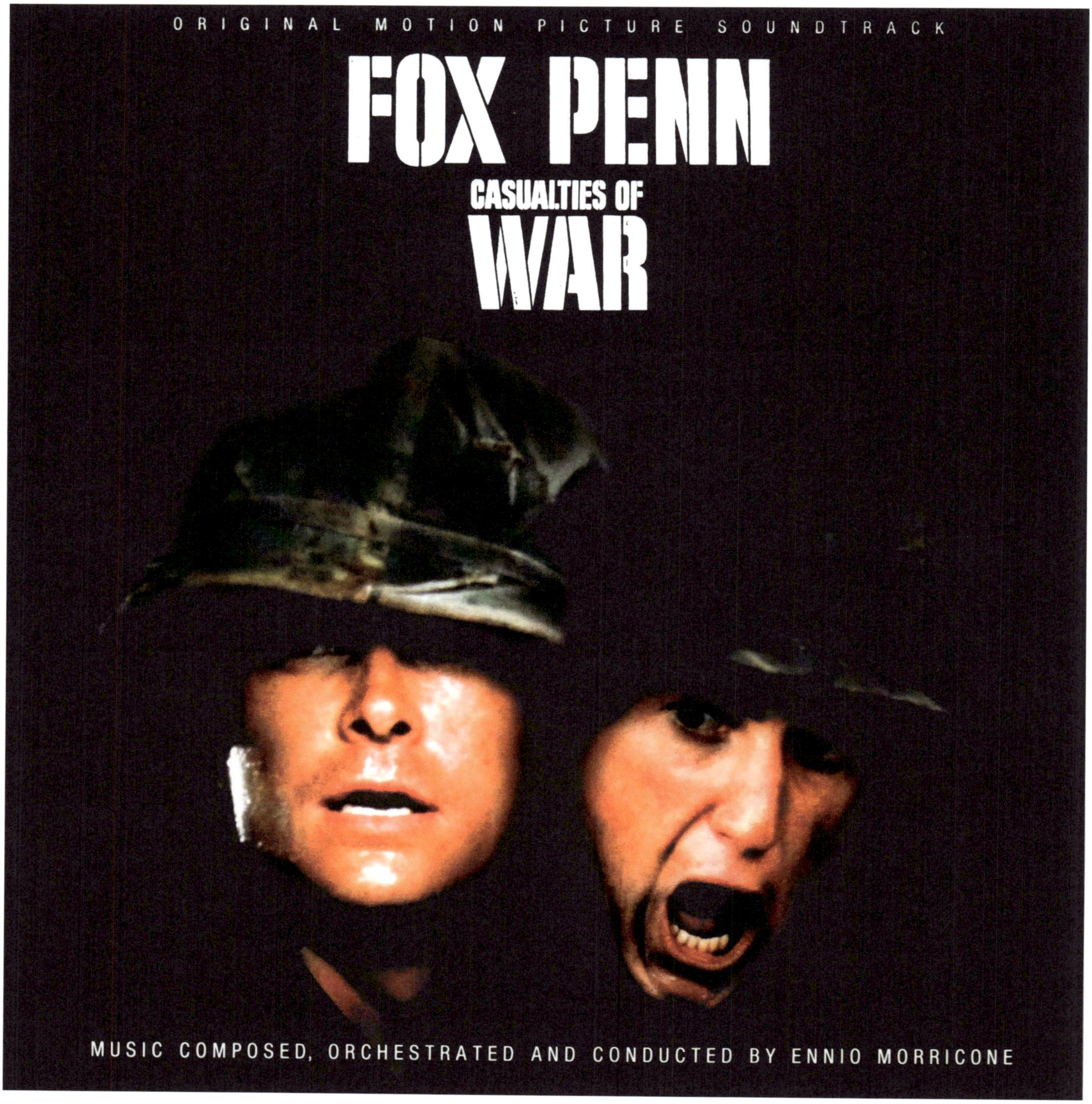

ORIGINAL MOTION PICTURE SOUNDTRACK
FOX PENN
CASUALTIES OF
WAR
MUSIC COMPOSED, ORCHESTRATED AND CONDUCTED BY ENNIO MORRICONE

MUSIC FROM THE PARAMOUNT MOTION PICTURE
FAT MAN AND
LITTLE BOY
COMPOSED AND CONDUCTED BY
ENNIO MORRICONE

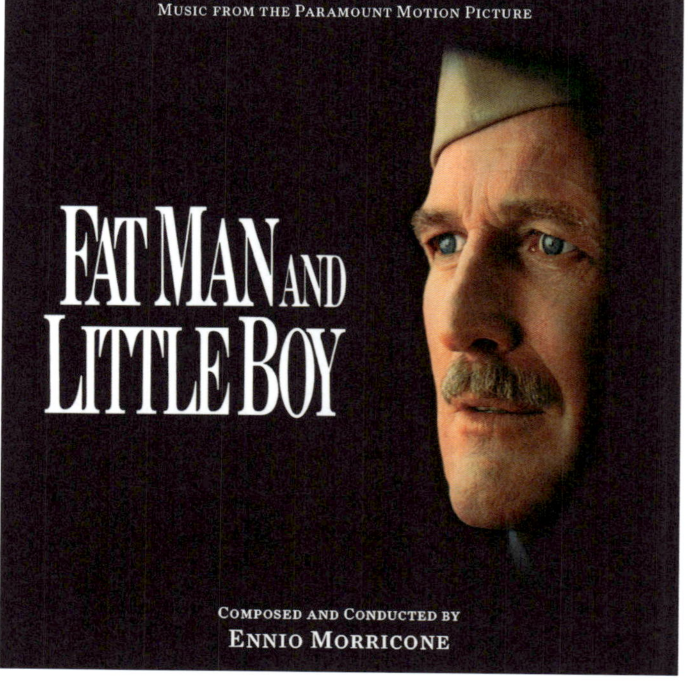

1989
Casualties of War
Vittime di guerra
Outrages
LP 33 rpm - CBS 466016

1989
Fat Man and Little Boy
L'ombra di mille soli
Les maîtres de l'ombre
CD - LA LA LAND RECORDS LLLCD 1196

1989
The Endless Game
Gioco senza fine
LP 33 rpm - VIRGIN V 2602

This music was for an English TV series but was recorded in Rome with the *L'Unione Musicisti di Roma* and the contribution of Edda Dell'Orso; and conducted by Morricone himself. Added to the soundtrack were two borrowed songs: *From Russia* from the film *The Prostitution Racket;* and *Silvia's Game* from the film *The Night Caller*; both of these movies were made in 1975.

1989
Tempo di uccidere
Time to Kill
Le raccourci
LP 33 rpm - EMI 66 7933231

1989
I promessi sposi
The Betrothed
Les fiancés
LP 33 rpm - FONIT CETRA LPX 245

Akin to other commissions during that period, Morricone used soloists and important orchestras such as *L'Unione Musicisti di Roma* and the RAI orchestra (Italian Radio Symphony Orchestra). That is what he chose to do here, for a television production that needs no introduction in Italy because it is based on Alessandro Manzoni's illustrious novel. It is captivating music that works for the story being told, and that was recorded on vinyl by Fonit Cetra. It is interesting to note that this record devolved from being highly valued and sought after to being of little interest to collectors.

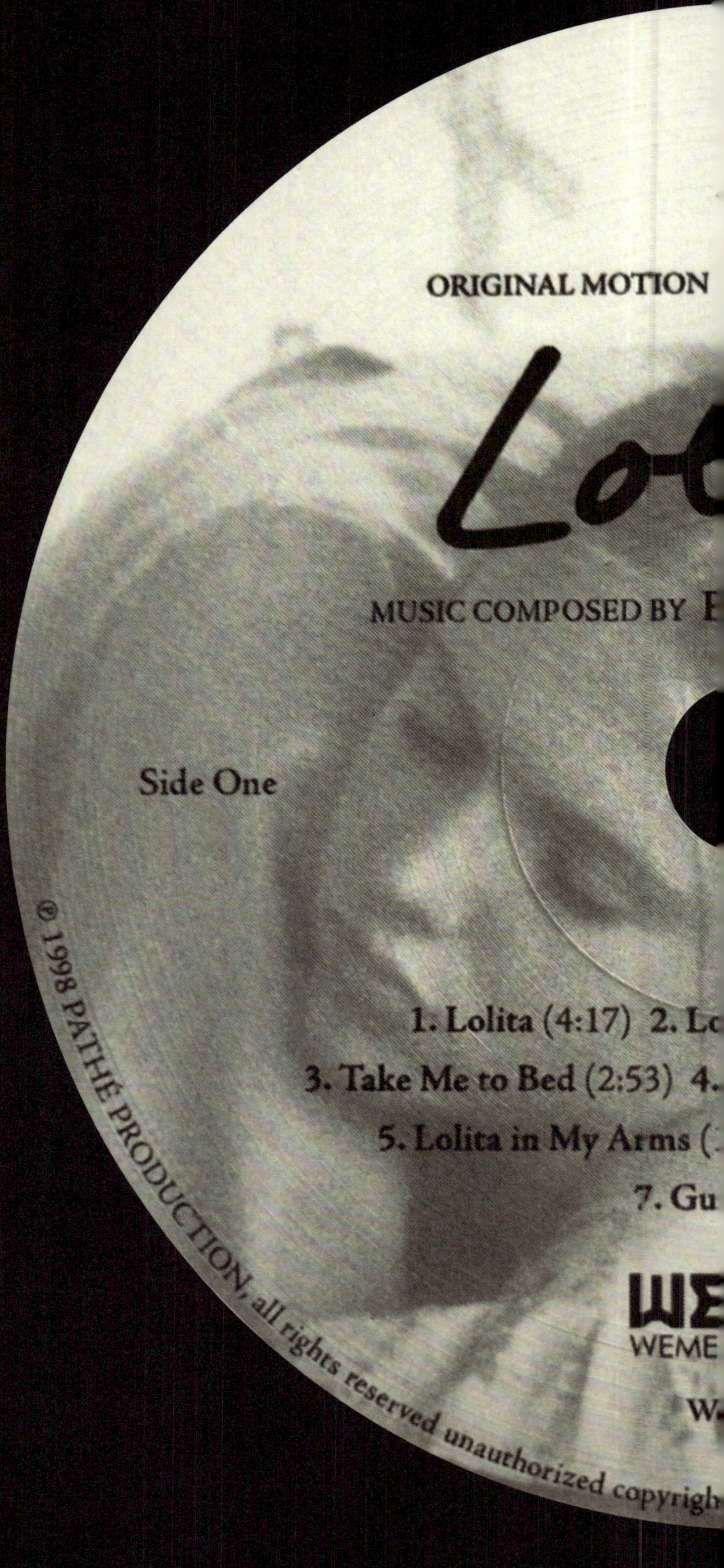

ORIGINAL MOTION

Lo

MUSIC COMPOSED BY E

Side One

1. Lolita (4:17) 2. Lo

3. Take Me to Bed (2:53) 4.

5. Lolita in My Arms (

7. Gu

WE
WEME

W.

1990 — 1999

RE SOUNDTRACK
ita
O MORRICONE
33⅓ Rpm
the Morning (3:38)
a on Humbert's Lap (3:36)
6. Requiescant (2:13)
:18)
ORDS
2
.mewelesite.be Picture John Seakwood © 1998 PATHÉ PRODUCTION.

Discography

1990—1999

1990

Crossing the Line. The Big Man, David Leland
Deutsches Mann Geil! Die Geschichte von Ilona und Kurti, Reinhard Schwabenitzky
Everybody's Fine, Giuseppe Tornatore
Hamlet, Franco Zeffirelli
Husbands and Lovers, Mauro Bolognini
La piovra 5. Il cuore del problema, Luigi Perelli
Money, Steven Hilliard Stern
Only One Survived, Folco Quilici
State of Grace, Phil Joanou
Tie Me Up! Tie Me Down!, Pedro Almodovar
The Bachelor, Roberto Faenza
The Palermo Connection, Francesco Rosi
Tre colonne in cronaca, Carlo Vanzina
Voyage of Terror, Alberto Negrin

1991

Bugsy, Barry Levinson
Especially on Sunday, Giuseppe Tornatore, Marco Tullio Giordana, Giuseppe Bertolucci
The Law of the Desert, Duccio Tessari

1992

City of Joy, Roland Joffé
Rapture of Deceit, Livia Gyarmathy
La piovra 6, Luigi Perelli
La signora delle camelie (1915), Gustavo Serena
Una storia italiana, Stefano Reali

1993

In the Line of Fire, Wolfgang Petersen
La Bibbia: Abramo, Joseph Sargent
Look to the Sky, Roberto Faenza
The Escort, Ricky Tognazzi
The Long Silence, Margarethe von Trotta
Palermo. Città dell'antimafia, Giuseppe Tornatore
Piazza di Spagna, Florestano Vancini

1994

A Pure Formality, Giuseppe Tornatore
Disclosure, Barry Levinson
La Bibbia: Genesi. La creazione e il diluvio, Ermanno Olmi
La Bibbia: Giacobbe, Peter Hall
La notte e il momento, Anna Maria Tatò
Love Affair, Warren Beatty
Missus, Alberto Negrin
Roma Imago Urbis, Luigi Bazzoni
The Baron, Enrico Maria Salerno, Richard T. Heffron
Wolf, Mike Nichols

1995

According to Pereira, Roberto Faenza
Con rabbia e con amore, Alfredo Angeli
L'uomo proiettile, Silvano Agosti
La Bibbia: Giuseppe, Roger Young
La Bibbia: Mosè, Roger Young
La piovra 7, Luigi Perelli
Lo schermo a tre punte, Giuseppe Tornatore
Roma: 12 novembre 1994, Francesco Maselli, Ettore Scola, Carlo Lizzani, Gillo Pontecorvo, Paolo e Vittorio Taviani
The Star Maker, Giuseppe Tornatore
Who Killed Pasolini?, Marco Tullio Giordana

1996

I magi randagi, Sergio Citti
Joseph Conrad's Nostromo, Alastair Reid
La lupa, Gabriele Lavia
Laguna, Francesco De Melis
Lolita, Adrian Lyne
The Nymph, Lina Wertmüller
The Stendhal Syndrome, Dario Argento
Strangled Lives, Ricky Tognazzi

1997

La Bibbia: Davide, Robert Markowitz
La Bibbia: Salomone, Roger Young
La Bibbia: Sansone e Dalila, Nicholas Roeg
The Fourth King, Stefano Reali
Naissance des Stéréoscopages, Stéphane Marty
Richard III (1912), André Calmettes e James Keane
U Turn, Oliver Stone

1998

Bulworth, Warren Beatty
Cartoni animati, Sergio e Franco Citti
In fondo al cuore, Luigi Perelli
La Bibbia: Geremia il profeta, Harry Winer
La casa bruciata, Massimo Spano
La città spettacolo, Giuliano Montaldo
The Legend of 1900, Giuseppe Tornatore
What Dreams May Come, Vincent Ward

1999

La Bibbia: Ester, Raffaele Mertes
The Phantom of the Opera, Dario Argento
The Sands of Time, Alberto Negrin
Ultimo, Stefano Reali
Ultimo 2. La sfida, Stefano Reali

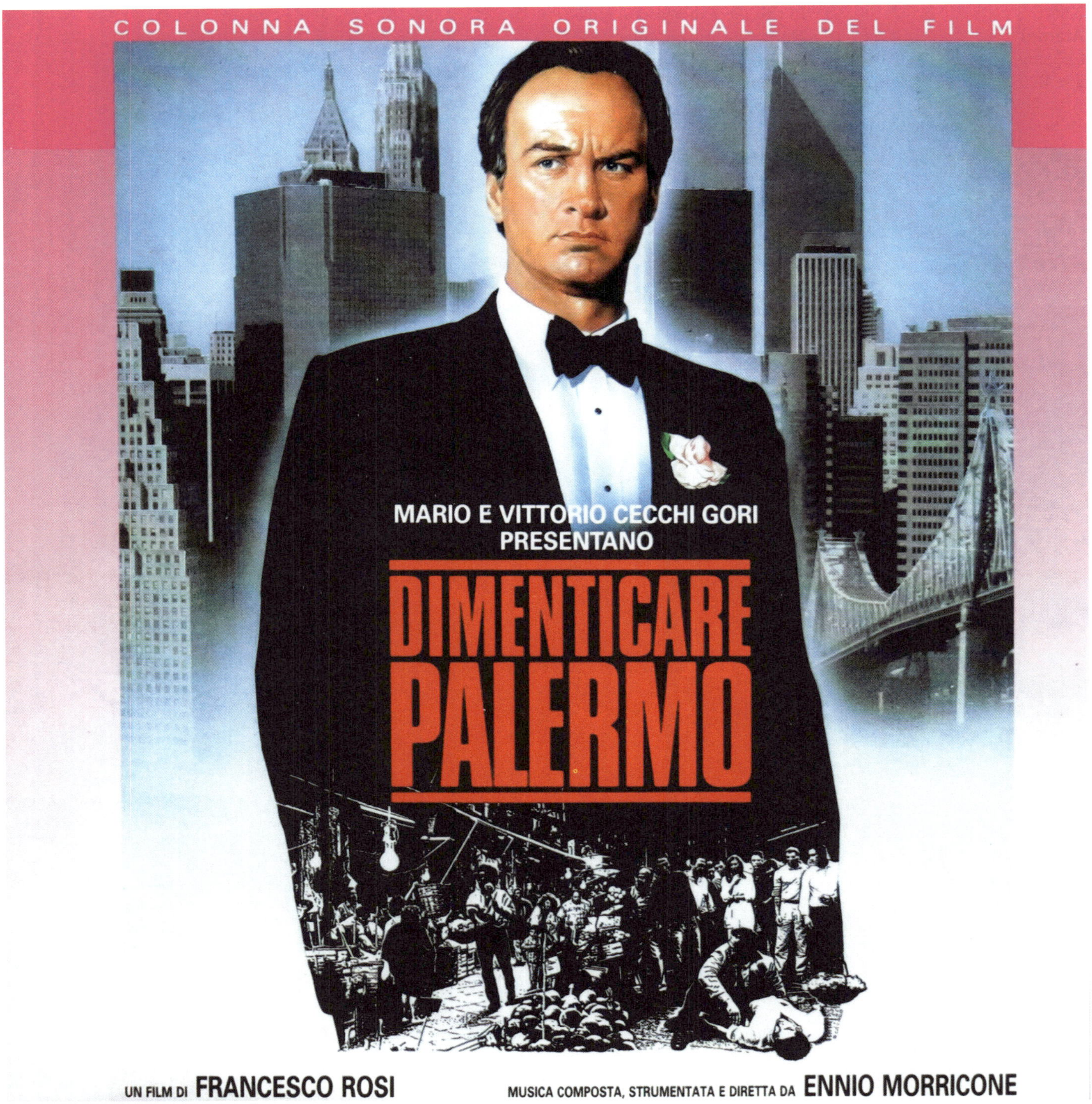
COLONNA SONORA ORIGINALE DEL FILM
MARIO E VITTORIO CECCHI GORI
PRESENTANO
DIMENTICARE
PALERMO
UN FILM DI FRANCESCO ROSI
MUSICA COMPOSTA, STRUMENTATA E DIRETTA DA ENNIO MORRICONE

Ennio Morricone
CACCIATORI DI NAVI

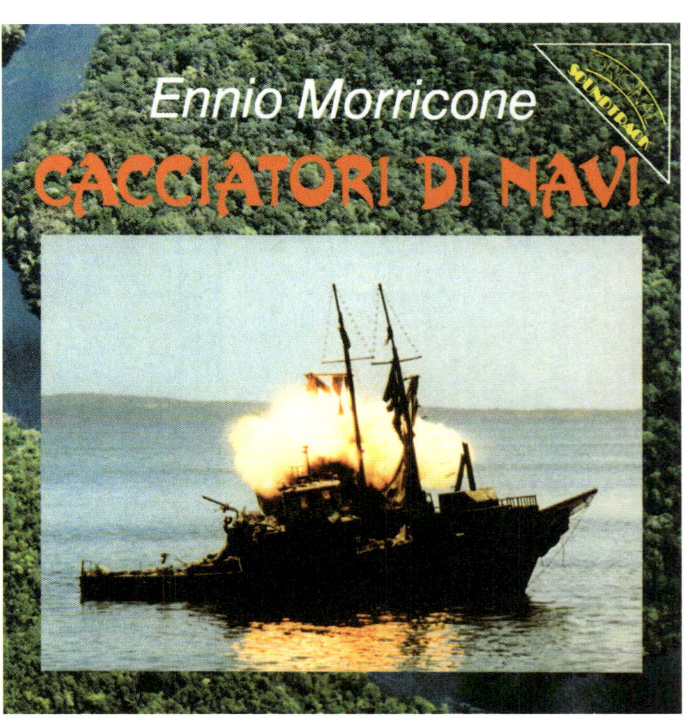

1990
Dimenticare Palermo
The Palermo Connection
Oublier Palerme
LP 33 rpm - PHILIPS 846 486-1

1990
Cacciatori di navi
Only One Survived
CD - RCA ORIGINAL CAST OST 109

1990
Atame!
Legami!
Tie Me Up! Tie Me Down!
Attache-moi!
LP 33 rpm - RCA BL 74524

In this piece of peaceful music, Morricone creates quiet yet intriguing conversations between the trumpets and the flutes against the background of a string section that indulges in crepuscular tonalities. It's a very enjoyable soundtrack even when separated from the movie. It was nominated for a Goya Award in 1991 for Best Original Music Score.

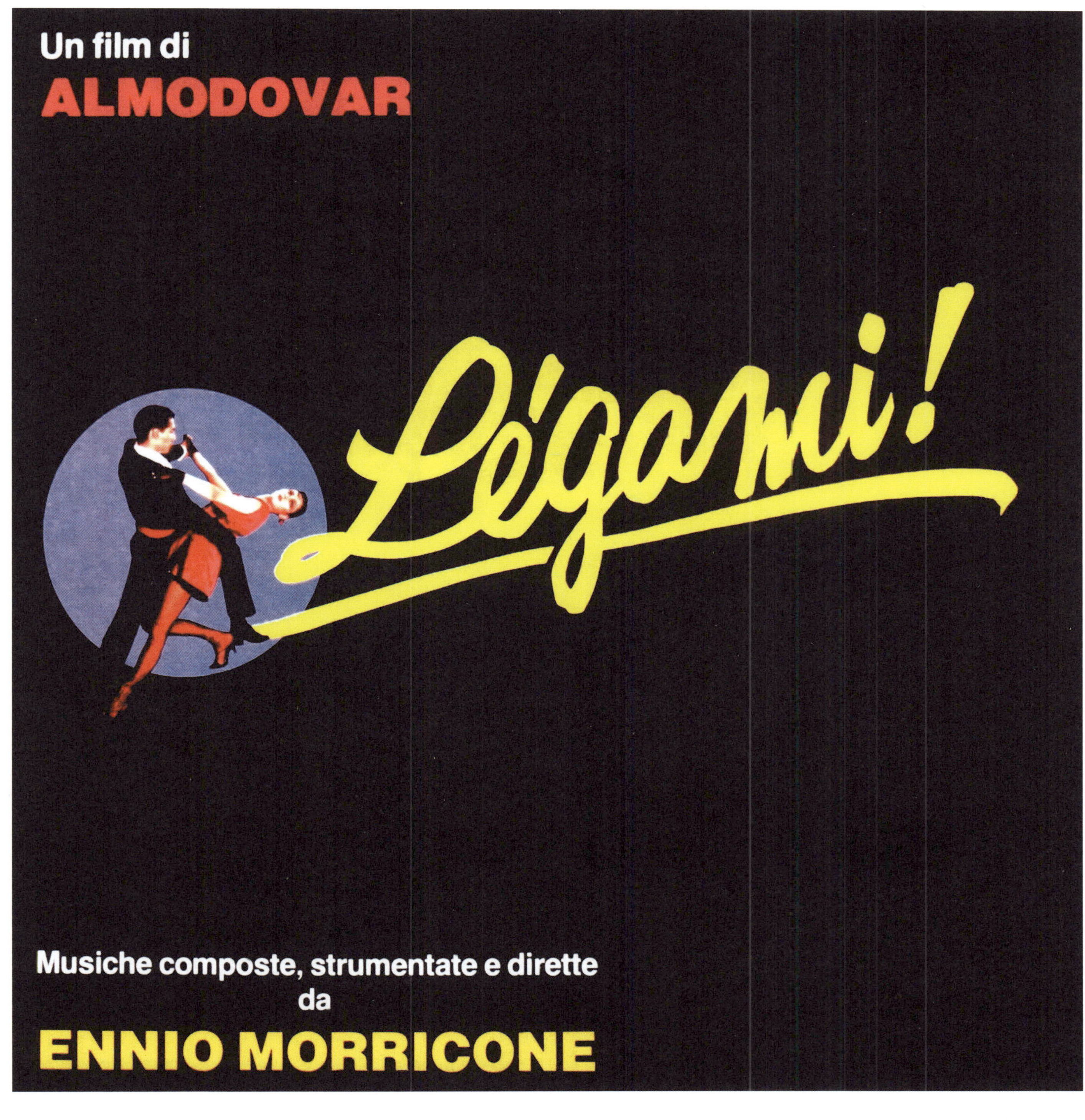

1990
Hamlet
Amleto
LP 33 rpm - VIRGIN V 211284

1990
State of Grace
Stato di grazia
Les anges de la nuit
CD - MCA MCAD 10119

While this was a notable film, it did poorly at the box office; and possibly was penalized by the timing of its release. The music score contributed little in this case; perhaps because of the long-windedness of Maestro Morricone who composed streams of music that seemed impersonal, repetitive, and lacking in inspiration.

1990

Mio caro dottor Grasler

The Bachelor

CD - CAM COS 003

This film was nominated for a David di Donatello Award for Best Original Music Score.

1990

Stanno tutti bene

Everybody's Fine

Ils vont tous bien!

with Andrea Morricone

CD - CAM SRC 001

This is a sad tale about an Italian family, but it could the story of a family anywhere. The film tells a story about the way in which illusions can sometimes help us cast aside doubt and forge ahead. These small victories are represented here by a folksy score and embellished with a beautiful dreamy theme composed by Andrea Morricone entitled *Sogno*.

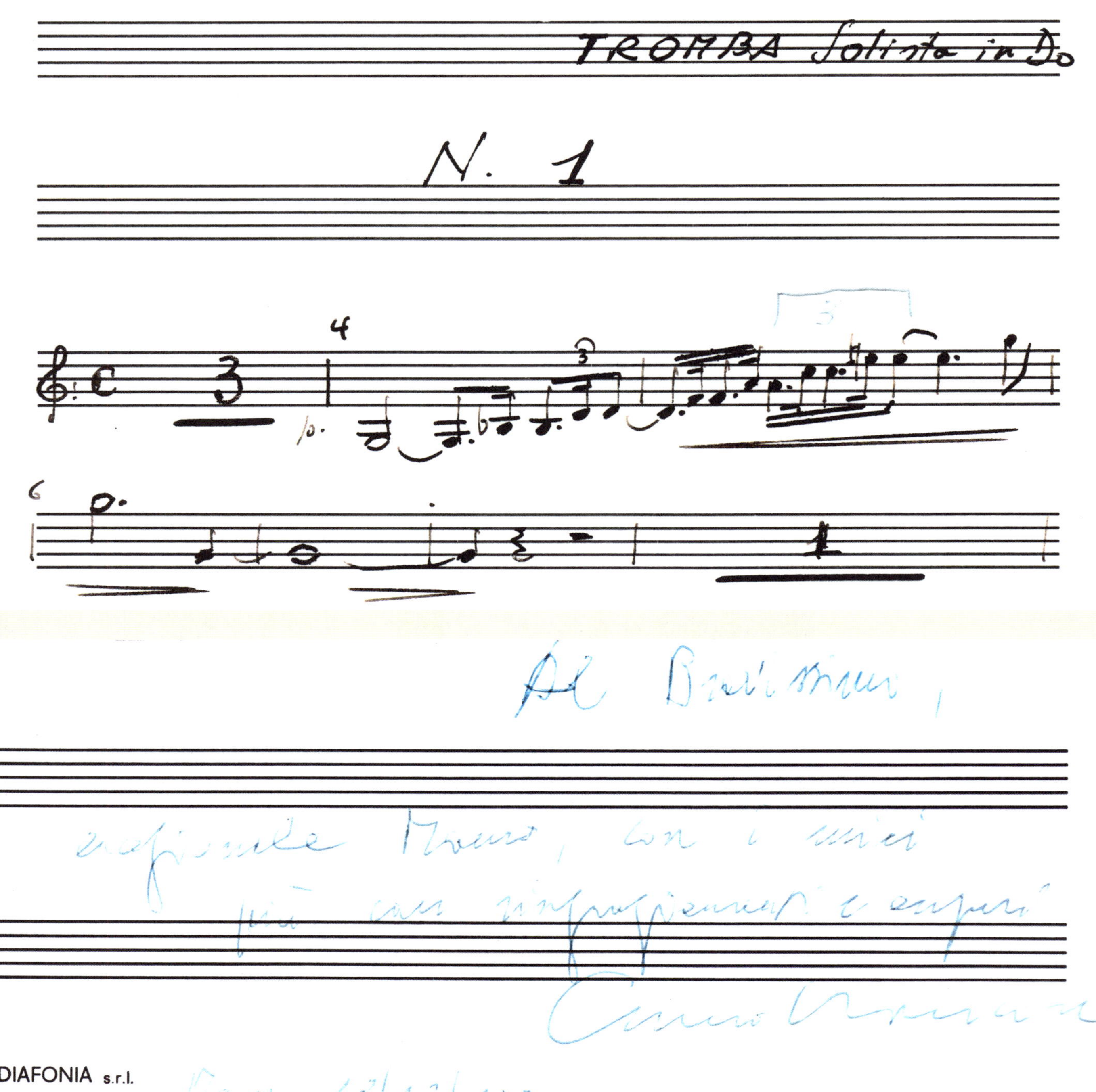

1990
Viaggio nel terrore: l'Achille Lauro
Voyage of Terror
Embarquement pour l'enfer
CD - RCA OST 101
CD - GDM CLUB 7108

This film was made for TV in cinematographic style about a dynamic real-life event that was reported in the international news. No surprises due to the well-known story but the music score is victorious with its use of wind instruments: Mauro Maur on trumpet, Gianni Oddi on sax, Marianne Eckstein on flute, and finally, the splendid voice of Amii Stewart; under the flawless direction of Maestro Morricone.

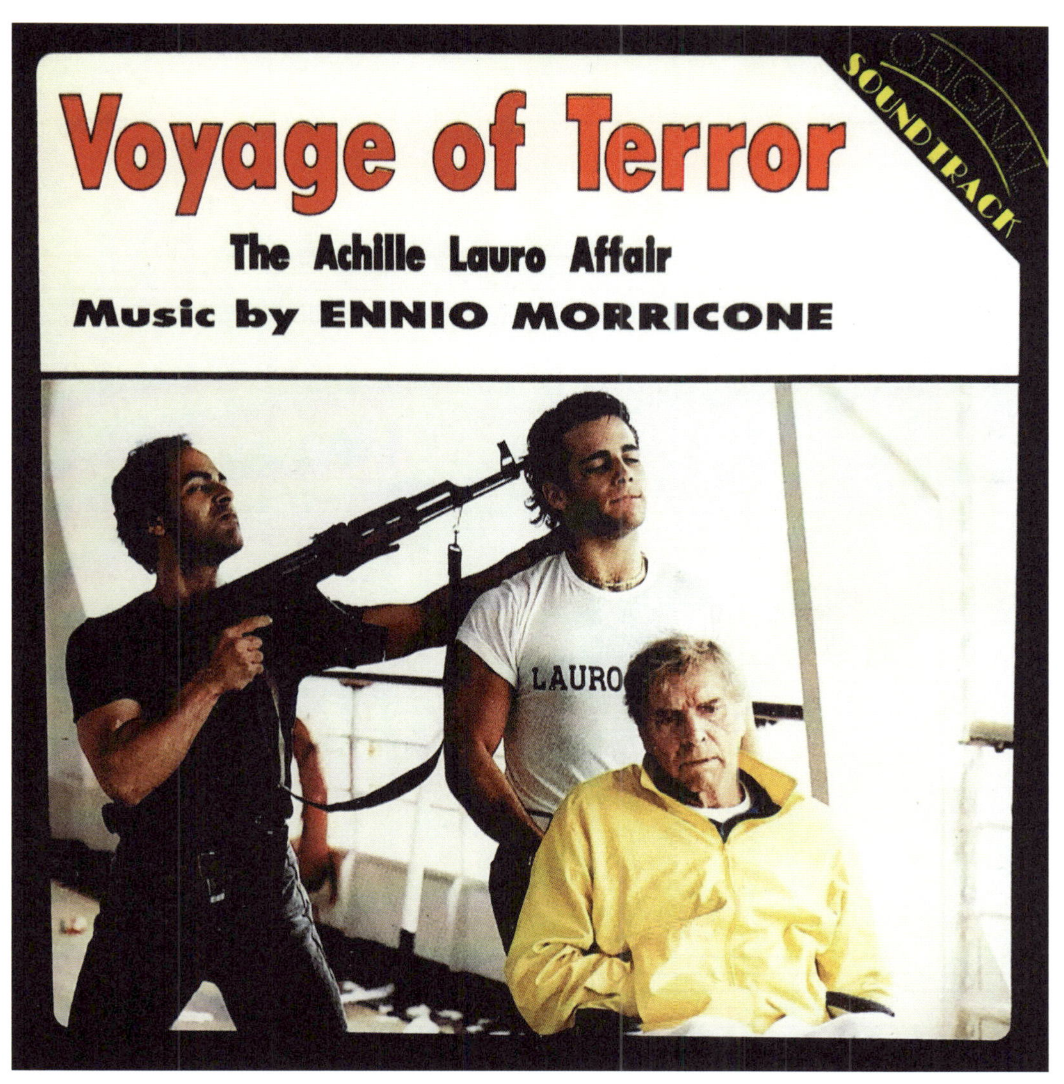
Voyage of Terror
The Achille Lauro Affair
Music by ENNIO MORRICONE
ORIGINAL
SOUNDTRACK
LAURO

colonna sonora originale - edizione speciale
VIAGGIO
NEL TERRORE
L'ACHILLE LAURO
musica di ENNIO MORRICONE

1990
Crossing the Line.
The Big Man
LP 33 rpm - V ARESE VSD 5296

1990
Deutsches Mann Geil!
Die Geschichte von Ilona
und Kurti
CD - MCP RECORDS 158.542

1990
Money
Money. Intrigo in nove mosse
CD - GDM CD CLUB 7060

1990
La villa del venerdì
Husbands and Lovers
CD - GDM CD CLUB 7022

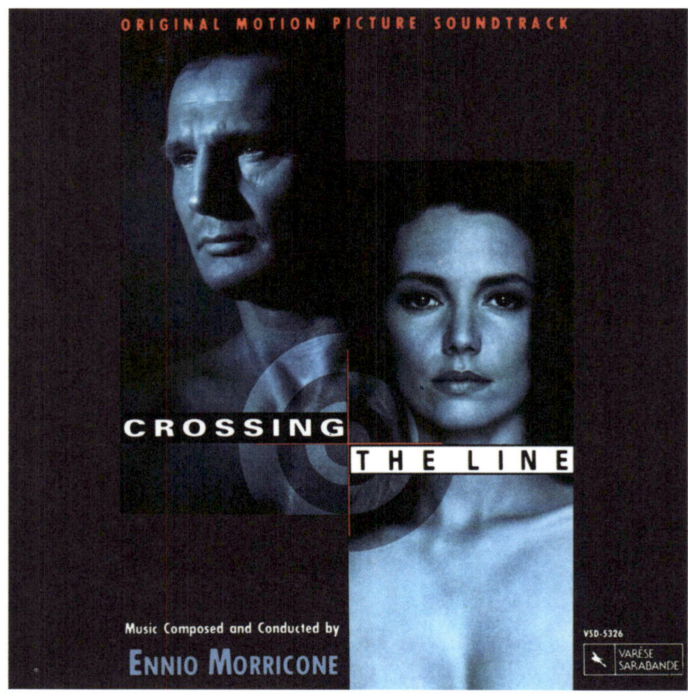

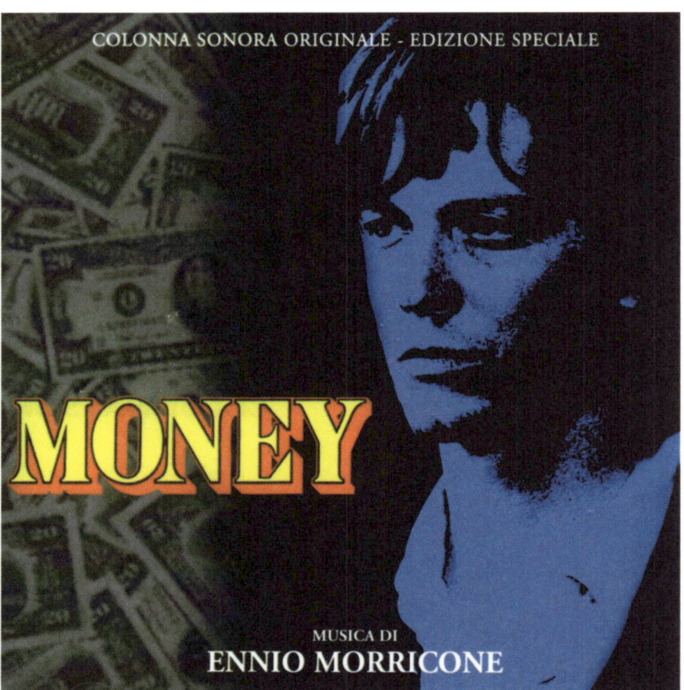

1990

Tre colonne in cronaca

LP 33 rpm - POLYGRAM 846485-1

The misdeeds of power told in Carlo Vanzina's film allow Ennio Morricone to exercise his creative talent. The Maestro is always scrupulous and attentive to the role of music at the service of the story. A violin plays a distorted drone note expressing suffering throughout the entire musical structure with a disturbing and impactful effect.

1991

Il principe del deserto

The Law of the Desert

Le prince du désert

LP 33 rpm - MERCURY 848 553

Adagio
BUGSY
di E. Morricone
sempre simile

1991
Bugsy
LP 33 rpm - MOVATM 132

This was the umpteenth nomination for an Oscar for Best Original Music Score and the umpteenth and by now, a smoldering disappointment. Some unpleasant theories have been suggested but never proven about the Maestro's failure to walk away from Hollywood with an Academy Award up to this point. (This changed in 2016 when he was awarded this prize for *The Hateful Eight*.) Nonetheless, the musical interpretation of North America and its heart-wrenching stories by Ennio Morricone here is perfect considering that he is not an American; and there was never any argument that the Maestro is a world-class musician. The theme song is remembered especially for the splendid solo trumpet played by Mauro Maur.

1991
La domenica specialmente
Especially on Sunday
Le dimanche de préférence
with Andrea Morricone
CD - CAM 9031 75428-2

1992
Una storia italiana
CD - RAI TRADE FRT 414

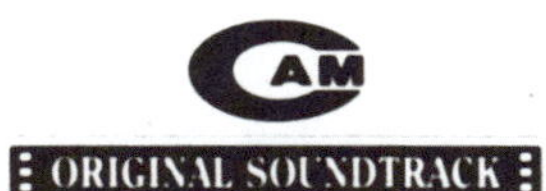

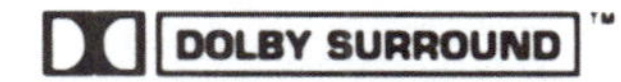

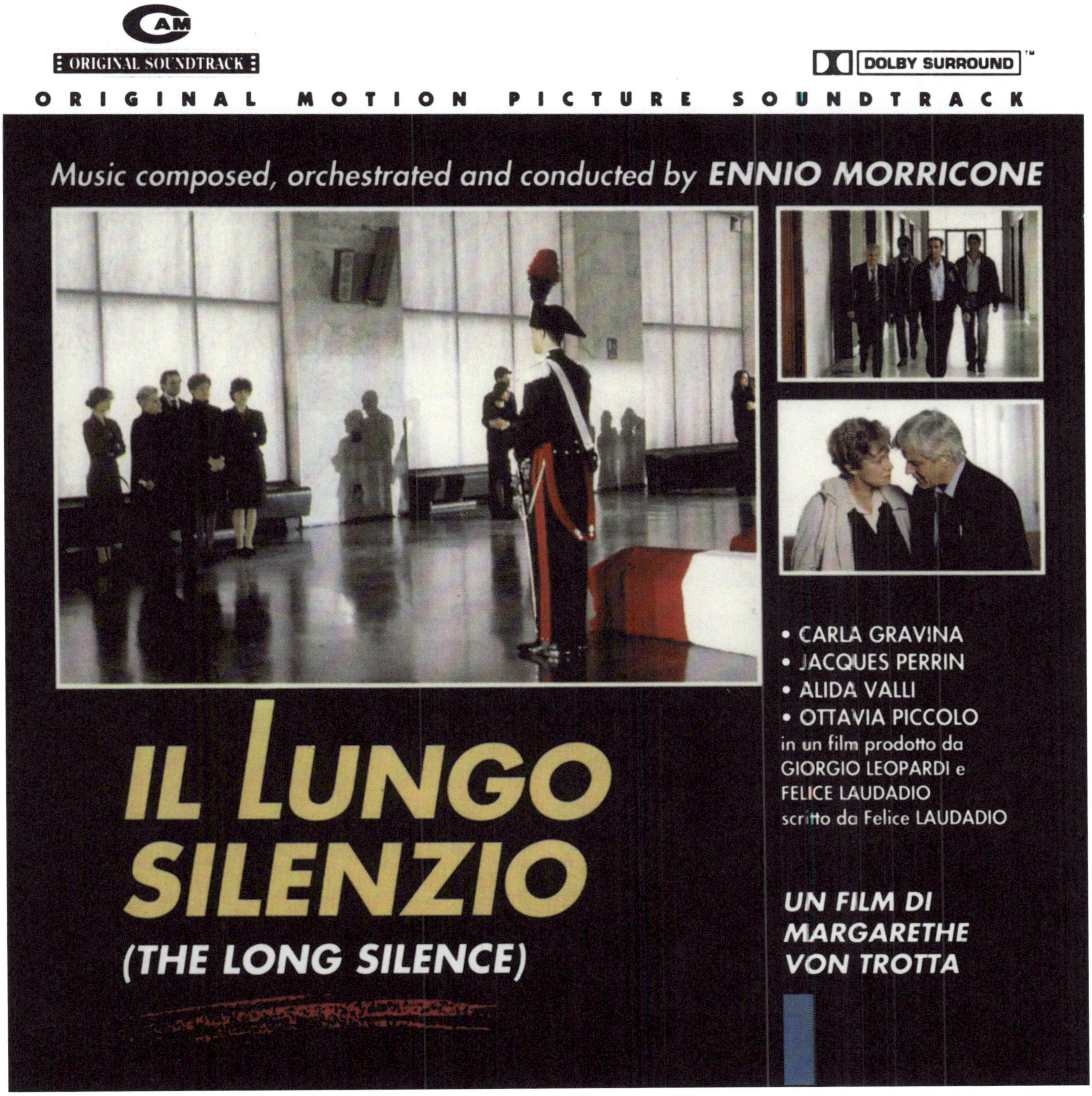
CAM
ORIGINAL SOUNDTRACK
DOLBY SURROUND ™
ORIGINAL MOTION PICTURE SOUNDTRACK
Music composed, orchestrated and conducted by ENNIO MORRICONE
• CARLA GRAVINA
• JACQUES PERRIN
• ALIDA VALLI
• OTTAVIA PICCOLO
in un film prodotto da
GIORGIO LEOPARDI e
FELICE LAUDADIO
scritto da Felice LAUDADIO
IL LUNGO SILENZIO
(THE LONG SILENCE)
UN FILM DI
MARGARETHE
VON TROTTA

ORIGINAL SOUNDTRACK RECORDING
PIAZZA DI SPAGNA
MUSIC COMPOSED, ORCHESTRATED AND CONDUCTED BY
ENNIO MORRICONE

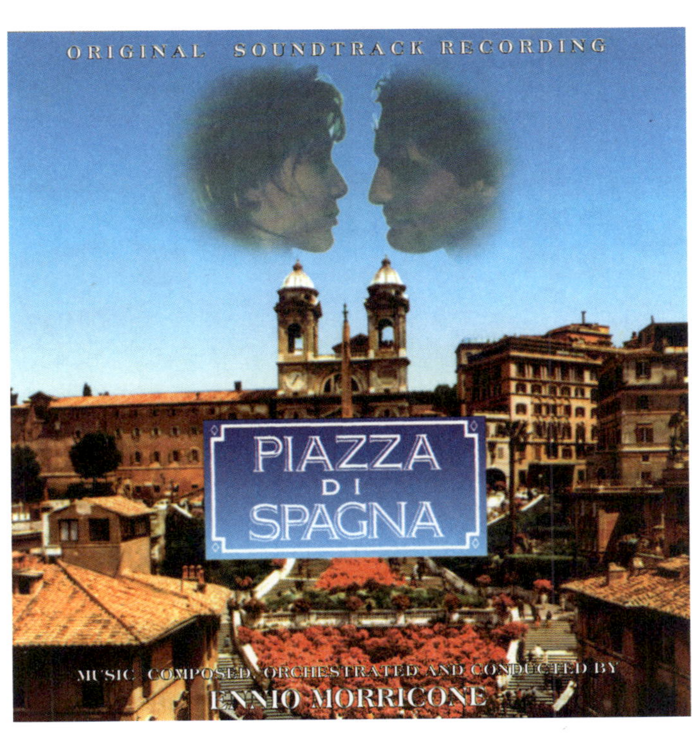

1993
Il lungo silenzio
The Long Silence
CD - CAM COS 014

1993
Piazza di Spagna
CD - POINT RECORDS PRCD 107

1992
City of Joy
La città della gioia
La cité de la joie
with Richard Blackford
LP 33 rpm - MOVATM 103

If the music composed by Ennio Morricone for this movie is supposedly limited by being a repetitive continuation of *The Mission*, as critics have claimed, then why not assert instead that in this film, the Maestro has created a renewed musical humanism at the service of cinema.

TROMBA Piccola
I Volta
3 Volte
Solo

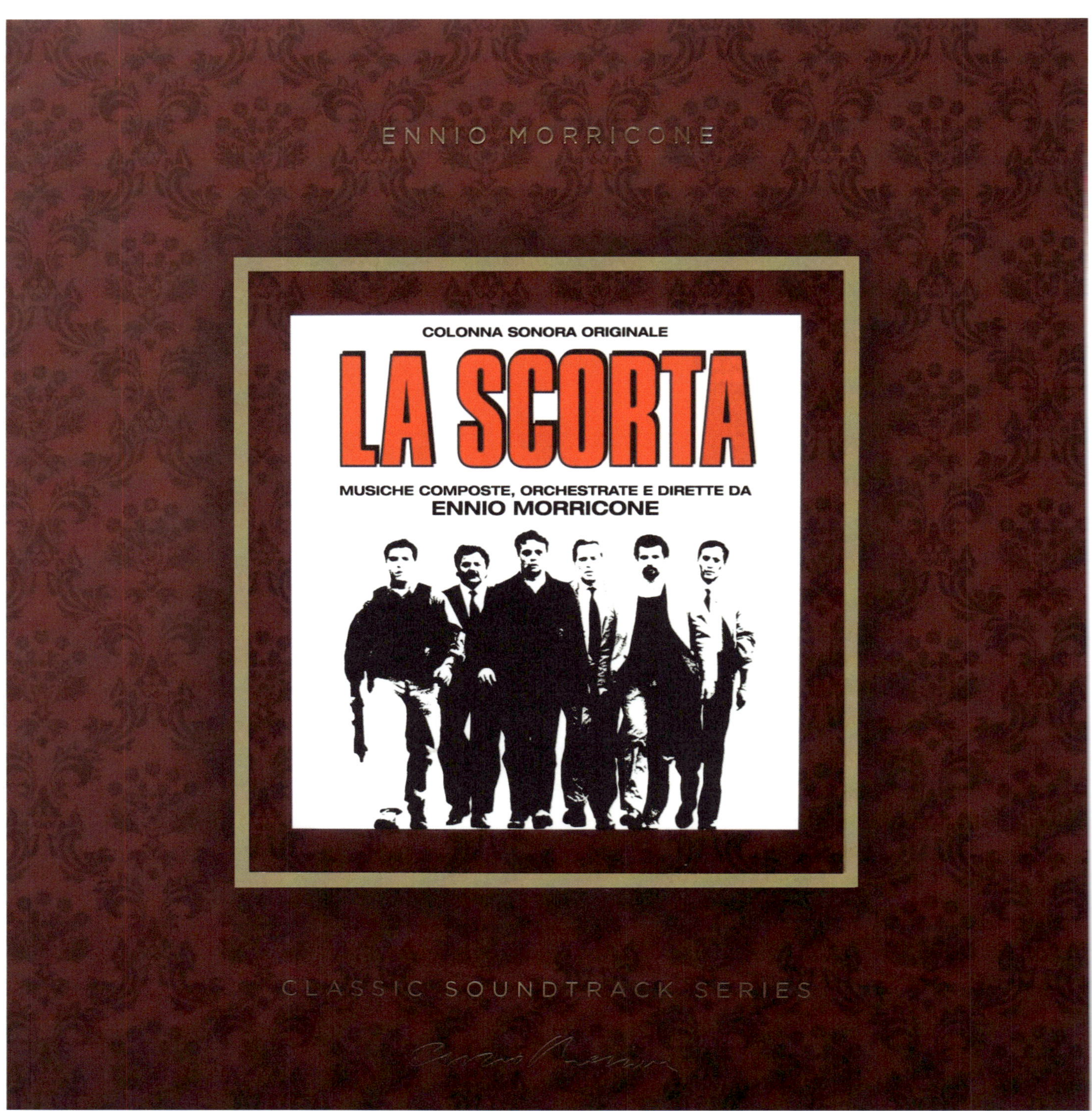

1993
La scorta
The Escort
L'escorte
LP 33 rpm - MOVATM 105

This film had another nomination for a David di Donatello Award for the original music score whose aim is perhaps disproportionate to its real value. While the music was clearly tragic and dramatic with distorted piano notes and an explosive woodwind section, unfortunately, we heard it all before.

1993
In the Line of Fire
Nel centro del mirino
Dans la ligne de mire
LP 33 rpm - MOVATM 104

Strangely missing from the soundtrack recorded on CD and vinyl is the *Main Theme* in this version of the opening credits. And while the composer's vast output is already full of gaps, Mauro Maur on trumpet expresses American style perfectly and with virtuosity; just what the story needs.

1993
Jona che visse nella balena
Look to the Sky
Années d'enfance
CD - CAM COS 015

Nominated for a David di Donatello Award for the Best Original Music Score, this deliberately intimate score was distinguished by its great emotion in spite of a story based on the terrible tragedy of imprisonment in Nazi concentration camps. Jazz musician Felice Clemente created a moment of intense feeling, caressing Pan's flute with his breath, rather than playing it.

▸

1994
Disclosure
Rivelazioni
Harcèlement
CD - VIRGIN CDVMM 16

1994
Il barone
The Baron
Le baron
CD - RCA 74321

1994
Missus
Nom de code 'Missus'
CD - RAI TRADE FRT 421

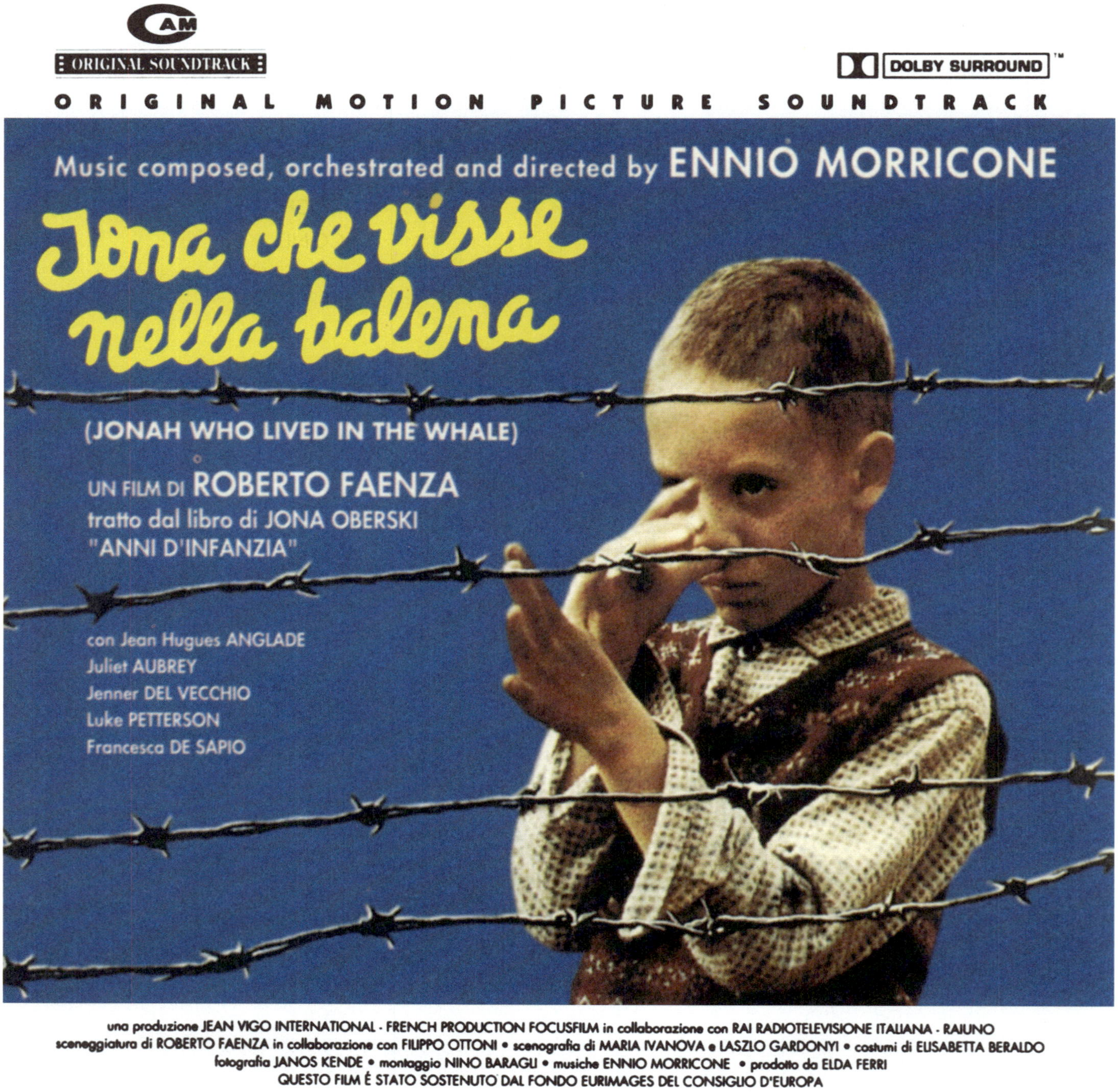

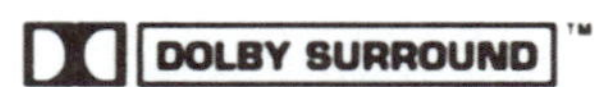

ORIGINAL MOTION PICTURE SOUNDTRACK

Music composed, orchestrated and directed by ENNIO MORRICONE

Jona che visse nella balena

(JONAH WHO LIVED IN THE WHALE)

UN FILM DI ROBERTO FAENZA
tratto dal libro di JONA OBERSKI
"ANNI D'INFANZIA"

con Jean Hugues ANGLADE
Juliet AUBREY
Jenner DEL VECCHIO
Luke PETTERSON
Francesca DE SAPIO

una produzione JEAN VIGO INTERNATIONAL - FRENCH PRODUCTION FOCUSFILM in collaborazione con RAI RADIOTELEVISIONE ITALIANA - RAIUNO
sceneggiatura di ROBERTO FAENZA in collaborazione con FILIPPO OTTONI • scenografia di MARIA IVANOVA • LASZLO GARDONYI • costumi di ELISABETTA BERALDO
fotografia JANOS KENDE • montaggio NINO BARAGLI • musiche ENNIO MORRICONE • prodotto da ELDA FERRI
QUESTO FILM È STATO SOSTENUTO DAL FONDO EURIMAGES DEL CONSIGLIO D'EUROPA

ORIGINAL
MOTION PICTURE
SOUNDTRACK
FROM THE FILM

MUSIC COMPOSED,
ORCHESTRATED AND
CONDUCTED BY
ENNIO MORRICONE

Il Barone
Colonna sonora dallo sceneggiato televisivo
Musiche di Ennio Morricone

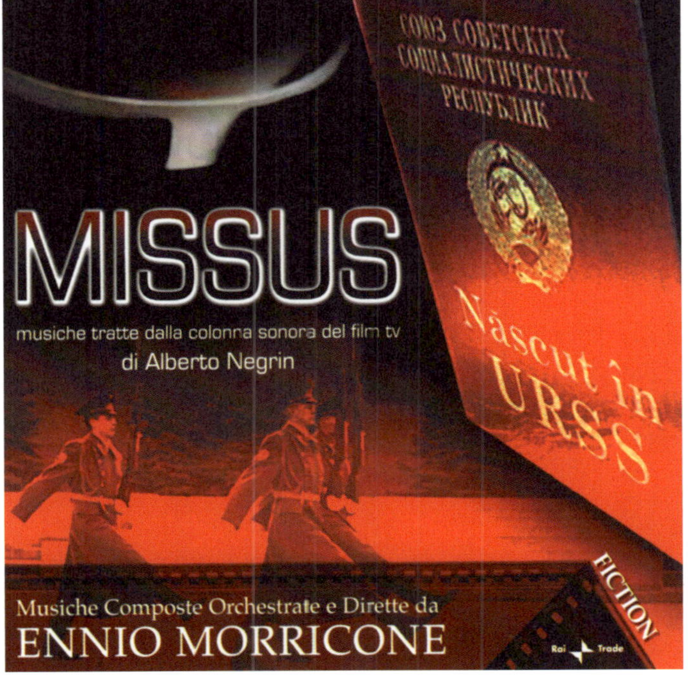

1994
Wolf
Wolf. La belva è fuori
LP 33 rpm - MOVATM 107

1994
La notte e il momento
La nuit et le moment
LP 33 rpm - MOVATM 108

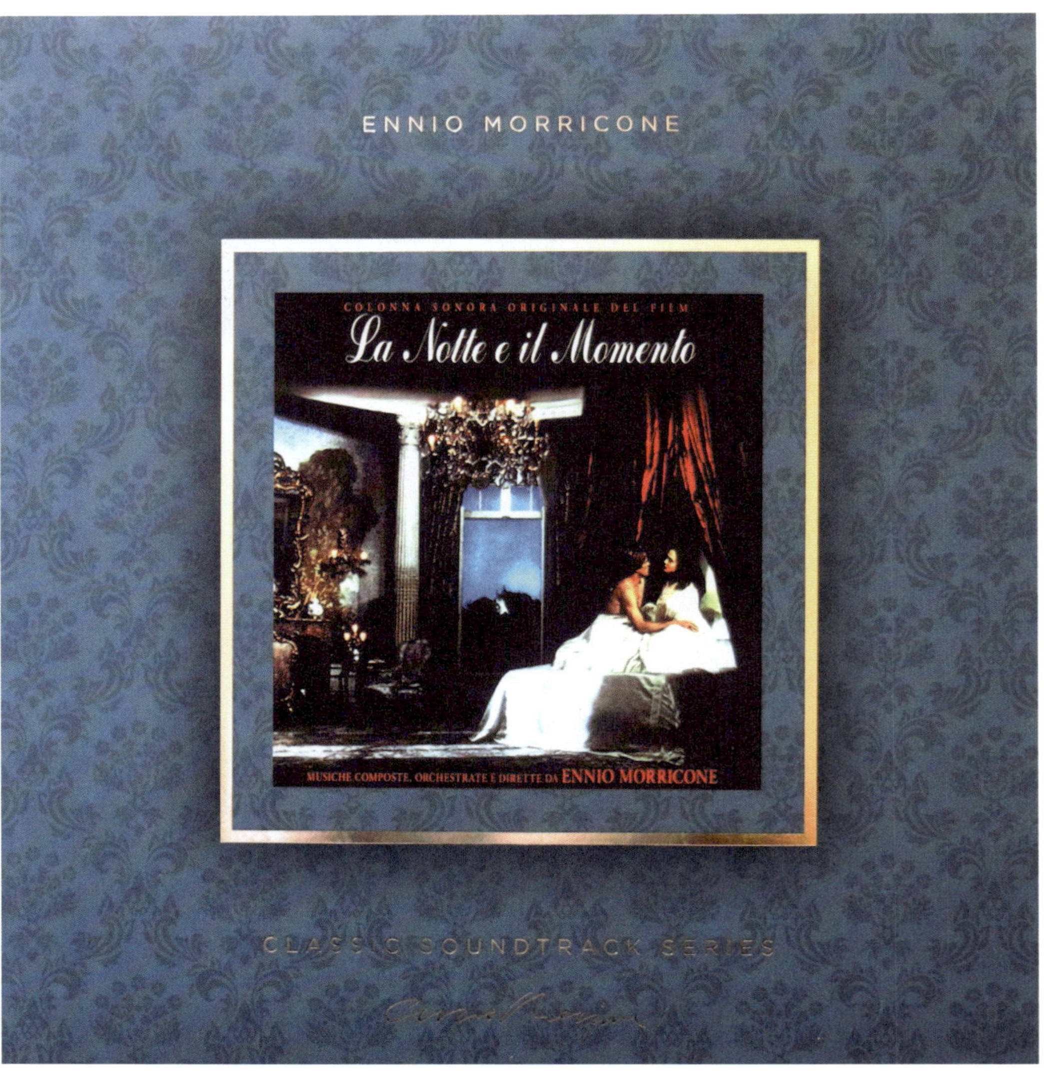

1994
Una pura formalità
A Pure Formality
Une pure formalité
with Andrea Morricone
LP 33 rpm - MOVATM 106

For the surreal and Kafkaesque story told in this movie directed by Giuseppe Tornatore, Maestro Morricone chooses to further intensify the protagonist's nightmare by writing a musical text that is melancholy and apparently resigned. He gave his son Andrea the task of creating a complementary leitmotif that is encompassed within the song, *Ricordare*, written by the director himself along with the author Pascal Quignard, and poetically sung by actor Gerard Depardieu.

1994
Love Affair
Love Affair. Un grande amore
Rendez-vous avec le destin
CD - REPRISE RECORDS 9 45810-2

This is another successful attempt at musical romanticism determined by a very sweet theme song written for piano, and although lightweight, has great emotional impact. A lovely version was sung by the Canadian singer-songwriter K. D. Lang (Kathryn Dawn Lang) and also used for the movie, *Twister*.

1995
Pasolini un delitto italiano
Who Killed Pasolini?
Pasolini, mort d'un poète
CD - CAM COS 700-026

1995
L'uomo delle stelle
The Star Maker
Marchand de rêves
CD - EPIC EPC 481463 2

Intriguing and subtle, in complete harmony with the bittersweet tale told by Giuseppe Tornatore in his film, the composer's commentary delves fully into the instrumental irony to freshen dreams and illusions that are as fleeting as they are deceptive. And he does this without forgoing the clear Mediterranean-ness that tints the music for this film, perhaps more than ever before. The score was nominated for a David di Donatello Award.

1995
Sostiene Pereira
According to Pereira
Pereira prétend
LP 33 rpm - MOVATM 159

Morricone's partner in this soundtrack is the impassioned Portuguese vocalist Dulce Pontes in the vibrant theme song, *A Brisa Do Coracao*. Her articulated and variable vocals make her voice a fully-fledged musical instrument.

1995
L'uomo proiettile
CD - GDM 2041

1995
Con rabbia e con amore
CD - GDM/EDEL 0194392ERE

1996
La lupa
CD - CAM COS 700-035

1996
La sindrome di Stendhal
The Stendhal Syndrome
Le syndrome de Stendhal
CD - IMAGE MUSIC IMG 11742

1993
La Bibbia: Abramo
with Marco Frisina
CD - CGD 4509 94978-2

1994
La Bibbia: Giacobbe
with Marco Frisina
CD - CGD RECORDS 4509 98939-2

There's something truly sobering in the simple musical structure of the song *Una tromba*, performed by Mauro Maur. It is also the theme song for various episodes in the Italo-European-American production of a made-for-television series, *La Bibbia*, which ran between 1993 and 1997. This TV series was based on the project, *Le storie della Bibbia*, a series of movies scored by important composers like Marco Frisina, Carlo Siliotto and others. Maestro Morricone directs no one, and actually, as is in keeping with his temperament, puts himself at the service of the project with rigor and professionalism. With the exception of the soundtrack of *Abramo* composed by both Ennio Morricone and Marco Frisina, the other parts of *La Bibbia* are done by other composers but they all contain the theme song, *Una tromba,* composed by Morricone.

LA BIBBIA
ABRAMO
Musiche di
Ennio Morricone e Marco Frisina

LA BIBBIA
GIACOBBE

1994
La Bibbia: Genesi. La creazione e il diluvio
with various authors
CD - CGD 4509 98927-2

1995
La Bibbia: Giuseppe
with Marco Frisina
CD - CGD 0630 10388-2

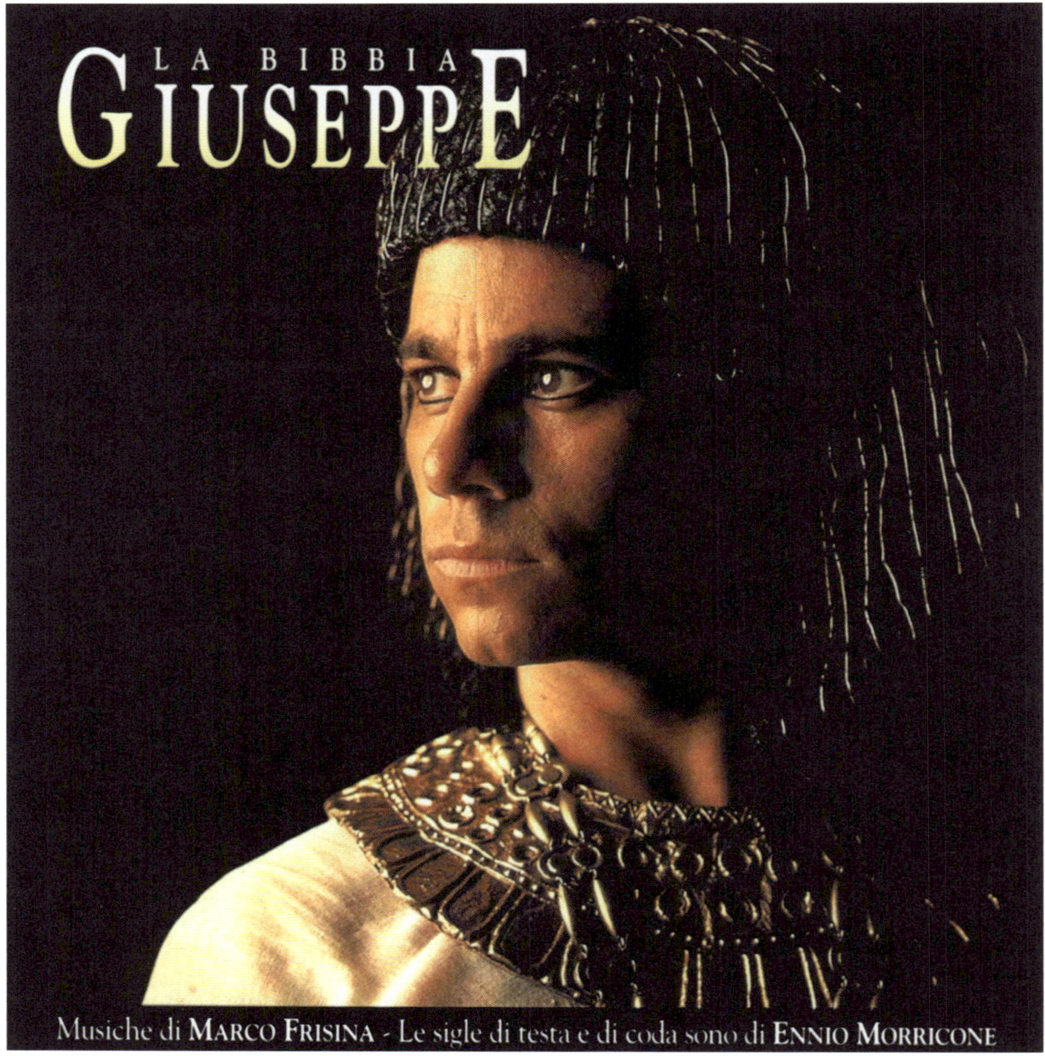

1995
La Bibbia: Mosè
with Marco Frisina
CD - CGD RECORDS 0630 13533

1997
La Bibbia: Sansone e Dalila
with Marco Frisina
CD - CGD EAST WEST 0630 17630-2

1997
La Bibbia: Davide
with Carlo Siliotto
CD - CGD EAST WEST 0630 19526-2

1997
La Bibbia: Salomone
with Patrick Williams
CD - CGD EAST WEST 39842 1822-2

Musiche composte e dirette da
Patrick Williams

1996
Lolita
LP 33 rpm - WéMé Records - WEME042

This work is particularly loved for its musical delicateness and smooth description of the intimate thoughts on sex kindled by the young and exuberant protagonist in her relationship with a professor, many years her senior. The allusions to other compositions by the Maestro are clearly audible and rather marked, but the musical context, which adheres perfectly to the story, is so involving that the self-referencing does not detract from the film's final form.

1996
Nostromo
Joseph Conrad's Nostromo
CD - SUGAR SGR D77800

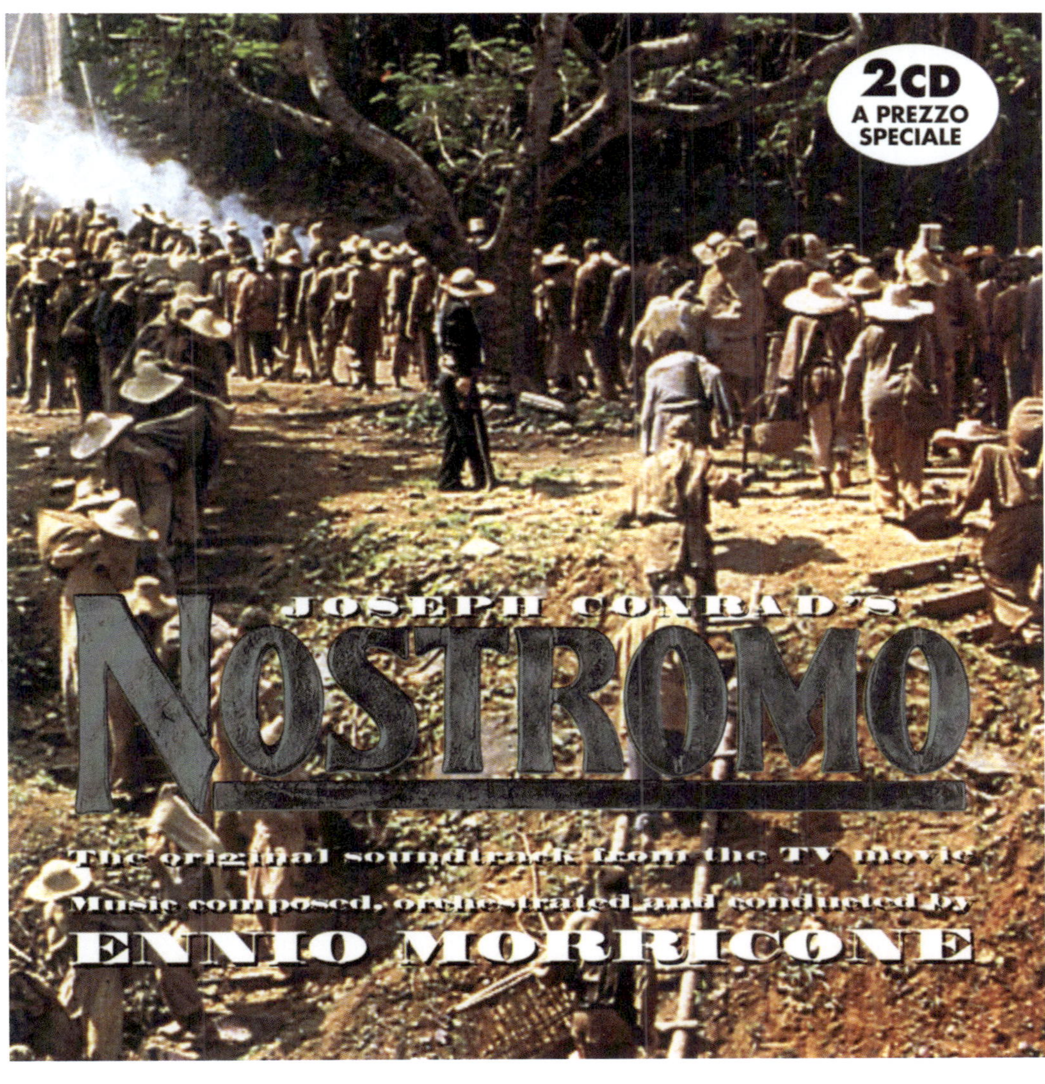

1996
I magi randagi
CD - CAM COS 700-040

1996
Ninfa plebea
The Nymph
CD - CAM COS 700-037

1996
Vite strozzate
Strangled Lives
Le jour du chien
CD - SCREEN TRAX CDST 312

For the squalid and detestable tale of blackmail and loan sharks in Ricky Tognazzi's dramatic movie, Ennio Morricone chooses the use of a musical noose weighed down by odious and strident sounds, which on the one hand affect the listening experience, and on the other influence the story in an important way, thus revealing a praiseworthy professional coherence, as well as being very brave.

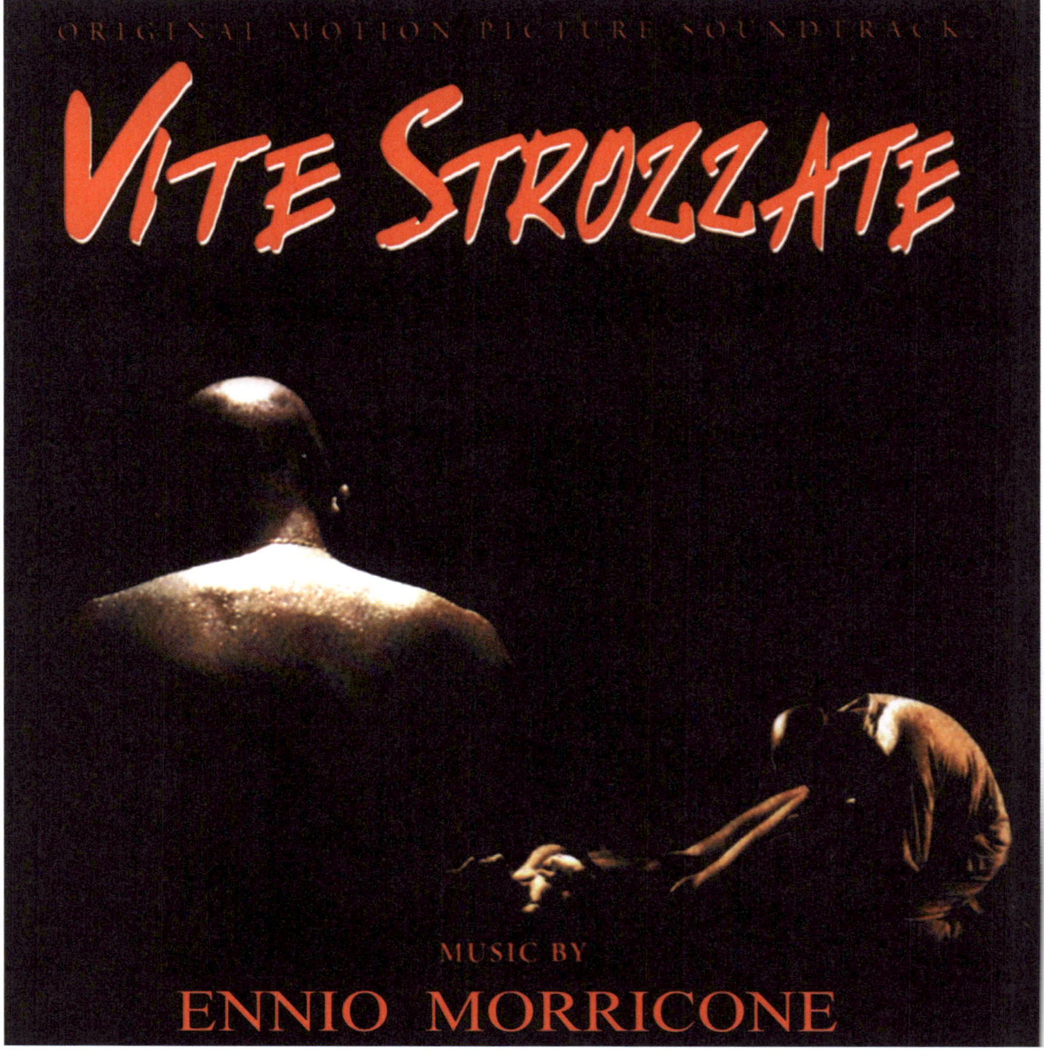

1997
U Turn
U Turn. Inversione di marcia
U Turn. Ici commence l'enfer
CD - EPIC EPC 489003 2

With this soundtrack, discussing only how the music works for the film would be simplistic. Morricone uses all of his creative talent to help tell a brutal tale with sensitivity and nuance. By squeezing atonal distorted sounds out of the orchestra, the composer's music tracks the unfolding of a horribly violent crime story, the terrible sounds as mangled and contorted as the lurking evil they represent.

1997
Richard III
Riccardo III
LP 33 rpm - MOVATM 109

1997
Il quarto re
The Fourth King
with Andrea Morricone
CD - IMAGE MUSIC IMG 11772

1998
La casa bruciata
CD - RAI TRADE - FRT 410

1998
In fondo al cuore
CD - RAI TRADE FRT 415

1998
Bulworth
Bulworth. Il senatore
CD - RCA VICTOR 09026-63253-2

1998
What Dreams May Come
Al di là dei sogni
Au-delà de nos rêves
CD - Bootleg - DREAM MUSIC RED CD359025

This score was rejected by the film producers. Paradoxically, even Maestro Morricone, like many of his illustrious colleagues, has had to suffer rejection, even when his work was already famous and prestigious. This was not the only time he suffered the ignominy of having his score rejected. Another important refusal occurred for the soundtrack of *La lettera scarlatta,* a 1995 film by Roland Joffè. It went from Morricone to Elmer Bernstein, who was also rejected; and finally to John Barry, who had to share it with the inclusion of classical music.

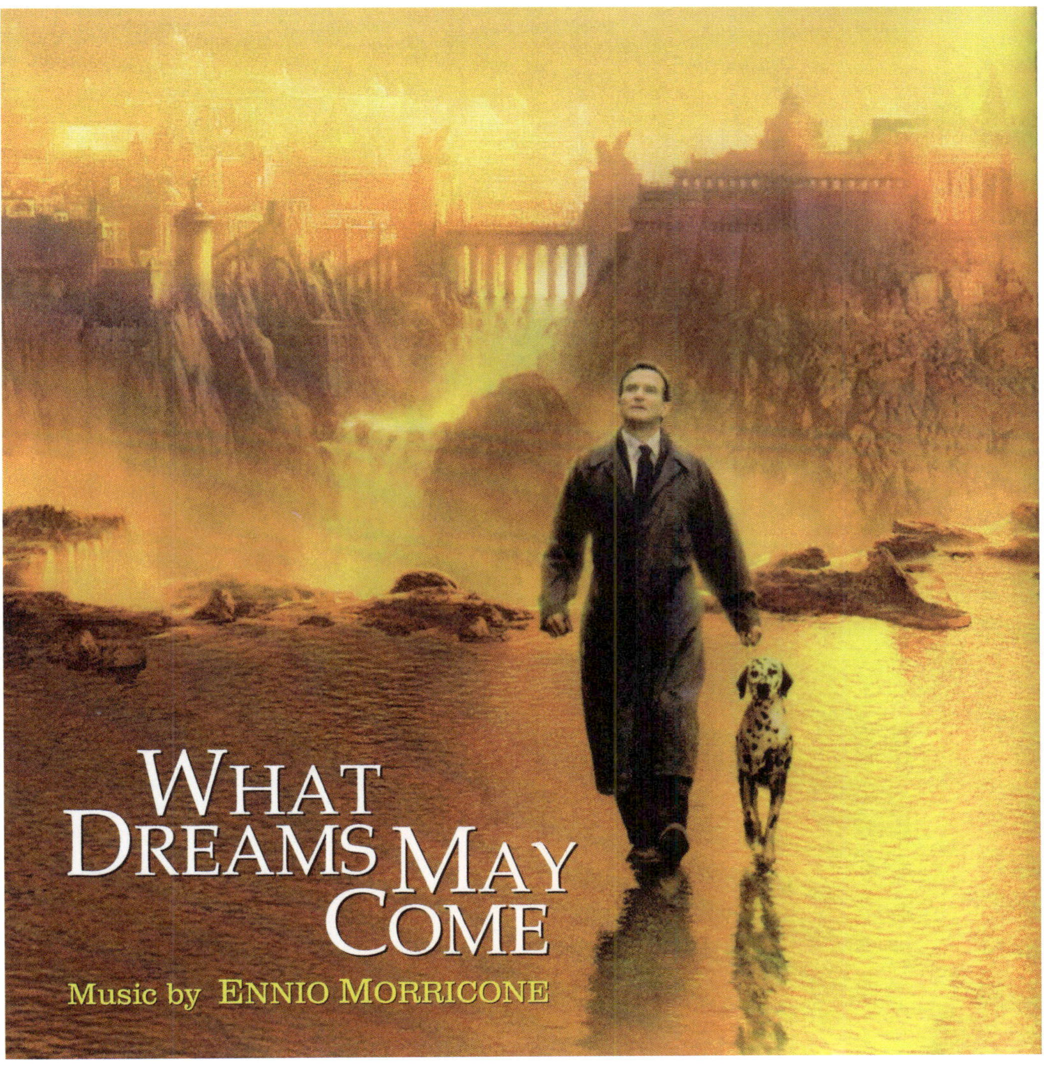

1998

La leggenda del pianista sull'Oceano

The Legend of 1900

La légende du pianiste sur l'océan

LP 33 rpm - MOVATM 110

In this modern fairy tale, Maestro Morricone's heartfelt participation follows a long period of preparing a score in which one can imagine while listening to it, that the composer lost himself in the story. It is a story that belongs to a relatively modern world, but one that is no longer our own. The composer interweaves his sensitivity as a human being and a musician with a timeless dimension. The top-notch musical cast includes the important contribution of the maestros Amedeo Tommasi and Gilda Buttà at the piano; the immortal Cicci Santucci and Gianni Oddi in the woodwind section, and Fausto Anzelmo with a solo on the viola. Inexplicably, the trumpeter Mauro Maur is not listed in the credits. The cameo is sung by Roger Waters, formerly of *Pink Floyd*, for *Lost Boys Calling*. Waters wrote this song to music by Morricone with a contribution by Eddie Van Halen on the electric guitar.

TRPT. Sib.
N. 1
con SWING
Bravissimo, grazie

1998
Cartoni animati
CD - GDM CD CLUB 7038

1999
Il fantasma dell'opera
The Phantom of the Opera
Le fantôme de l'opéra
CD - IMAGE MUSIC IMG 13382

1999
Ultimo
Ultimo. Première mission
with Andrea Morricone
CD - IMAGE MUSIC IMG 496873 2

1999
I guardiani del cielo
The Sands of Time
La tour secrète
CD - BMG / RCA ORIGINAL CAST 74321720502

QUENTIN T

THE
HAT
EIGHT

SI

20. NOW YOU'RE ALL A
21. SANGUE E NEVE BY
22. L'INFERNO BIANCO (OTTO
23. NEVE #3 BY EN
24. DAISY'S SPEECH
JENNIFER JASON LEIGH
25. LA LETTERA DI LINCOLN (STRU
26. LA LETTERA DI L
27. THERE WON'T BE MANY CO
28. LA PUNTU
BY ENNIO M

2000
2016

ANTINO'S

FUL

D

BY DAVID HESS – 1:30
O MORRICONE – 2:05
Y ENNIO MORRICONE – 3:31
ORRICONE – 2:02
ALTON GOGGINS,
ICHAEL MADSEN – 1:32
ALE) BY ENNIO MORRICONE – 1:41
N (CON DIALOGO)
HOME BY ROY ORBISON – 2:44
LLA MORTE
CONE – :27

Discography 2000—2016

2000
Malèna, Giuseppe Tornatore
Mission to Mars, Brian De Palma
Padre Pio. Tra cielo e terra, Giulio Base
The Inverse Canon, Ricky Tognazzi
Vatel, Roland Joffé

2001
Aida degli alberi, Guido Manuli
La piovra 10, Luigi Perelli
Nanà, Alberto Negrin
Ripley's Game, Liliana Cavani
The Sleeping Wife, Silvano Agosti
Un altro mondo è possibile, Autori vari

2002
Black Angel, Tinto Brass
Il Papa buono, Ricky Tognazzi
Musashi, Mitsunobi Ozaki
Perlasca, un eroe italiano, Alberto Negrin
The End of a Mystery, Miguel Hermoso
Un difetto di famiglia, Alberto Simone

2003
Al cuore si comanda, Giovanni Morricone
Guardians of the Clouds, Luciano Odorisio
Ics. L'amore ti dà un nome, Alberto Negrin
Kill Bill Vol. 1, Quentin Tarantino
Maria Goretti, Giulio Base

2004
72 Meters, Vladimir Khatinenko
E ridendo l'uccise, Florestano Vancini
Fateless, Lajos Koltai
Kill Bill Vol. 2, Quentin Tarantino
The Doll (1919), Ernst Lubitsch
Ultimo 3. L'infiltrato, Michele Soavi

2005
Cefalonia, Riccardo Milani
The Heart in the Well, Alberto Negrin
Karol. Un uomo diventato Papa, Giacomo Battiato
Lucia, Pasquale Pozzessere

2006
A Crime, Manuel Pradal
Gino Bartali. L'intramontabile, Alberto Negrin
Giovanni Falcone. L'uomo che sfidò Cosa Nostra, Antonio e Andrea Frazzi
Karol. Un Papa rimasto uomo, Giacomo Battiato
La provinciale, Pasquale Pozzesere
The Unknown Woman, Giuseppe Tornatore

2007
Death Proof, Quentin Tarantino
Men of Corleone, Alberto Negrin
The Demons of St. Petersburg, Giuliano Montaldo
Tutte le donne della mia vita, Simona Izzo

2008
Baarìa, Giuseppe Tornatore
Bread and Freedom, Alberto Negrin
Resolution 819, Giacomo Battiato

2009
Inglourious Basterds, Quentin Tarantino
Mi ricordo Anna Frank, Alberto Negrin

2010
Angelus Hiroshimae, Giancarlo Planta
Filumena Marturano (TV), Franza Di Rosa
L'ultimo gattopardo, Giuseppe Tornatore

2011
Come un delfino, Stefano Reali
Napoli milionaria (TV), Franza Di Rosa
Questi fantasmi (TV), Franza Di Rosa

2012
Come un delfino, Raoul Bova
Django Unchained, Quentin Tarantino
Il suono delle fontane di Roma, Massimo F. Frittelli
L'isola, Alberto Negrin
Paolo Borsellino. I 57 giorni, Alberto Negrin
Sabato, domenica e lunedì (TV), Massimo Ranieri

2013
The Best Offer, Giuseppe Tornatore
Ultimo 4. L'occhio del falco, Michele Soavi

2014
American Sniper, Clint Eastwood

2015
Mayday, Christian Carion
The Hateful Eight, Quentin Tarantino

2016
The Correspondence, Giuseppe Tornatore

Vl. solo
Pf.
ff
f

2000
Canone inverso. Making Love
The Inverse Canon
LP 33 rpm - MONTE STELLA RECORDS
MSR 13-20006

The structure of the inverted or retrograde canon is perhaps the boldest form of the musical counterpoint that in this case takes on an implicit and close link to the story recounted by Ricky Tognazzi in his film. The second solo instrument, in this case the violin, traces backwards over the melody generated by the first instrument in a classical manner. This apparently bizarre musical composition by Maestro Morricone intrinsically becomes a *trait-d'union* between a story that re-emerges from the past and another time; indeed with thanks to the sound of the violin.

2000
Vatel
CD - VIRGIN 8493652

We can describe in this film a Baroque expressionism, refined and elegant but not too mannered, gracious and at times discreet. If in the soundtrack, the musical lyricism conceived for the images by Maestro Morricone becomes passionately integrated and strongly descriptive, when listened to live in concert under his direction it expands majestically; it grows airy and alienating. And in that moment, if you close your eyes, it can seem as though nothing else exists.

2000
Mission To Mars
CD - HOLLYWOOD RECORDS HR 62257-2

This music has a dry and abstract symphonism halfway between the unluckily rejected score by Alex North for *2001: A Space Odyssey* and a vague echo in the style of John Williams. Such influences to the Maestro's style might stem from American standards for composing and make the great music by Morricone somewhat difficult to recognize.

2000
Malèna
CD - RTI MUSIC 850811 2

Here, our Maestro fully identifies with the melodramatic story of femininity in Sicily that director Tornatore conjures in his film *Malèna*. Morricone eases the narrative along with a recurring theme rich with both tenderness and disillusionment. The music was not as successful as the film itself, boosted by the presence of Monica Bellucci, but in hindsight we wonder if it might have been a completely different picture without Morricone's imprint. Though it was nominated for an Oscar for the Best Original Music Score, once it again it failed to win the prize.

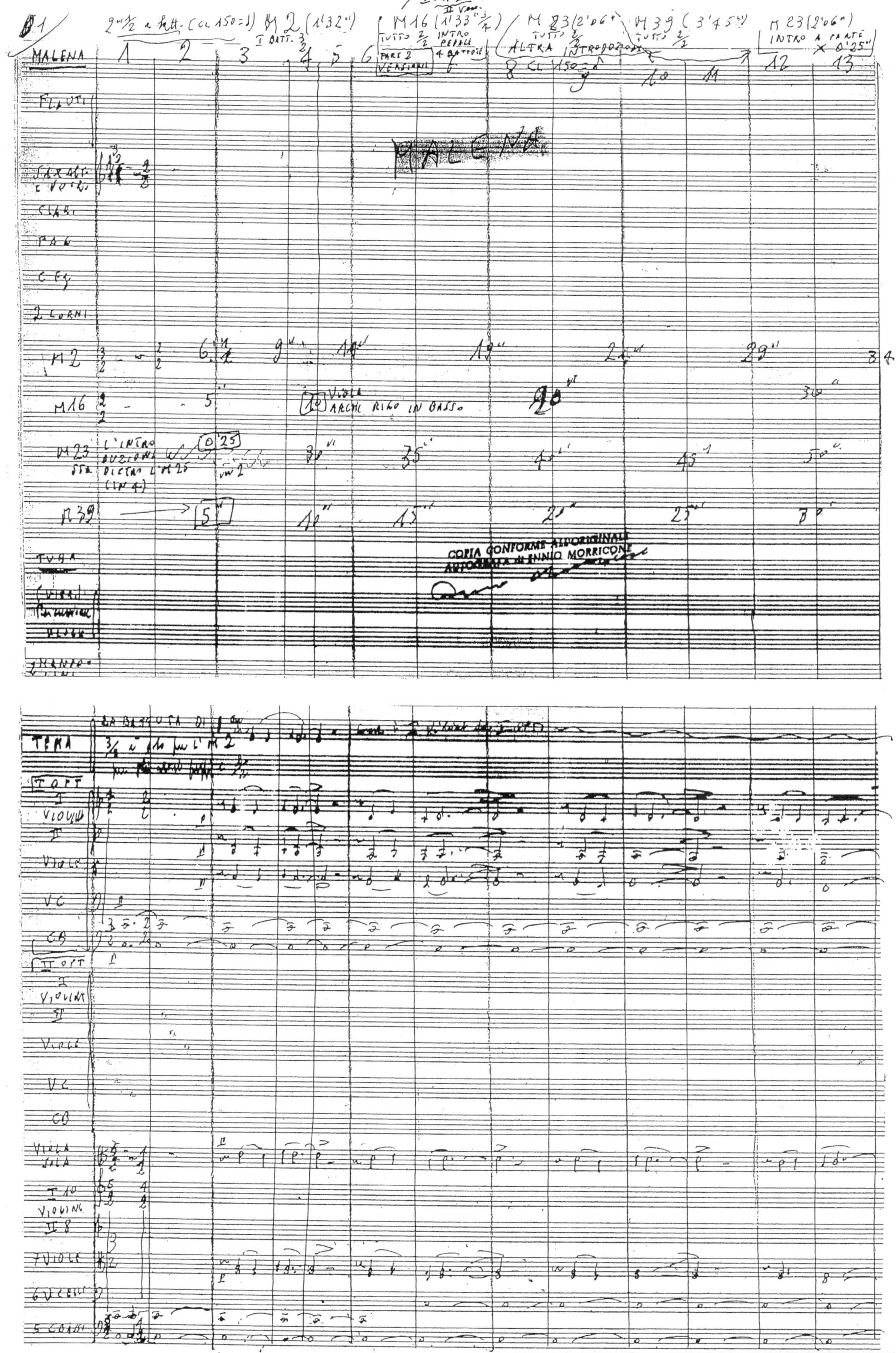
MALENA
M2 (1'32")
M16 (1'33")
M23 (2'06")
M39 (3'45")
INTRO A PARTE
ALTRA INTRODUZIONE
FLAUTI
2 CORNI
M2
M16
VIOLA
ARCHI RIGO IN BASSO
M23
M39
TUBA
COPIA CONFORME ALL'ORIGINALE
AUTOGRAFA DI ENNIO MORRICONE
TEMA
VIOLE
VC
CB
VIOLA SOLA
VIOLINI
VIOLE

2000
Padre Pio. Tra cielo e terra
CD - W ARNER STRATEGIC 092740386-2

2001
Nanà
CD - IMAGE MUSIC 4996582

2001
Aida degli alberi
CD - SUGAR 300377-2

2001
La ragion pura
The Sleeping Wife
La femme qui rêve
CD - GDM - GDM 4167

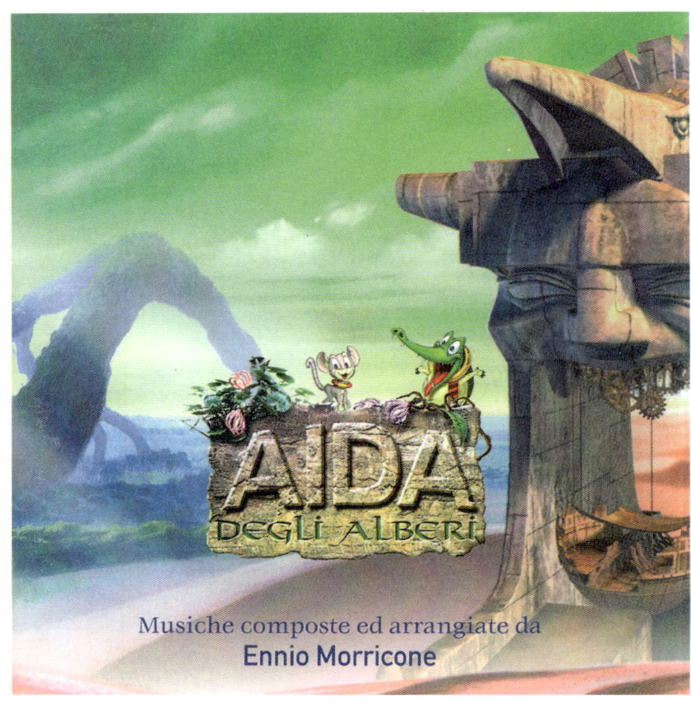

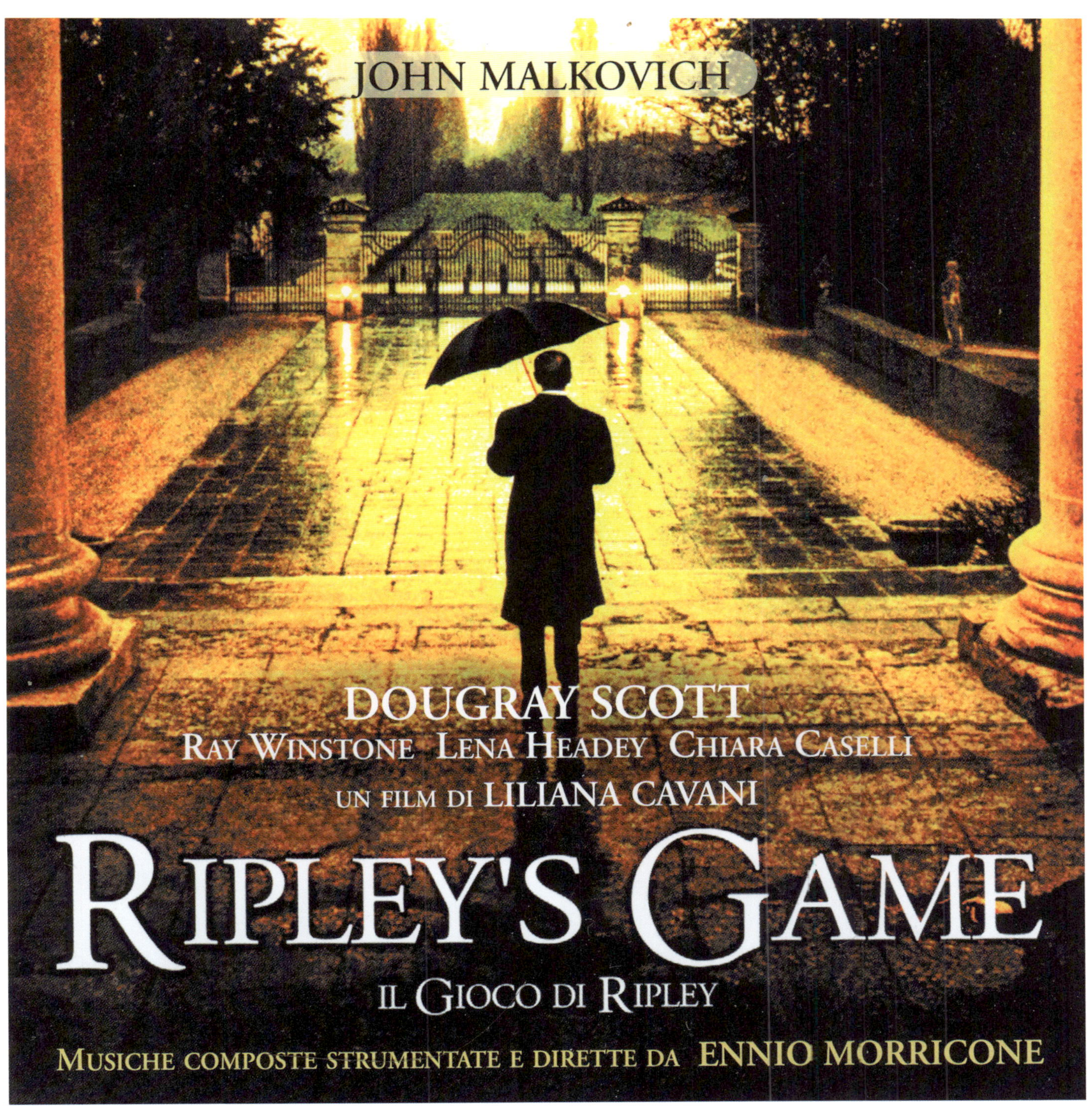

2001
Ripley's Game
Il gioco di Ripley
CD - WARNER STRATEGIC 256460072-2

Although it does not adhere to 'Morriconian' models, the music for this successful film subject that had already been tried and tested could have been entirely based on jazz, with the hypothetical, unlikely, and unrealizable collaboration between Ennio Morricone and Miles Davis. It is a *monstre sacré* of composition, and an indomitable wild panther of jazz. Ultimately, in spite of huge musical distance between the two artists, they have their instrument in common: the trumpet.

2002
Perlasca
CD - RAI TRADE FRT 402

2002
Un difetto di famiglia
CD - BMG RICORDI 74321934912

2002
La luz prodigiosa
La fine di un mistero
The End of a Mystery
CD - CONCERTONE CO 03001

2002
Il Papa buono
CD - IMAGE MUSIC IMG 5101362

2002
Senso '45
Black Angel
CD - CONCERTONE 74321934922

2002
Musashi
CD - VICTOR VICP-62176

2003
Al cuore si comanda
con Andrea Morricone
CD - GDM 2039

2003
Guardiani delle nuvole
Guardians of the Clouds
CD - UNIVERSAL 987 641-7

2004
72 метра
72 metri
72 Meters
CD - 1 VIDEO 145 CD

2004
Sorstalanság
Senza destino
Fateless
Être sans destin
CD - EMI 7243 860308

Beatitude and musical solemnity are expressed in the pain of childhood interrupted by the protagonist's cruel imprisonment in a Nazi concentration camp. Lisa Gerrard's voice/instrument modulates from darkness to light in a commentary that appears to move strongly against these tragic events, but that in truth seems to keep a thin yet vivid glimmer of hope alive.

2003
Kill Bill Vol. 1
with RZA and various authors
LP 33 rpm - MAVERIK 48570

2004
Kill Bill Vol. 2
with RZA and various authors
LP 33 rpm - MAVERIK 48676

Quentin Tarantino first attempted to involve Ennio Morricone in the music for his blood-stained saga; a proposal that seems to have been amicably declined by the Maestro but was nonetheless resolved by using various fragments taken from Italian Western music by Morricone and others.

2004
E ridendo l'uccise
CD - BEAT RECORDS CDCR 73

2005
Karol.
Un uomo diventato Papa
CD - EDEL ITALIA 0180642ERE

2005
Il cuore nel pozzo
The Heart in the Well
CD - RAI TRADE FRT 407

2005
Lucia
CD - RAI TRADE FRT 412

2005
Cefalonia
CD - RAI TRADE FRT 408

2006
Gino Bartali.
L'intramontabile
CD - RAI TRADE FRT 416

2006
Giovanni Falcone.
L'uomo che sfidò
Cosa Nostra
CD - RAI TRADE FRT 417

2006
Karol.
Un Papa rimasto uomo
CD - IMAGE MUSIC ERE 0171292

LA SCONOSCIUTA

un film di giuseppe tornatore

musiche composte, strumentate e dirette da ennio morricone

2006

La sconosciuta

The Unknown Woman

L'inconnue

CD - RCA 88697027922

A gloomy squalor characterizes a story of crime that resembles something that might have come from a collaboration between Franz Kafka and Bram Stoker, but in a modern version. Giuseppe Tornatore narrates it ruthlessly, supported by a melancholic, downcast musical contribution from Ennio Morricone. A David di Donatello Award went to the director and the composer.

2006
La provinciale
CD - RAI TRADE FRT 418

2007
L'ultimo dei Corleonesi
Men of Corleone
CD - RAI TRADE FRT 424

2007
I demoni di San Pietroburgo
The Demons of St. Petersburg
CD - BEAT RECORDS BCM 9551

2007
Tutte le donne della mia vita
CD - ATLANTIC 5041442046120

2008
Pane e libertà
Bread and Freedom
CD - RAI TRADE FRT 430

2008
Résolution 819
Risoluzione 819
Resolution 819
CD - IMAGE MUSIC 0195252

2008
Baarìa
CD - SILVA SCREEN SILCD 1322

Ennobled by the intention to turn this into an epic opera telling the story of the inventor's native Sicily, *Baarìa* (Bagheria, the name in Sicilian dialect of Tornatore's birthplace) was hit by harsh criticism and was a flop at the box office. It cost too much and it was accused of plagiarism and attacked by the animal rights movement. Also, it was not convincingly supported by the music composed by Ennio Morricone. Many believed it was missing something that should have characterized, not just the real Sicily, but also the historical-temporal nature of the narrative. It garnered numerous nominations but none for the Academy Award; and then received only a handful of prizes. The fate of this film lies in a re-evaluation that it will no doubt have in the future.

2007
Death Proof
Grindhouse. A prova di morte
Boulevard de la mort
with various authors
LP 33 rpm - WB 106172-1

2009
Inglourious Basterds
Bastardi senza gloria
with various authors
LP 33 rpm - WB520377

This was yet another missed opportunity to involve Ennio Morricone for this homage to Italian cinema by the pyrotechnical filmmaker, Quentin Tarantino. This director loves cross-referencing but had to be content using existing pieces taken from other films: *The Big Gundown Colorado*, *Blood in the Streets,* and *Allonsanfàn*.

2011
Come un delfino
CD - SONY MUSIC 88697887602

2012
L'isola
CD - RECORDING ARTS 2x905

2012
Django Unchained
with various authors
LP 33 rpm - REPUBLIC RECORD 15703

In this soundtrack, we see the relationship between Morricone and Tarantino continue to move towards their triumphant Oscar-winning collaboration for *The Hateful Eight* in 2016. In this case however, the director continued to pull from the back catalog with the exception of the sole original tune *Ancora qui*, written by Elisa Toffoli to music by Morricone.

2014
American Sniper
with various authors
Available on streaming services

In times of rancorous debate about political partisanship, Clint Eastwood's movie is like a painful thorn in the side, loved and hated depending on the ideology of the critic. The heart-rending sound of Michele Lacerenza on the trumpet in Morricone's reinterpretation of *Taps*, borrowed from *The Return of Ringo* and entitled, *The Funeral*, was chosen by the director for the closing credits and tends to leave an audience speechless. The lump in our throats when we listen to this piece makes it impossible to say anything trivial about it.

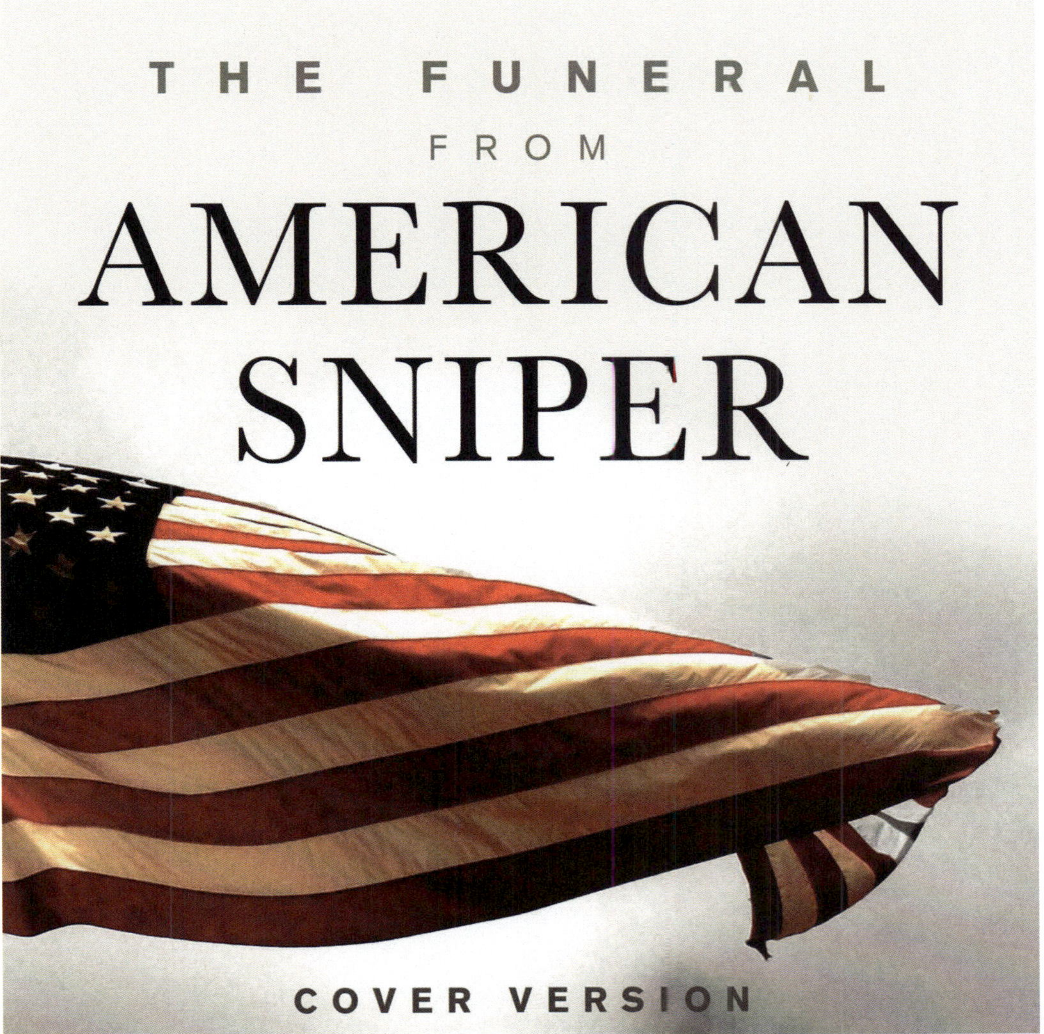

2013

La migliore offerta

The Best Offer

CD - WARNER CHAPPELL 2564 64755-3

The brilliant, engaging plot tells the story of a love affair that melts the ice through mystery, even with crime as a backdrop. A truly ingenious movie in terms of its architecture, one in which Morricone, in his own way, constructs fitting musical support.

2015
En mai, fais ce qu'il te plaît
Accada quel che accada
Mayday
CD - QUARTET RECORDS QR 207

2016
La corrispondenza
The Correspondence
CD - WARNER CHAPPEL 0825646485338

This surreal love story with existential and cosmic elements offers special appeal for female audiences and sensibilities. In addition to exploring emotional themes, the passage of time is central to the narrative. Likewise, the musical theme for the piano exerts a cadence like the slow incessant dripping sound of water. The film was nominated for a David di Donatello Award.

2015

The Hateful Eight

LP 33 rpm - THIRDMAN TRM 364

The long musical journey for the cinema by Ennio Morricone reached a destination in 2016 that was not an end, but rather a point of arrival. Now long into his career, he received the most sought-after and prestigious award for film music in the world, the Academy Award for Best Original Music Score. Much has been said and written about the Maestro's previous Oscar, an Academy Honorary Award which was given to him in 2007. That tribute was surrounded by controversy and criticism for the Academy's not giving him an award before this despite five exceptional previous Oscar nominations. For his lifetime achievement, the Academy appeared to be clearing its conscience about Ennio. Maestro Morricone welcomed the honor with disarming gratitude and moving humility. He, who is widely considered to be the greatest living film music composer, would finally silence any doubts once and for all with this glorious and unexpected late success. The film score is a memorable work – a highly creative and professional one that deserved to win the top prize. Of all the songs written for the movie, the piece, *Neve,* alone would justify an Oscar. The music for the film, produced by Tarantino himself, was wholly composed, orchestrated, and conducted by Morricone. It was recorded at the historic Abbey Road Studios in London and cut on CD and on a vinyl double album in a sumptuous edition with a tri-gatefold cover and supplementary material that included photos and a movie poster. The soundtrack of *The Hateful Eight*, besides winning an Oscar, also won a British Academy of Film and Television Arts (BAFTA) Award, a Golden Globe, and a host of other accolades that testify to the appreciation for this film's music and its prodigious composer, Maestro Ennio Morricone.

QUENTIN TARANTINO'S

THE HATEFUL EIGHT

a Maurizio
dedicato a Maurizio
per la sua splendida
iniziativa. AUGURI!
Ennio Morricone

ORIGINAL MUSIC COMPOSED AND ORCHESTRATED BY
ENNIO MORRICONE

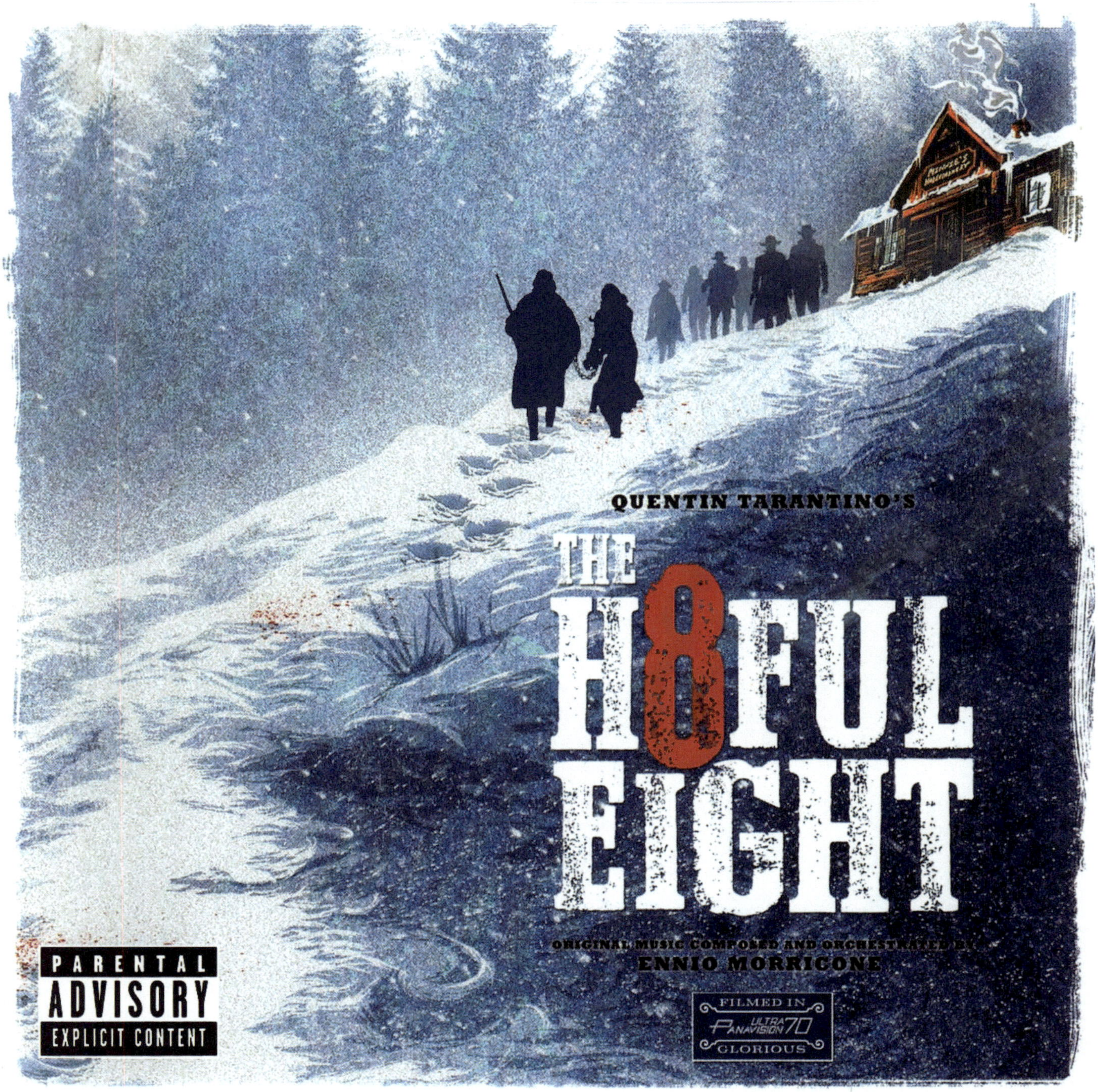
QUENTIN TARANTINO'S
THE H8FUL EIGHT
ORIGINAL MUSIC COMPOSED AND ORCHESTRATED BY
ENNIO MORRICONE
FILMED IN
ULTRA PANAVISION 70
GLORIOUS
PARENTAL ADVISORY
EXPLICIT CONTENT

QUENTIN TARANTINO'S
THE HATEFUL EIGHT
SIDE I
1. L'ULTIMA DILIGENZA DI RED ROCK #2 BY ENNIO MORRICONE – 2:37
2. RAGGI DI SOLE SULLA MONTAGNA BY ENNIO MORRICONE – 1:41
SIDE J
1. JIM JONES AT BOTANY BAY BY JENNIFER JASON LEIGH FEATURING KURT RUSSELL – 4:10
TMR-365-I/J

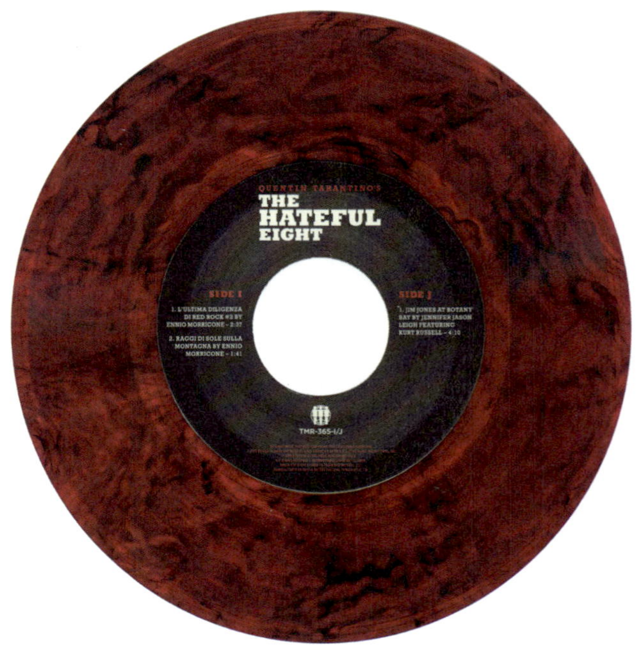

LP 33 rpm - DECCA 4769494
8 x Vinyl, 7", 45 rpm, Limited Edition,
Special Edition 2 x Vinyl, LP, Album
EP - THIRDMAN
TMR-365-I/J -E/F -C/D -O/P -G/H -A/B

List of illustrations for EP/45rpm/LP records and CDs

Authors

Maurizio Baroni

A native of Castelfranco Emilia, he began collecting movie posters and soundtrack albums when he was 11 years old. Since then, he has met almost all the most important figures in Italian cinema, among them actors, directors, producers, musicians, poster designers; he has written books, taken part in television shows, organized festivals, exhibitions and events. Most importantly, he has put together an important and well-organized collection (over 25,000 items) of posters, soundtracks, documents, and other trivia which he entrusted to the Cineteca in Bologna a few years ago. He has curated several books and mounted exhibitions.

— Books (incomplete)
Platea in piedi, Vol. 0, Bolelli, 1996
Platea in piedi, Vol. 1, Bolelli, 1995
Platea in piedi, Vol. 2, Bolelli, 1996
Stelle sui muri, MGE Communication, 2004
Victor Mature, (con Roberto Festi), Stampalith, 2000
C'era una volta il… western all'italiana, (con Roberto Festi), Stampalith, 2001
Alfred Hitchcock, (con Roberto Festi), Stampalith, 2002
Alberto Sordi, (con Roberto Festi), Stampalith, 2003
Morricone Bossa, (con Marco D'Ubaldo), Mediame, 2005
Morricone Western, (con Marco D'Ubaldo), Mediane, 2006
Morricone Awards, (con Marco D'Ubaldo), Mediane, 2007
Pier Paolo Pasolini, (con Marco D'Ubaldo), Mediane, 2007
Bernardo Bertolucci, (con Marco D'Ubaldo), Mediane, 2007
Mario Monicelli, (con Marco D'Ubaldo), Mediane, 2007
Dario Argento, (con Marco D'Ubaldo), Mediane, 2007
Armando Trovajoli, (con Marco D'Ubaldo), Mediane, 2007
Brigitte Bardot, (con Marco D'Ubaldo), Mediane, 2008
Castelfraco Emilia nei ricordi, (con Maurizio Benassi), Multimedia, 2000
Ernest Borgnine, Un carpigiano da Oscar, (con Roberto Festi e Odoardo Semellini), Comune di Carpi, 2002
Il mio paese, MB, 2012
Pittori di Cinema, Lazy Dog, 2018

— Exhibitions (incomplete)
Il Cinema, Castelfranco Emilia, 1981
Il Cinema e la musica, Castelfranco Emilia, 1988
La vertigine del delitto: Alfred Hitchcock, Modena, 1990
I cari estinti, Modena, 1991
Attenti al cielo, Modena, 1991
Il sipario strappato, Modena, 1992
Platea in piedi, San Marino, 1993
I grandi manifesti del cinema, San Polo D'Enza, 1993
L'uomo che amava il cinema: François Truffaut, Ferrara, 1994
Rocce e insegne al neon, Modena 1994
Michelangelo Antonioni, Ravenna, 1994
Stelle sui muri, San Marino, 1994
Festival Cinema Italiano, Annecy, 1995
Valerio Zurlini, Ravenna, 1995
I 400 colpi, Modena, 1995
Il contributo dell'Emilia Romagna al cinema, San Marino, 1995
Federico Fellini, Roma, 1995
Victor Mature, Madonna di Campiglio, 2000
C'era una volta il… western all'italiana, Madonna di Campiglio, 2001
Alfred Hitchcock, Madonna di Campiglio, 2002
Alberto Sordi, Madonna di Campiglio, 2003
Sogni di carta. Bernardo Bertolucci, Rovereto, 2007
Fellini dall'Italia alla luna, Bologna, 2010
Tutti De Sica, Roma, 2013
Pais al cinema, Cervia, 2014
Tracce di cinema: Bernardo Bertolucci, Parma, 2014
Il Boom, Castelfranco Emilia, 2015
Pasolini e Salò, Castelfranco Emilia, 2016
Omaggio a Ennio Morricone, Bologna, 2016
Il genio di Federico Fellini, Castelfranco Emilia, 2016
The Beatles, Castelfranco Emilia, 2017
Come noi non c'è nessuno, Castelfranco Emilia, 2017
Brigitte Bardot, Bologna, 2017
Il était un fois Sergio Leone, Paris, 2018
Marcello Mastroianni. Una vita tra parentesi, Roma, 2018

Germano Barban

Born in Ferrara in 1955, he studied graphics and printing and has had a long career in the world of publishing where he has curated the publication of thousands of art books and facsimiles for the most important museums in the world, and monographs of the great twentieth-century photographers like Richard Avedon, Henri Cartier-Bresson, Sebastião Salgado, James Nachtwey, and Josef Koudelka, some of whom have become close friends. At the same time, he has written numerous essays of a technical nature on the quality of printing for the graphic industry. He has traveled far and wide for work, and has published numerous reportages on his adventure trips to Africa and the Middle East in specialized magazines. He has always been a music fan with a preference for rock and film music, and in addition to being a keen collector, he is considered by many to be one of Italy's greatest experts. For over fifteen years he has been writing articles about his field for music magazines distributed both in Italy and abroad. Having retired from work he now lives in Milan with his wife, with whom he has had two children.

Acknowledgments

Andrea Savoia
Anna Fiaccarini
Baba Richerme
Carlo Verdone
Cesarina Marchetti
Christopher Frayling
Daniele Furlati
Dario Argento
Edda Dell'Orso
Ennio Morricone
Francesco Ceccarelli
Franco Nero
Françoise de Clossey
Germano Barban
Gino Paoli
Giuliano Montaldo
Giuseppe Tornatore
Guido Lombardo
John Boorman
John Carpenter
Liliana Cavani
Lisa Gastoni
Luca Barcellona
Luciano Parmeggiani
Maria Vittoria Melchioni
Mauro Maur
Nicola Piovani
Paolo Zelati
Renato Sperandini
Quentin Tarantino
Renzo Ansaloni
Riccardo Bello
Roberto Faenza
Rosaria Gioia
Stefano Galeone
Valerio Barbati

Maurizio Giora Vinyl, Alessandria
Nicola Simi, Pianeta Musica, Castelmassa (RO)
Roberto Dallari HF, Reggio Emilia
Achille de Il Disco D'oro, Bologna
Crocodisc, Paris
Nostalgia, Paris
La Violetera, Paris
Yeti's Records, Paris

This book could not have been made without the collaboration of the masters:
Ennio Morricone, Mauro Maur, and Daniele Furlati, who kindly provided me with manuscripts, musical scores, and precious advice.

I am grateful to:
Germano Barban, whom I asked to write the texts. We worked together on a daily basis for over a year to choose the images and to draft a list of film titles.
Renzo Ansaloni, a vinyl LP enthusiast and meticulous researcher, who helped me to find the material that was needed to complete the collection. His contribution was truly priceless.
Christopher Frayling, for kindly giving us the permission to use his valuable interviews and his precious help.
Francesco Ceccarelli, my tireless companion of Roman adventures, for the very patient work of the editorial project design.

Dedicated to my niece Giulia, may music always accompany her in life.

Credits

First published under license in October 2019 by
GINGKO PRESS

First Edition

Gingko Press Verlags GmbH
Schulterblatt 58
D-20357 Hamburg
Germany
Tel: +49 (0)40-291425
Fax: +49 (0)40-291055
Email: gingkopress@t-online.de

Gingko Press Inc
2332 Fourth Street, Suite E
Berkeley, CA 94710
USA
Tel: (510) 898 1195
Fax: (510) 898 1196
Email: books@gingkopress.com

www.gingkopress.com

ISBN: 978-3-943330-33-5

English translation:
Sylvia Adrian Notini
Cover and book design:
Bunker
Copyediting:
Meri Furnari, David Lopes
Reprographics:
UnoUndici

Printed in Italy

Original title: *Morricone*
First published by
Lazy Dog Press, Italy

Texts by:
Germano Barban, Maurizio Baroni and by Dario Argento, John Boorman, John Carpenter, Liliana Cavani, Edda Dell'Orso, Roberto Faenza, Christopher Frayling, Daniele Furlati, Lisa Gastoni, Giancarlo Giannini, Guido Lombardo, Mauro Maur, Giuliano Montaldo, Franco Nero, Gino Paoli, Nicola Piovani, Quentin Tarantino, Giuseppe Tornatore, Carlo Verdone
© 2019 Their authors

Photos:
Maurizio Baroni, 362
Renato Sperandini, 6
© Their authors
Tommaso Bonaventura, 32-41
© Contrasto
Ferdinando Scianna, cover, 2
© Magnumphotos/Contrasto

ARCHIVIO MB
All the images of the CD and vinyl covers belong to the archives of: Maurizio Baroni, Germano Barban and Valerio Barbati.

"I wish to thank the Academy for the honor it has given me by awarding me with this prestigious prize, but I also wish to thank all those who worked to help me receive this award and did so from the bottom of their hearts. Truly, I want to thank my directors, the directors who trusted me to work for them, to write the music for their movies. Truly, I would not be here if it weren't for them. My thoughts also go to all those artists who deserved this same award and did not receive it. I hope they do receive it in the near future. I believe that this award is not a point of arrival, but a point of departure, so that I may continue to improve at the service of the cinema and also at the service of my personal aesthetic as concerns applied music. I dedicate this Oscar to my wife Maria, who loves me dearly [...] and whom I love just as dearly. This prize is for her as well."

Ennio Morricone's words to the audience at the Academy Awards Ceremony in 2007 on the night he received an Academy Honorary Award which was presented by Clint Eastwood, "for his magnificent and multifaceted contributions to the art of film music."